The New Queer
Aesthetic on Television

ALSO EDITED BY JAMES R. KELLER AND LESLIE STRATYNER

*Almost Shakespeare: Reinventing His
Works for Cinema and Television* (2004)

ALSO BY JAMES R. KELLER

Queer (Un)Friendly Film and Television (2002)

*Anne Rice and Sexual Politics:
The Early Novels* (2000)

ALL FROM MCFARLAND

The New Queer Aesthetic on Television

Essays on Recent Programming

Edited by
JAMES R. KELLER *and*
LESLIE STRATYNER

McFarland & Company, Inc., Publishers
Jefferson, North Carolina, and London

LIBRARY OF CONGRESS CATALOGUING-IN-PUBLICATION DATA

The new queer aesthetic on television : essays on recent programming / edited by James R. Keller and Leslie Stratyner.
    p.   cm.
Includes bibliographical references and index.

ISBN 0-7864-2390-0 (softcover : 50# alkaline paper)

1. Homosexuality on television.   2. Homosexuality and television.   I. Keller, James R., 1960–   II. Stratyner, Leslie.
PN1992.8.H64N49   2006
791.45'653 — dc22   2005029556

British Library cataloguing data are available

©2006 James R. Keller and Leslie Stratyner. All rights reserved

No part of this book may be reproduced or transmitted in any form or by any means, electronic or mechanical, including photocopying or recording, or by any information storage and retrieval system, without permission in writing from the publisher.

On the cover: (foreground) couple watching television, *©2005 Photodisc;* (background) *©2005 PhotoSpin.*

Manufactured in the United States of America

McFarland & Company, Inc., Publishers
  Box 611, Jefferson, North Carolina 28640
    www.mcfarlandpub.com

Contents

Introduction — 1
    James R. Keller and Leslie Stratyner

What Do Gay Men Desire? Peering Behind the Queer Eye
    Robert Benjamin Bateman — 9

Queer Eye on the Prize: The Stereotypical Sodomites of Summer
    W. C. Harris — 20

Embattled Sex: Rise of the Right and Victory of the Queer in *Queer as Folk*
    Rebecca Clare Beirne — 43

Queering the Straight World: The Politics of Resignification in *Queer as Folk*
    Esther Peeren — 59

A Trip to the Queer Circus: Reimagined Masculinities in *Will & Grace*
    Richard J. Conway — 75

Straight and Crazy? Bisexual and Easy? Or Drunken Floozy? The Queer Politics of Karen Walker
    Danielle Mitchell — 85

Desire and the "Big Black Sex Cop": Race and the Politics of Sexual Intimacy in HBO's *Six Feet Under*
    Guy Mark Foster — 99

"We cannot afford to keep being so high-minded": Fighting the Religious Right on *The L Word*
    Margaret McFadden — 113

Contents

Politics of the Sitcom Formula: *Friends, Mad About You,* and
the Sapphic Second Banana
Kelly Kessler 130

Masculinity and Male Intimacy in Nineties Sitcoms: *Seinfeld*
and the Ironic Dismissal
Margo Miller 147

Gay Performativity and Reality Television: Alliances,
Competition, and Discourse
Christopher Pullen 160

Altar Ego: GLAAD Sacrifices Male Intimacy and Commitment
Ceremonies to the Media Gods
James Black 177

Lesbians and Serial TV: *Ellen* Finds Her Inner Adult
Becca Cragin 193

About the Contributors 209

Index 213

Introduction

James R. Keller and *Leslie Stratyner*

The essays in this volume explore the politics of representation, the clash of progressive and regressive social agendas, and particularly the effort to negotiate a space for Gay, Lesbian, Bisexual, and Transgendered (GLBT) individuals and communities within the mainstream media. The contributors here trace the successes and failures within the culture wars that determine the current measure of tolerance and visibility afforded to the queer collective. They applaud television when it is daring, revile it when it exhibits cowardice, and demonstrate that while GLBT individuals and communities share a common interest in equal rights for those who do not/cannot conform to the normative sexual proclivities of the dominant culture, those same GLBT individuals do not always uniformly agree on either the most efficacious and desirable means of accomplishing the said goal or the specific shape of that success once it has been achieved.

The problem of gay/lesbian representation on television can be traced in part to the fictitious, oversimplified notion of a single unified community. There are many GLBT communities. Perhaps the most dramatic display of schism within the queer collective occurred during the celebration of the 25th anniversary of the Stonewall riots when two separate parades with opposing ideologies snaked through the streets of Manhattan. Because organizers of the official parade excluded groups that it had deemed too radical for the very public celebrations, ACT UP and Radical Fairies created an alternative procession to accommodate those judged too embarrassing or too potentially damaging to the safe and hygienic image that official organizers hoped to create.

While a legion of subdivisions exists within the queer classification, there are many subjects in which the queer populace maintains a common interest, such as the establishment and codification of marital and parental rights, protections against discrimination in employment and housing, and the repeal of draconian and discriminatory laws privileging the heterosexual and punishing any manifestation of its converse. But the methods of achieving the desired progress and even the shape of that success can create acrimonious debate. While queer television attempts to address many of these unifying issues within the diverse GLBT communities, the relative accuracy of any portrayal is determined exclusively by the priorities and preoccupations of the producers and viewers. The frankness of gay male sexuality within *Queer as Folk* may make many GLBT viewers cringe, particularly those who are concerned with its potentially reckless image of gay male promiscuity. This image in the 1980s might have provoked condemnation by rightwing demagogues arguing that AIDS infection was an inevitable and deserved consequence of just such a hedonistic lifestyle. On the other end of the spectrum, the entirely sexless life of Will Truman is infuriating to many who feel that gay men are being publicly neutered in the interest of heterosexist pacification. Perhaps most vexing is the idea that each of these portraits can be considered both an advance and a retreat in a progression/regression dialectic where each representation generates its own antithesis and synthesis. Perhaps, then, the next evolution of queer television may be derived from a compromise of these oppositional gender performances, creating a new standard that manufactures its own antinarratives.

At the heart of the conflicting agendas represented above is the antagonism between the residual "gay" and emergent "queer" priorities. The appropriation/recuperation of the term "queer" from homophobic discourse was not undertaken to generate a new acceptable synonym for "gay" and "homosexual," although the terms are frequently used interchangeably — both here and elsewhere. The term "queer" signifies a broader range of illicit sexualities than the expression "gay," including but not limited to bisexual and transgendered people, not all of whom can be accurately invoked with the appellation "gay." Born in the desperate and contentious environment of the early AIDS crisis, "queer" adopted a more confrontational and radical political stance than was typical of the gay liberation movement at that time — a movement that has been characterized as essentially capitulationist, seeking to portray gays and lesbians as safe and bourgeois, not so much a challenge to as an emulation of heterosexual conventions and values.

"Gay" seeks to assimilate into the mainstream by eliding difference, both in its relationship to the heterosexual dominant culture and in the representation of sexualities within its own margins. "Queer" is revolutionary, demanding an alteration in the draconian values that legitimize continued discrimination against people with alternative sexual identities. "Gay" does not want to scare the straights into a still more defensive stance, one that would result in more repression of sexual diversity, but seeks to demonstrate that there is no danger to the collective values of the heterosexual community/communities if cultural and legal prohibitions against same sex desire are lifted. "Queer" does not sugarcoat its intentions and desires in order to appear less radical or demanding, but insists upon recognition and equal rights on its own terms.

However, the inherent contentiousness of the queer collective is not a liability but its strongest asset, for that contentiousness embodies its intellectual vigor and rigor — its determination to fashion a prominent and visible place within the mainstream American media. It demonstrates that gays and lesbians have always been an unappreciated yet important intellectual and aesthetic catalyst behind a culture that has systematically elided their presence, and that queer television may constitute the long awaited acknowledgement of the queer cultural contributions.

Many of the contributors to this volume discuss the new commerciality of the gay aesthetic. Having discovered in gay communities a yet untapped market of professional people with a good deal of disposable income, advertisers and subsequently television executives have overcome their former reticence about sponsoring gay-friendly programming, and the result is a gay media market that, like all markets, is irrevocably fettered to the commercial viability of a product. The subsequent exploitation only places gays and lesbians in the same predicament as the rest of the populace (a position that every gay or lesbian person already occupies in some other category of humanity) who were long ago identified and commodified according to their market potential. However, this may be a small compromise for the abundant benefits of greater visibility. It goes without saying that in American culture, nobody gets respect as quickly as those with money, and once the bidding begins, if there is enough money in play, the buyer can choose those products that are most appealing and banish those that are not. Such an environment may seem mercenary, but it is also very American, guaranteeing competition that is eventually going to benefit the buyer, though its first few efforts may be painfully inadequate for some. Perhaps soon, the same economic imperative that determined the success of *Will & Grace* and *Queer Eye for the Straight Guy* and the failure of *Normal, Ohio*, will legitimize more courageous televisual ventures into the present queer underground. The recognition of gay and lesbian financial power may (from a Marxist point of view) resemble (or even be) exploitation, but it is also a very powerful facilitator of civil rights in a culture that values nothing more than materialism and consumerism. From the stereotyping and overt commercialism of *Queer Eye*, one could argue that gay men are the quintessential Americans.

GLBT narratives are only aired on television after significant compromises and concessions have been made — concessions intended to coddle a still reticent public, to render queer sexualities safe, invisible, or agreeable. The essays that follow identify and interrogate the politics of these negotiations and conciliations, bringing attention to the relative benefit or damage that is sustained when partial or truncated representations of queer lifestyles are televised.

In his essay "What Do Gay Men Desire? Peering Behind the Queer Eye," Robert Benjamin Bateman criticizes *Queer Eye*'s use of gay stereotypes, its prioritization of heterosexual relationships, and its inattention to gay ones. To do this he focuses on the "spectatorial arrangement" at the end of each show — an arrangement that privileges the straight participants and marginalizes the "queer eye." Through this ordering, "queer men are positioned comfortably outside the spectacle; they are onlookers, accomplices, facilitators, but alas, not participants." Conversely, W. C. Harris' essay, "Queer Eye on the Prize: The Stereotypical Sodomites of Summer," serves as a counterpoint to Bateman's, examining charges that the show "promotes reductive stereotypes (analogous to those of minstrelsy)" and serves only as a tool to promote product. Harris believes that critics of the show advocate assimilationism, and he seeks to illuminate "the unexamined attitudes lurking beneath the surface of this outcry that pose a more insidious and significant threat to the attainment of equity and the integrity of queer identity."

In "Embattled Sex: The Rise of the Right and Victory of the Queer in *Queer as Folk*," Rebecca Claire Beirne demonstrates how *Queer as Folk* "registers the victory of queerness over those forces that oppose it." To do this she examines the representation of assimilationism in the Showtime series, differentiating between "those who try to integrate homosexuals into the mainstream ... and those who intervene in, sexualize, and "queer" the mainstream."

Esther Peeren, in her discussion of *Queer as Folk*, "Queering the Straight World: The Politics of Resignification in *Queer as Folk*," considers the drama in its original British incarnation, as well as its American counterpart. Her essay is an examination of resignification, which is "never a straightforward practice that can be kept completely under control." Peeren explores how both versions "remake practices of linguistic resignification to challenge the dominant politics of representation in their respective national contexts."

Richard J. Conway's "A Trip to the Queer Circus: Reimagined Masculinities in *Will & Grace*," applies Bakhtinian carnival theory to the popular NBC series *Will & Grace*, arguing that the potentially subversive representations of masculinity embodied in Will and Jack are contained, rendered harmless by the limits of the sitcom genre, which erases the consequences of disorder at the conclusion of each episode. *Will & Grace* creates a privileged space within which the unconventional characters are allowed to flaunt their gender eccentricities while all their revolutionary potential is restricted by the spatial and temporal limitations of the televisual medium.

In "Straight and Crazy? Bisexual and Easy? Or Drunken Floozy? The Queer Politics of Karen Walker," Danielle Mitchell discusses same-sex marriage, arguing that "*Will & Grace* plays a significant role in the production of sexuality," and that "Karen Walker ... symbolizes the program's most progressive political work." Karen, according to Mitchell, queers marriage itself, and in doing so "challenges the same-sex marriage movement to produce counter-discourses that depart from hegemonic nuclear family structures."

Guy Mark Foster, in "Desire and the 'Big Black Sex Cop': Race and the Politics of Sexual Intimacy on HBO's *Six Feet Under*," analyzes the HBO series' approach to the concept of "color blindness." According to Foster, though *Six Feet Under* seems to offer a critique of this idea, its "representational politics have not completely departed from this dominant, postwar strategy for dealing with race"—a strategy that "is inadequate to the task of resolving the crisis of difference that has long plagued our collective national life."

In "'We cannot afford to keep being so high-minded': Fighting the Religious Right on *The L Word*," Margaret McFadden addresses *The L Word*'s contention that queers and progressives need not emulate "the values and morality of conservative cultures." *The L Word*'s analysis and critique of the strategies of fundamentalist Christian activists marshals viewer support for the pro-gay position—a position asserting that homoerotic art and lesbian and gay lives are neither shameful nor indefensible.

Kelly Kessler examines the lesbian characters in two popular situation comedies. In "Politics of the Sitcom Formula: *Friends*, *Mad About You*, and the Sapphic Second Banana," she addresses "issues such as aesthetics, romantic involvement, motherhood, community, and conflict avoidance," proving how such secondary status "inhibits significant progressive representations of marginalized groups." In the end, she asserts, such representations actually accomplish the opposite of their apparent intentions. They do not embody progress, but are rather "ineffective or [even] destructive."

In "Masculinity and Male Intimacy in Nineties Sitcoms: *Seinfeld* and the Ironic Dismissal," Margo Miller traces the "comic denials of perceived homosexuality whenever male bonds [are] confirmed or prioritized." She finds *Seinfeld* the "notable exception to this trend" because the show not only refuses to conflate effeminacy with homosexuality, but also "refuses to retract or reject its characters' intimacy in order to confirm heterosexuality."

Among the more unusual contributions to this collection are Christopher Pullen's "Gay Performativity and Reality Television: Alliances, Competition, and Discourse" and James Black's "Altar Ego: GLAAD Sacrifices Male Intimacy and Commitment Ceremonies to the Media

Gods." In the former, Pullen discusses *Boy Meets Boy* within the context of other reality shows involving openly gay characters. His essay delineates the "strategies of alliance" between gay and straight characters, and the effect they have on related alliances of producer and performer in the show. Offering an abbreviated history of the role of gays in previous reality programming, such as *The Real World* and *Survivor*, Pullen maintains that such environments have become a place of welcome for gay subjectivities, "overturning negative stereotypes about alternative sexual identities." James Black's essay interrogates the homophobic narrative structure within World Wrestling Entertainment's 2002 season in which two hypermasculine wrestlers, Billy and Chuck, feigned a romantic involvement only to repudiate both their personal bond and alternative lifestyles as a whole in a climactic display of masculine dominance. Black further discusses the constructedness of gender, particularly masculinity, which he describes as relationally constituted within American culture.

The final chapter of the volume, Becca Cragin's "Lesbians and Serial TV: *Ellen* Finds Her Inner Adult," addresses that pivotal moment in television history when Ellen Morgan came out, becoming the first lesbian character central to a primetime narrative. Cragin seeks to explore the volatile politics of this television moment, explaining the seeming incongruity between the growing fascination with lesbian chic in the popular media of the eighties and the wide public uproar over the creation of a lesbian sitcom star. Cragin examines *Ellen*'s queer apotheosis and subsequent cancellation in relation to the trepidation of television producers, as well as the evolving activism of its star.

What Do Gay Men Desire? Peering Behind the Queer Eye[1]

Robert Benjamin Bateman

Queer Eye for the Straight Guy has elicited a panoply of responses, both positive and negative, from individuals both gay and straight, liberal and conservative. Heralded as a sign of increased tolerance towards gays and derided as a purveyor of pernicious homosexual stereotypes, *Queer Eye* attests to the ambivalence surrounding gay representation. Given the historical marginalization of gays and lesbians in popular culture and in the public sphere more generally, it is tempting to view any representation as positive. But one must always ask: what is being represented, and does this representation challenge the norms and preconceptions of heteronormative society or simply reaffirm them?

In what follows, I lay out a critique of *QE* that reiterates, but also builds upon, criticisms made by others in popular media. Before proceeding, though, I wish to register my own ambivalence with this project. Like many others, I have derived pleasure from *QE* and chuckled at the Fab Five's hilarious antics and bawdy humor; moreover, I consider the show's success a provisional sign that American society has warmed to gay culture and that the Fab Five have wormed their way into the hearts of individuals who might otherwise have little day-to-day contact with gays and lesbians. That said, I am troubled by several features of the show, including its use of well-worn gay stereotypes, its inattention to the everyday lives and desires of gay men (including the Fab Five), and its privileging of heterosexual bonds through a spectatorial arrangement in which the Fab Five are figured as facilitators of, but more importantly, outsiders to the spectacle of heterosexual romance and matrimony.

In his 1987 book, *When Men Meet: Homosexuality and Modernity*, Danish scholar Henning Bech, a relative unknown in American queer theory, argues that the homosexual form of existence is quintessentially modern in its reliance upon chance, anonymous encounters, stolen looks, and urban spaces. According to Bech, the homosexual's gaze, his crafty ability to pick up men through surreptitious glances and superficial encounters, prefigures contemporary practices of consumption that rely heavily on window shopping and careful manipulation of the eye (104–110). For Bech, homosexuality signifies a highly stylized and aestheticized mode of existence; and inasmuch as more and more individuals are adopting this mode of existence, society is undergoing a process of homosexualization or, as Bech terms it, homo-genization (195–196).

How prescient Bech's insights strike us today. The discursive construction of the metrosexual, college hook-up culture, the countless one night stands on primetime television, the trendiness of bisexuality and, of course, the popularity of *QE*, all suggest that homosexuality has gone mainstream. But to what end and in what form? To be sure, there *is* something subversive and contestatory in *QE*'s message. Traditional masculinity and heterosexuality are made to appear inept, insufficient, and, at times, downright fatuous. Moreover, the show highlights some of the absurdities around which heterosexual courtship is organized and maintained. And to the extent that the Fab Five succeed in transforming their clueless protégés into dapper aesthetes, the show nicely denaturalizes and renders mutable supposedly stable sexed and gendered categories. But the question remains, what does homosexuality signify in all of this? In what follows, I show how sex, desire, and the bodily needs of gay men drop out of contemporary homosexual representation, leaving only an aesthetic apparatus; a way of perceiving the world, in short, an eye; furthermore, I explore how the performances delivered by the Fab Five speak to larger debates about identity and performativity in queer theory and gender studies.

In any discussion of *QE*, one must bear in mind that while homosexuality is indeed discussed and represented, perhaps even encouraged, the perfection of heterosexual romance is each episode's ultimate goal. Fashion unconscious straight men enlist the Fab Five to overhaul their wardrobes, refashion their lives, and impress the women whom, in some instances, they want to marry or live with. In other words, *QE* puts gay men to the task of making heterosexual relationships work. We need not worry over the heightened visibility of gay men, their desires, or the alternative lifestyles they lead because, after all, their primary objective is to cement the bonds between men and women.

What *QE* neglects to represent are gay relationships, gay desires, and the homophobia that all too often makes these things unrealizable. The Fab Five do not discuss their personal lives, nor does the show's website provide any information on the matter. And while the men engage in playful sexual banter and continually allude to their desire for men, none of this is taken very seriously, in large part because the men they desire, which in most cases are the men they makeover, are emphatically heterosexual. In this respect, *QE* merely incorporates into reality television a problem that has long beset *Will & Grace*. Rightfully praised for its portrayal of two openly gay men, *Will & Grace* nevertheless fails, time and again, to depict Will and Jack's involvement in homosexual activity, whether it be one night stands or lasting relationships. Again, one might reply, hey, chat about sex ceaselessly, but let us bear in mind Foucault's insight in *The History of Sexuality: An Introduction*, that endless sexual talk does not equal sex, nor sexual liberation, nor the absence of gay erotophobia. In one of his late, notorious interviews, *Friendship as a Way of Life*, Foucault also remarked that what society truly fears from homosexuality is not the idea of two men fornicating, but of two men loving each other, specifically, of two men loving each other in yet unimagined or unanticipated ways (308–309). Neither *QE* nor *Will & Grace*, not even *Queer as Folk*, attempts such a project.

Although *QE* projects a desexualized, desireless image of gay men, does it nevertheless serve a progressive function by blurring the gay-straight binary through its transference of queerness from homosexuals to heterosexuals? Perhaps, one might argue, heterosexuals first need to see gays as something other than totally "other" before they can accept gay sex and gay relationships. In the show's very title, it is the straight man that gets to be the guy; the gay man is reduced to an eye. One might argue that this formulation nicely denaturalizes sexuality by implying that anyone can possess the queer eye, but this is not the case; it is the Fab Five, all of whom are gay, who possess the queer eye and the category "guy" remains uninterrogated, the true guys being those real men whose hardwiring prevents them from seeing the world in the same way as their gay counterparts.

This view may be a bit pessimistic. In certain episodes, the straight men appear to have seen the light after their makeovers, as if the Fab Five had actualized the queerness inside them. But in many of the episodes, what we find hilarious and what the wife or girlfriend frequently finds unamusing is the unnaturalness of the straight man's new persona; the dissymmetry between his actual self and the self imposed on him by the Fab Five. How frequently do we witness the Fab Five either laughing or expressing displeasure at the straight man's inability to pull off or perform his nascent queerness? In the final analysis, *QE* defines queerness as an essential property of homosexuality far more than it emphasizes its transmitability.

What is at stake in turning homosexuality or queerness into an aesthetic? While homosexuality has long been associated with style, surfaces, and the aestheticization of life (consider the nineteenth century figure of the dandy or the *flaneur*), homosexuality must not be reduced to a mere aesthetic form or a highly aestheticized mode of existence, but must involve an evaluation of real bodies, real desires, and real sex acts. Rita Felski has pointed out that the dandy's celebration of female artifice and style was often accompanied by a misogynic discomfort with the female body more generally. Along the same lines, the reduction of queer men to an eye in almost complete disembodiment might function as a disavowal of gay sex and of the very real problems gay men experience in reconciling their desires and bodily needs with the prevailing desire structure of heteronormative society.

Felski also shows how the dandy's appropriation of femininity might be read as an attempt to neutralize or control what was taken to be minatory, because of the excessively unruly, sensual, and corporeal female body (105–114). That the current appropriation might constitute a similar effort to render the queer body anodyne merits consideration when we take into account our culture's recent antipathy towards and terror of the gay body expressed through countless moral panics over AIDS and HIV transmission. It is interesting that after years of stigmatizing and quarantining the gay body, straight culture has finally found an aspect of homosexuality to which it wishes to be exposed. The gay man can now be absolutely infectious, absolutely contagious, so long as we are speaking of his fashion sense and not his pathological desire. Aestheticizing homosexuality, by this account, allows heterosexuals to dabble in homosexuality, to experience the delights of the other without jettisoning the gay erotophobia underwriting their sense of sexual and moral superiority.

One might fault me for my constant invocation of the real here, but I find it important to retain what I take to be homosexuality's fundamental principle: a love for and a desire to have sex with men. Any queer project must put this undeniable fact front and center. Aestheticization and all the talk about queering this and queering that threaten to erase the specific needs of gay people in a society that only recently decriminalized sodomy and in a consumer market whose language and products (specifically condoms and lube) still pretend that penises never come into contact with anuses.

What Marx finds so queer (319) about commodities[2] is their ability to take on a life of their own and to appear independent of the social relations, or relations of production, upon which they depend. In the case of *QE*, the gay man's sensorial attunement to superficialities, surfaces, and style is untethered from homosexuality and transferred to heterosexuals; erased in this process, however, is the troubling fact of the gay man's desire and the social recognition and respect it so urgently needs. Heterosexuals in this arrangement get to experience homosexuality without having to attend to the facets of homosexuality they find most threatening or having to inhabit the second-class status to which gays are relegated.

Almost a decade ago, Danae Clark penned a fascinating article entitled *Commodity Lesbianism*, in which she explored how companies attempt to reach gay consumers without offending their more populous heterosexual clientele. But today, just ten years later, the landscape of consumer culture appears radically different. In the age of *QE*, companies employ gay spokespeople to sell their wares to heterosexual consumers. Recently Pier 1 Imports replaced the tabloid-hounded Kirstie Alley, its longtime spokesperson, with a member of the Fab Five; in fact, the Fab Five frequently endorse products at the conclusion of *QE*, and, to my knowledge, no business has balked at such endorsements, nor has *QE* struggled to fill advertising space. In contemporary American culture, the gay man has become an exotic whose endorsement imbues the commodity with mystery, allure, excitement, and danger. Companies continually struggle to convince consumers that their products are unique and that the consumption of their product will give the consumer a radical edge. Just as companies like Nike and Sprite have used elements of hip-hop culture to entice white audiences, companies like Pier 1 are beginning to spy the marketing potential of gay culture and gay alterity.

There is no doubt that straight society has become fascinated with gay men, even if this fascination is often accompanied by a strong repulsion. One might hope that this fascination would eventually engender and give way to tolerance, acceptance, and the diminution of homophobic sentiment. But even as gays make their way into the mainstream, they remain marked as radically other and distinct from their heterosexual counterparts. Highlighting this distinction, moreover, has become an effectual means of winning social acceptance for gays and lesbians. In a section entitled Jews and Society from *On the Origins of Totalitarianism*, Hannah Arendt argues that the nineteenth century German Jews who were most successful at currying favor with the social elite were not those Jews who attempted assimilation by masking their Jewishness, but who proudly performed and played up their Jewishness. The stereotypically theatrical and flamboyant Jew, according to Arendt, became an object of fascination for a bourgeoisie in desperate need of entertainment and of opportunities to demonstrate his self-congratulatory universalism and humanism. Rather than explore exotics abroad, the German elite created its own domestic exotic

> Eager to stress the basic unity of mankind, they wanted to show the origins of the Jewish people as more alien, and hence more exotic, than they actually were, so that the demonstration of humanity as a universal principle might be more effective [78].

QE appears to present a similar ambition. Viewers allow the Fab Five into their homes on the condition that they exhibit conventional gay stereotypes, such as effeminacy, theatricality, and an obsession with superficiality (another prerequisite, of course, is that they not speak too freely of their sexual desires). This practice generates entertainment for heterosexuals while simultaneously satisfying their need to associate with exotic others. Whether the heterosexual forms enduring, communal bonds with actual gay men or participates in politics beneficial to gays does not matter. Watching *QE* reaffirms his liberal-minded, unprejudiced humanism; thus the armchair quarterback is replaced by the armchair humanist. But the straight man's investment may be more insidious than this. Arendt also suggests that the dominant group — whether it is the bourgeoisie or heterosexuals — must seek out others not only as sources of entertainment, but also as foils against and upon whom they can establish and consolidate their superiority. A straight individual's interest and investment in *QE* therefore may testify less to his acceptance of homosexuality than to his need for shoring up his own heterosexual identity and masculinity vis-a-vis a homosexual foil. In other words, we should not assume that a straight man's fascination with *QE* signifies progress or the erosion of sex/gender barriers. It might, in fact, signify the opposite.

How do we make sense of a system in which heterosexuals seek out homosexuals as foils and as objects of amusement and in which homosexuals give them what they desire in exchange for social tolerance? *QE* constitutes only the most gratuitous instance of this phenomenon. The Fab Five hyperinflect their speech with a feminine lisp and exaggerate their flamboyant gestures and mannerisms in return for overnight celebrity and multimillion dollar contracts. But every day, less conspicuously and on a smaller scale, gay men engineer and micromanage their self-presentation to meet heterosexual demands. To be clear, I am not suggesting that gay effeminacy and theatricality are completely imputable to a desire for social acceptance; nor am I claiming that these behaviors naturally belong to the female gender; to the contrary, I find the gay man's blurring of gender lines politically and theoretically productive. Nevertheless, it would be a mistake to regard the nelly behavior as necessarily more natural or more radical than the behavior of the gay man whose gender performance corresponds more closely to traditional masculine ideals. Effeminate behavior, however unconsciously generated, may derive from an unspoken social demand for the gay man to be different. One more caveat: I am not suggesting that the Fab Five are somehow unconscious of their theatricality or effeminacy, merely that their behavior might constitute an extremity of histrionics that in everyday life is slightly less volitional.

Too frequently it is assumed that straight men want gay men to act straight and that their hatred or fear derives from the gay man's womanish behavior. But what may terrify straight men most is the gay man's pretension and proximity to masculinity; his ability to appear, for all purposes, straight like a real man, when in fact, at least in the heterosexual imagination, his perverse desires disqualify him from that category. Desiring social acceptance but realizing the threat he poses to straight men, the gay man may consciously or unconsciously alter his behavior — that is, make it more feminine — to prove his harmlessness to traditional masculinity. His self-transformation suggests that he is no threat because he is really more like a woman than a man; and if that is not sufficient to allay fears, he is an alien creature whose difference and foreignness charms, disarms, and entertains. At the same time, the gay man's move toward femininity may allow him a greater degree of intimacy with women, whose company can then substitute for the camaraderie he has lost with men (and here I would again cite the gay man's transmutation into a commodity or status symbol — an upper-class white female can no more do without her gay best friend than she could without her Gucci bag or Prada shoes).[3]

This perspective, whose provisional nature and only partially explanatory power, enables us to see how the performance of difference may constitute not only a way of expressing one's marginality, but also of selling oneself to a dominant group whose acceptance one craves.[4] Of course, the unconscious or subconscious character of this performance should be stressed. Furthermore, as Judith Butler explains in her introduction to *Bodies That Matter*, though identity may be performative, the performances constitutive of all identities are compulsory in nature. Our example here illustrates how gay identity in all its manifestations, whether it is the gay man who passes for straight or the gay man who flaunts his femininity and flamboyance, is a reaction to — though perhaps not entirely a product of — compulsory techniques of one form or another.

QE points up the limits of homosexuality's power to undermine stable gender categories. According to Butler, homosexuality denaturalizes gender by relocating a trait purportedly constitutive of female identity — that is, the desire for men — to men. But if a culture can convince itself that gay men are more like women, or women trapped in men's bodies, or a third species whose particularity cannot be captured by either category, can homosexuality really serve a deconstructive function? Moreover, the production of difference is also the logic of consumer capitalism, which may explain the gay man's recent annexation to and complicity with American commodity culture.

In an effort to tie together several of the observations, I want to conclude by reflecting on *QE*'s spectatorial arrangement. At the end of each episode, having completed their project, the Fab Five retire to a comfortable living room where, by television, they watch as their aesthetically reconstituted straight man reunites happily, though at times ambivalently, with his spouse or girlfriend. The viewers witness not only this reunion but also the Fab Five witnessing this reunion. Thus, *QE* serves up the image of gay men looking longingly at the spectacle of heterosexual romance. Queer men are positioned comfortably outside this spectacle; they are onlookers, accomplices, facilitators, but alas, not participants. The Fab Five are ultimately portrayed as desiring beings, but their desire, it appears, is to be straight or to have the type of relationships straight people have, or maybe, to have no relationships at all.[5] Or perhaps their desire is for the straight man whom they must regretfully relinquish to his female paramour. On the other hand, with the depiction of gay men staring longingly at heterosexual romance, perhaps *QE* is urging a social recognition of the need for cultural institutions that would enable gay men to have the same type of intimate relationships. Maybe, just maybe, *QE* betrays sympathy for something like gay marriage. However, I am more inclined to argue that *QE* views gay men as radically exterior to and incapable of such relationships.[6]

Call this story "The Story of the Eye." Like George Bataille's pornographic novel of the same name, this narrative recognizes the importance of the eye in initiating, cultivating, and even conveying sexual desire. Yet, Freud argues that scopophilia can become pathological if one becomes more interested in looking than in pursuing the actions to which such spectatorship might lead. To be sure, the *QE* is a desiring eye; it desires beauty, fashion, social approval and an endless array of commodities; in fact, the queer eye thirst for material goods is apparently insatiable. But does the queer eye desire something carnal or romantic — like bodies, like sex, like love, like sustained intimate relationships? Or has the queer eye been thoroughly appropriated by consumer capitalism and by aesthetically impoverished heterosexuals? Where is the gay man in all of this? Where is his body? Where is his desire for other men's bodies? Is there a gay body that remains to be liberated; that cannot afford to be robbed of its eye? Is it possible that the proliferation of queers on television is in fact inimical to a truly contestatory queer politics? What, I finally ask, do gay men desire?

Notes

1. A shorter version of this paper was presented at the 2004 PCA/ACA conference in San Antonio, TX. Thanks go to Rita Felski for reading a first draft and offering criticism and to Eleanor Kaufman and Patrick Roberts for helping me think through several ideas in advance.

2. I'm indebted to Danae Clark article for pointing out Marx's characterization of the commodity as queer.

3. Indeed, the Fab Five are thoroughly commoditized. Without personal lives, intimate relationships or articulated desires, they exist, at least in the phantasmic world of QE, for the sole purpose of ornamenting the lives of others. How perfectly docile and innocuous!

4. We should use caution in embracing the multiculturalist "be yourself" mantra and the contemporary celebration of difference. As Arendt explains, dominant groups need others to be different in order to consolidate their superior identities and to exercise their self-congratulatory humanism. Furthermore, as Alain Badiou has recently cautioned (*Saint Paul*, 2003), capitalism can all too easily appropriate new identities manufactured by contemporary identity politics and turn them into profitable consumer groups.

5. In some episodes, to be sure, the hetero couple appears too ridiculous to be desirable; nonetheless, by positioning the Fab Five as spectators, *QE* offers no glimpse into the type of intimate relationships gay men might develop or how these relationships might challenge traditional heterosexual coupling.

6. I realize I'm waffling here over whether gays should be included in heterosexual institutions or should challenge these institutions with alternative relational configurations. On this question, I haven't a strong opinion, as I find both strategies desirable and not mutually exclusive. The point is that whatever position one takes, one is likely to be disappointed by gay representation in shows like *QE* and *Will & Grace*.

Works Cited

Arendt, Hannah. "Jews and Civilization." *The Portable Hannah Arendt.* Peter Baehr, ed. New York: Penguin, 2000. 75–103.

Bech, Henning. *When Men Meet: Homosexuality and Modernity.* Chicago: University of Chicago Press, 1997.

Butler, Judith. *Bodies That Matter: On the Discursive Limits of Sex.* New York: Routledge, 1993.

Clark, Danae. "Commodity Lesbianism." *Out in Culture.* Corey Creekmur and Alexander Doty, eds. Durham: Duke University Press, 1995.

Felski, Rita. *The Gender of Modernity.* Cambridge: Harvard University Press, 1995.

Foucault, Michel. "Friendship as a Way of Life." *Foucault Live.* New York: Semiotext(e), 1996. 308–312.

―――. *The History of Sexuality: An Introduction.* New York: Vintage, 1990.

Marx, Karl. Das Kapital, Volume I. *The Marx-Engels Reader.* Robert C. Tucker, ed. New York: Norton, 1978. 294–438.

Queer Eye on the Prize: The Stereotypical Sodomites of Summer

W. C. Harris

Since the summer 2003 premiere of the Bravo network's runaway hit *Queer Eye for the Straight Guy*, in which five gay men, dubbed the Fab Five, make over the world, "one straight guy at a time," there has been an inordinate amount of hand-wringing over what this new makeover show represents or fails to represent about gay men as well as the potential boon or harm it poses to the struggle for GLBT rights in America.[1] For example, according to sociologist Melinda Kanner, the show "presents us with a preparation in which gayness has become domesticated, unthreatening, and constructive to the interests of heterosexual fulfillment" (37); similarly, Terry Sawyer, music and TV critic for *PopMatters*, complains that "Bravo seeks to show gay men as materialistic vamps, style clowns with cock-centered worldviews who see conversation as opportunity for *Three's Company*-level double entendres" (par. 2). Negative reactions of industry critics and everyday viewers,[2] or at least the volume of such reactions, may have been fueled by unfortunate (or, to others, perhaps felicitous) timing. For the summer of 2003 also witnessed a landmark Supreme Court decision: *Lawrence et al. v. Texas* struck down sodomy laws as discriminatory and unconstitutional, thus correcting *Bowers v. Hardwick*, the Court's 1986 decision that upheld sodomy laws and gave the Court's imprimatur to the treatment of gays and lesbians as second-class citizens. Then, in November 2003, Massachusetts's Supreme Court handed down an equally groundbreaking decision asserting the legality of same-sex marriage. Most often, naysayers to *Queer Eye for the Straight Guy* attacked the show for relying on gay stereotypes. Although the connection was not voiced,[3] perhaps the fear was that the dissemination of what some felt to be stereotypical images of gayness — and on a tremendously popular show with straight as well as gay viewers — would precipitate a backlash and deal a fatal blow to revived debates about GLBT equality and same-sex marriage at the very instant when progress on those issues seemed within reach.

This chapter examines responses to *Queer Eye*—sharp critiques along with sometimes heady accolades — and examines in particular claims that the show promotes reductive stereotypes (analogous to those of minstrelsy) and that it is a market penetration device devoted to hawking merchandise and little else. My overall claim is that the show's most vehement critics — whether they balk at stereotypes, sexual innuendo, or merchandising — are advocating assimilationism, advocating the maintenance of what Michael Warner in *The Trouble with Normal* (1999) calls "hierarch[ies] of respectability" and "shame" (49, 24). This policing action is not always conscious, is often far from malicious, and may perhaps be necessary to guard the snail-like progress of gay rights from the whiplash of ignorant homophobes. And the motives behind negative responses to sissies like Carson Kressley and Jai Rodriguez may be as diverse and complex as "'internalized homophobia,' in-group hostility, or simply ... the [heteronormative] perspective unconsciously embedded in so much of our thought and perception" (Warner 89). But motive and awareness make little difference. The effect is the same.[4] Rather than take individuals to task merely for their opposition to the show, it is important to note not just the analytical or historical errors that undermine their critiques, but the unexamined attitudes lurking beneath the surface of this outcry that pose a more insidious and significant threat to the attainment of equity and the integrity of queer identity.

Pagan Adoration

Allegations of commercialism are as exaggerated as they are baseless. Richard Goldstein, writer for *The Village Voice*, insists "[t]here are more product placements in this show than on the Home Shopping Network" (par. 2). Terry Sawyer is equally hyperbolic: "Every scene involves a close-up on a store front, a label, or a smartly designed tube of styling gel. I hope that most gay people are rich as well as peerless aesthetic fascists, because *Queer Eye* consistently equates good taste with ridiculous expense" (Sawyer par. 10). Aside from the exaggerations that weaken their point, Goldstein, Sawyer, and others seem to have forgotten (one wonders how) the corporate marketing forces that structure every single televised moment on any show. It is true that, in a moment of high-end excess, food and wine expert Ted supplies pricey foie gras for a wife's belated birthday party. On the other hand, Thom Filicia, an interior designer, consistently takes the straight men to midmarket chains like IKEA, Hold Everything, and Pier 1. And if some of the spas and furniture and clothing stores the Fab Five patronize are high end, one cannot forget that *Queer Eye* is filmed in New York not Des Moines. (How seriously would viewers take a makeover show that has its hosts rooting around in bargain bins?) The charge that the show hawks predominantly high-end businesses makes little sense if we consider that most of its audience lives outside Manhattan or other areas where such specialty stores or branches of regional chains exist.

It might seem that part of the worry over *Queer Eye*'s commercialism stems from the gay and lesbian community's recent love affair with mainstream corporate culture. This heady courtship over the last decade or so has purchased mainstream visibility and economic clout with the coin of diminished (or at least less confrontational) calls for political equity. As Alexandra Chasin points out in *Selling Out: The Gay and Lesbian Movement Goes to Market*, the queer community has been a marketing target since the early 1990s spawned the myth of the "DINK" (Dual Income, No Kids): because lesbians and gay men have no children (supposedly), any queer, partnered or not, has a significantly larger chunk of disposable income than a heterosexual couple with children.[5] Of course, economic clout does not necessarily translate into political clout. Swimming in the mainstream market, queers become as anesthetized as heterosexuals, focused more on the best cell phone plan than the cost of healthcare, an illusory middle-class tax cut, or "compassionate" moves to segregate gays and lesbians in the separate-but-equal corral of civil unions.

Surprisingly, critics of *Queer Eye* hold the show responsible for prostituting gay men to corporate America, apparently single-handedly. Kanner writes,

> the underlying premise of the show [is] that all it takes to lead a happier romantic life and have greater personal fulfillment is an improved ability to consume goods.... The growing link between gayness and consumerism is disconcerting. The gay movement of the 1970s and 80s found gay people acting as a potentially disruptive force, challenging the straightjacket of compulsory heterosexuality and fixed gender roles. If, in contrast, our energies are focused on finding the perfect sofa or optimizing our highlights, can we still be acting as a progressive force for necessary social change? [37].

"*Growing* link?" Kanner seems not merely to have forgotten the developments of the 1990s and to have avoided opening a mainstream gay or lesbian magazine, but also to have assumed the show is aimed solely at gay viewers. Sawyer, apparently attempting to rescue gay men from being portrayed as materialistic, errs on the side of excess: "It would be better to broaden the representations and deny that being gay has any consistent content at all than to write a show that portrays gays as moral savages who live their entire lives in pagan adoration of high end hair products" (par. 13). Aside from evoking an offensive image of primitive societies as backward worshippers of inert objects ("moral savages" in "pagan adoration"), Sawyer ignores the fact that, thanks to marketing machinery, a significant number of straight men currently use gel or other hair products. Alonso Duralde, reviewing the *Queer Eye* CD, which includes the *Queer Eye* theme song along with other pop music tracks, snidely dismisses the show's "you-should-buy-this ethos"—a profoundly ironic observation to make in the slick, ad-glutted pages of *The Advocate*. What distinguishes *Queer Eye* from any other network show, straight or gay, or from queer media organs like *The Advocate* and *OUT*, both of which devote more space than *Queer Eye* to the hawking of pricey merchandise and the creation of consumer needs?

Consumerism has certainly levied a deadening weight on the American republic (if a word that implies a sense of public debate is still applicable), but it makes no sense—indeed, it seems perceptually impossible—

to single out *Queer Eye* as the lone culprit. Unfortunately, the illusion that a television show, whatever its content, is not always also a market-penetration device is no longer sustainable. Nonetheless, the presence of product placements on *Queer Eye*, which constitute an urban, semi-affluent style that not all gays or all men desire, does not invalidate the transformation each week of one heterosexual man's self-image. What matters in this transformation is not so much a trendier haircut as it is the modeling of alliances between two groups (straight and gay men) whose acknowledged mistrust, ignorance, or fear of one another has helped keep homophobia faceless, monolithic, and powerful.

Lispin' and Swishin' for the Heterosexual Massa

The second recurrent criticism is that *Queer Eye* trades on stereotypes, disseminating reductive images of gay men and providing visibility only in clichéd forms regularly used to sustain homophobic cultural attitudes. Like other minorities, queers harbor a long-standing, warranted paranoia regarding stereotypical representation. Equally strong, though perhaps unwarranted, are the pressures that weigh on mainstream representations of a minority, particularly the imperative of diversity — with the result that any single image is, by default, reductive, exclusive, and (so the logic goes) stereotypical.[6] Yet to compare *Queer Eye* to the minstrelsy of Stepin Fetchit, as more than one observer has done, seems alarmist and indefensible. Kanner cautions, "Perhaps gay people are next to be relegated to the status of an entertainment class, much as black performers have been throughout the twentieth century..." (37). When Christopher Kelly, writing for *The Miami Herald*, "[w]elcome[s us] to the rise of the gay minstrel show," it is true that he has *Will & Grace* and *Queer as Folk* in his sights along with *Queer Eye* (par. 3), but the latter draws the heaviest fire:

> It may seem a bit unfair to compare shows like *Queer Eye* ... to the minstrel show tradition, which, in its best-known form, featured white actors in blackface, grossly exaggerating African-American stereotypes and dialects for the amusement of mostly white audiences. But much like, say, the 1950s television version of *Amos 'n' Andy*—

which featured black actors — shows like *Queer Eye* peddle entirely in stereotypes and then write off their offensiveness as good fun [pars. 10–11].

The accusation of minstrelsy is historically inaccurate and analytically unsound. Camp, unlike minstrelsy, has usually been enacted by gay men for other gay men (or for a gay-friendly audience). Minstrelsy was rarely performed by African-Americans for an African-American audience. Furthermore, the object of camp is not the denigration of an entire race (as when performed by whites in blackface), and its result is not self-denigration (as with the black stars of the television version of *Amos 'n' Andy*). Minstrelsy's only purpose is the maintenance, by ridicule, of an image of black Americans as childlike fools who deserve the second-class citizenship that a biased polity assigns them. The aim of camp, by contrast, is to trouble — always at the hands of queers — the naturalized categories of gender and sexuality and the presumed hegemony and integrity of those categories in a heteronormative culture.[7]

At times, camp humor may seem little more than sophomoric. For instance, when Carson squeezes a tube of skin ointment too hard and accidentally squirts ointment all over Ted and that week's guest, John Zimmerman IV, Carson's tag line is, "Oh, I had no idea ... I was that close." But this is gross-out humor with a difference: two of the participants are gay, and their graphic projection of queer sexuality — literally — onto other male bodies, gay and straight, provides the edge, the inflection, which is part of what defines camp. More often than not, however, camp turns on gender inversion (which raises the specter of stigma so disconcerting for many straights and some queers). When Carson originally discovers a large collection of creams and ointments among a professional male skater's toiletries, designer Thom Felicia quips, "He's got a dry vagina." Some jokes, apparently sophomoric, are camp because they accentuate gay desire, if only humorously, as when Ted, referring to an unwashed jockstrap found and soaked in a pot of water, says, "We're gonna fry that. Would you like some soy sauce with that?" and Carson replies, "There was already some soy sauce on it. Was it soy sauce or *boy* sauce?" ("Hair Today, Art Tomorrow"). The frank sexuality of the Fab Five, which deserves its own analysis, is the subject of the final section of this essay.

And while in *Queer Eye* camp humor might seem to have been drafted in service of the norm (commercialism or heterosexuality), is it possible for camp irreverence to maintain its integrity within the matrix of popular consumer culture, which Goldstein and Sawyer portray as absolutely oppressive? Since the time of Oscar Wilde, if not before, camp humor has been one of gay men's strongest weapons against hypocrisy and the concept of normal. The Fab Five's camp humor is not only important in terms of gay history, but also crucial to the success of the show's project. I would argue that irony and innuendo are in fact responsible for the success of *Queer Eye*, and for its central achievement: keeping open (within a heteronormative consumer/pop culture) a space in which authentic connections between straight and gay men and culture can be forged and sustained — and not just between the show's participants but between the homo- and heterosexual men and women who bond while watching it together or talking about it at work the next day.

Another version of the complaint about stereotypes is that the show confines its gay stars to the role of "body servants" to heterosexual men (Goldstein par. 7). I find this interpretation, which quickly becomes a refrain in commentary about *Queer Eye*, uniquely puzzling, not just in its origin but in the tenacious grip this trope seems to have on some version of gay communal memory. Goldstein, Kanner, and others hold that because gay men have been enslaved for too long (to straight women, apparently), *Queer Eye* constitutes a step backward in queer history. Goldstein sarcastically supposes, "It's a sign of progress that this interchange [between gay and straight men] looks plausible, but it's a measure of how far we *haven't* come that the meeting must be staged on stereotypical ground" (par. 6). He continues:

> The makeover show is a perfect setting for this hedged entente. It offers the illusion of a power exchange within very stylized confines. The queers fuss while the straight guy gets fussed over. Aside from a requisite hug when the work is done (and a playful slap when homo hands stray below the belt), the attended one never touches his attendants. Doesn't this resonate with the most primitive view of gay men? Haven't fags always been consigned to the role of body servant? Aren't they supposed to have a doting eye for the straight guy? And as faux women, aren't they expected to be obsessed with style? [Goldstein par. 7].

It is unclear what period or context Goldstein has in mind, in which gay men served as straight body servants (although his choice of words recalls the stereotypically predatory gay man, precisely the "primitive view of gay men" to which Goldstein objects). Goldstein's reaction to what he views as distasteful sexual baiting is significant, and I will return to this topic in the concluding section.

Writing in *The Gay and Lesbian Review Worldwide*, Kanner attempts a more informed analysis:

> For many decades, some otherwise marginalized gay men have found their way into the mainstream, into the seats and rooms of money and influence, as mascots, mostly for theamusement of straight women. Straight society seems to be able to tolerate a certain amount of gayness, but only in confined quarters. We need theatre, we need dance, we need hairdressers and florists, after all, to enhance the lives of heterosexual married women and their men. Traditionally, gay men serve, entertain, and please. But the accomplishments of gay men outside these domains have rarely been celebrated in the public forum of the mainstream media [36].

One of the flaws in Kanner's position is a striking blindness to those gays who were not stylists, interior designers, or confidants, and so who were always marginalized. Even if the "mascot" (or lapdog) scenario were accurate, would not interacting with straight men — the traditional bogeymen for gays — be an advance? What is most offensive about this analysis is the failure to consider that these mascots did not live their entire lives performing for straight society but had lives and, more emphatically, a subculture of their own and that these highly visible gay men were well paid for their services, wielding a certain amount of expertise and power within their domains. This male underclass which exists only to "serve, entertain, and please" does not resemble the interior designers and stylists I knew as a child and a gay youth. And if one's definition of a mascot is someone who exists merely to enhance the lives of a more privileged set, then those in the swelling ranks of the American service sector equally qualify as lapdogs.[8]

Inspiration for applying the "lapdog" myth to *Queer Eye* may be partly due to the fact that these gay men appear to play second fiddle to their straight counterparts, allowing their skills to be co-opted in service of the tedious heterosexual narrative: getting the girl. Kanner describes it as a sort of homosexual serfdom:

> After sprucing up the straight man's body, house, and cuisine, the Fab Five return to their loft — a sort of queer superhero Bat Cave — to eavesdrop on the unfolding of a gaily enhanced straight romance. Now, as in earlier times, the powers and talents of gay men are being pressed into the service of heterosexual privilege. Remedial therapy in personal care, fashion savvy, and dating service are all directed at a straight guy's romantic life [36].

Christopher Kelly, in part quoting Bob Thompson, director of the Syracuse University Center for the Study of Popular Television, concurs with Kanner:

> The straight couple whose home they have invaded looks upon them with both superiority and delight. They are the ersatz king and queen, welcoming their jesters to court....
>
> Talk about reaffirming heterosexual primacy: the Fab Five are the literal fairy godmothers who help straight dudes hook up and who then return to their own beds alone.
>
> ... "In the end, who's the hero...?" Thompson asks. "It's the straight guy. He's the guy who needs to be rescued so he can either get the girl or the gallery showing. And then they leave before the climax, and they have to watch it on the periphery. Talk about being marginalized — they literally have to watch the climax of the show from the margins.
>
> ... They can't even stay to take their bows" [pars. 2, 7, 22].

Among the oddities in this passage is the monarchical imagery (few of the houses and apartments look anything like a "court" when the Fab Five first arrive) and the insinuating tone (is Kelly indignant, or is he suggesting that the Fab Five should be indignant, about being banished from the straight man's presence without "hook[ing] up"?). Although Kelly takes exception with *Queer Eye*'s use of stereotypes, he himself evokes one of the oldest and most homophobic: the oversexed gay man, incapable of interacting with a straight man without making sexual advances.

Questions of tone aside, if one accepts the premise of the show and further recalls that impressing a girlfriend is not the goal every week (several desire an improved image for career advancement purposes), Kanner's statement requires qualification. And a gallery showing, which Kelly mentions, is hardly the standard telos of the heterosexual male narrative. To be fair, there are a lot of girlfriends involved. Yet both Kelly and Kanner fail to acknowledge the fact that monogamous romantic pairing is the heterosexual narrative, not the Fab Five's invention. Carson, Thom, Kyan, Jai, and Ted are helping heterosexuals fulfill their own quest (unexamined as it may be) to reenact the heteronormative ur-text. Further, a makeover show hardly seems the appropriate forum for serious debate about civil rights and equity.

It is my contention that those who disparage the show so vehemently are — unconsciously or not, no doubt unintentionally, and in fact counter to their declared intentions — advocates for assimilationism. While it seems unwise to conclude that allegations of stereotyping necessarily have assimilationist underpinnings, in this instance it seems true. Assimilation into the mainstream is a common strategy of minorities attempting to gain legal equality by winning social acceptance. For the GLBT community at least, acceptance has all too often been translated into acceptability; the latter is easier to obtain, but becoming acceptable is surreptitiously more costly than being accepted. Presenting a nonthreatening, desexualized, unflamboyant face to the public may be politically expedient, but it is also incompatible with the gay and lesbian community's commitment to diversity, tolerance, and openness, unless that commitment is to be jettisoned. And yet for decades before Stonewall, being versed in style and culture was gay men's province, artistically and socially.

Hemal Jhaveri, writing for *PopPolitics.com*, exemplifies the way in which concern over stereotyping may mask nervousness about traits, behaviors, and personalities that jeopardize assimilation because they are socially (read, publicly) unacceptable:

> By clinging to existing stereotypes, and mainly seeing all gay people as savants of style, we marginalize them and dilute the complicated lives of many. In ignoring gay men's sexuality, we project a condescending tolerance of a lifestyle, implying that homosexuality is well and good, unless it actually involves sex [par. 8].

If I may bracket for a moment the question of the Fab Five's asexuality, it is illuminating to note that Jhaveri, in speaking out against marginalization, is doing some marginalizing of his own. (The use of "we" is vague and worrisome, regardless of Jhaveri's sexuality, which is not indicated.) Is there no longer a place for interior decorators and hairdressers in representations of GLBT persons?[9] Are men who happen to have stereotypically gay occupations not rounded in other, individualized ways? Is effeminacy still unacceptable, even within a queer setting? Leanne Potts, reporting on negative reactions to the show, suggests not: "Critics say the show panders to the widely held belief that all gay men are flaming style mavens. Tom Shales of the *Washington Post* [sic] said the show encouraged a 'patronizing mentality' while Latisha Frederick, an attorney active with the Albuquerque Lesbian and Gay Chamber of Commerce, says the show 'perpetrates stereotypes, both gay and straight'" (par. 23). Accusations about stereotyping are yet more disconcerting, more perniciously dismissive, when one considers, as surprisingly few seem to have done, that in spite of their moniker the Fab Five are not fictional characters — they are real people. The fact, then, that Jhaveri speaks in the same breath of real people (the Fab Five, Chip and Reichen from *The Amazing Race*) and fictional characters (Jack from *Will & Grace*, Keith and David from *Six Feet Under*) suggests either a facile confusion between reality and representation or a discomfort with realities that he passionately does not want represented.

Assimilation into the mainstream appears to require both a near total erasure of difference and a kind of identitarian eugenics to weed out traits, occupations, or behaviors that have been deemed too embarrassing for public view. As gay software engineer Fred Jarina says, "Of course there are some gay stereotypes represented on the show. But there are gay people like that out there. Why should we as gay people be embarrassed by it?" (qtd. in Potts par. 24). If anyone is advocating stereotypes, it seems to be the very individuals who criticize the Fab Five for embodying them; these critics would have us reject a whole host of negative stereotypes for the sake of a single, blanched image: what David Leavitt, in his short story "The Marble Quilt," calls the "'good faggot'" — someone who is not an embarrassment to those at the head of the table or to those who have just recently gained a place at it (495). The recent outcry about *Queer Eye* proves that assimilationism is alive and kicking:

it requires that diversity, the watch cry of the GLBT movement, be absorbed into uniformity — heterosexual or straight-acting uniformity. No nellies, femmes, or lispers need apply. I would argue that what is occurring in *Queer Eye,* by contrast, is not assimilation but integration, an interleaving of gay and straight lives and sensibilities: the creation of a new landscape whose only threat is its novelty, its bravura navigation of what many gays and lesbians assumed for so long — and it seems, sadly, still assume — to be forbidden territory. Goldstein evinces most clearly this uneasiness, as well as the reactionary stigmaphobia from which it issues, when he observes that *Queer Eye* "allows straight and gay men to relate to each other with an ease that seems at once moving and strange, like a sci-fi film from the '50s. But this is not a forbidden planet; it's a world in the making" (par. 10). Despite what Goldstein says, it still in some way feels forbidden.

"Homo Hands" and the Activism of Camping

If the mood evoked by *Queer Eye* is "moving and strange," however, it is so because of the show's flirtation with the forbidden. The show's genius is the way its stars establish a richly ambivalent and complex — to many critics, downright frustrating — relation to stereotypes of gay effeminacy and sexual predation. The American Film Institute ranked the show as one of 2003's nine "moments of significance" because it "brought gay culture to the national fore by spoofing *and* celebrating stereotypes, and unlike other reality shows, [doing] so in a winning and genuine manner that developed a bond between the gay and straight men" ("AFI's Top Film, TV Moments of 2003" par. 26; emphasis added). As Michael Giltz reports for *The Advocate,* "Thom [Filicia] ... resisted being an interior designer because he thought it would embarrass his parents, while Carson [Kressley] avoided fashion because it seemed too gay. [Both are] excited that a new generation of kids, both gay and straight, can grow up seeing their careers celebrated..." (44). By highlighting men whose occupations' stereotypical gayness brands pariahs in a nominally diverse gay and lesbian movement, *Queer Eye* is activist in the best tradition of queers re-appropriating images and words (including "queer") which have been used to stigmatize gays as well as occupations (like hair stylist or interior designer), which gays themselves have marginalized. Bruce Steele, also in *The Advocate*, suggests that

> By playing into gay stereotypes, the Fab Five, paradoxically, lay them to rest. They're so personable and sharp and real that the clichés they embody are magically reconstructed as richly human without the tiniest swatch of shame.... Winning gay and lesbian marriage rights ... will be an uphill effort for years to come, but in a few short weeks *Queer Eye* has high-glossed over centuries of prejudice and fear. It's "We're here, we're queer" with a sensible dose of altruism....
>
> And one of the ultimate joys of *Queer Eye* is this: The Fab Five are reshaping how America sees gay people not because they chose to be activists but because they chose to be designers and gourmets and groomers — to straight eyes, the gayest jobs on the planet. They don't even seem to know or care that they're fighting the good fight, which makes them elusive targets for our enemies.
>
> Who would have thought throw pillows and chocolate mousse could be among the most powerful weapons of social change? [43].

Although Steele gets right the covert activism of focusing the public's attention on five men with "the gayest jobs on the planet," it seems hasty to say the show has "high-glossed over centuries of prejudice and fear," or much less, could attempt to do so. In their rush to crown the Fab Five the new Great Gay Hope, Steele, along with other critics like Jhaveri, Johnson, and Potts, is quick to characterize these goodwill ambassadors as wholly and unrealistically nonthreatening. While I am certainly not questioning the sincerity (or success) of the show's attempt to reach straight viewers, to view the project as anodynic is to miss what makes it a unique and especially promising meeting ground for straights and gays: the overt sexuality which, along with camping, makes a significant portion of both audiences so deeply, if unadmittedly, nervous.

The fear is that sexualized homosexuality will only exacerbate the historic estrangement between hetero- and homosexual men. The straight men are "subjected to no small amount of ribbing and flirtation," "alternately poked at and shoved aside by the team's flood of energy" (Johnson par. 4); the Fab Five constitute a "slashy bitchpit," whose "hissy onslaught" their "makeover candidates ... weather ... with steel-plated patience and courtesy" (Sawyer par. 6). Among the most vocal is Kelly, who denounces *Queer Eye* as "execrable — a catalog of homosexual stereotypes played to a throbbing, techno-disco beat, that also systematically denies its gay stars their complexity and their sexuality. From first scene to last, they trill and fuss, displaying their talents at traditionally effeminate tasks. The straight guy ... stands back, endures some innocuous flirting and emerges as the ultimate hero stud" (par. 6). Kelly's nervousness about the show's humor leads to the odd conclusion that the Fab Five are at once oversexed ("trill and fuss") and neutered ("denie[d] ... their sexuality)—an ambivalence best summed up in the phrase "innocuous flirting." Dismissing flirtation with straight men as "innocuous" misses the reality that it is still taboo, inappropriate, and, around the wrong crowd, dangerous. The implication is that the straight man is embarrassed, while the Fab Five have embarrassed an entire community by reinforcing the stereotype of the sex-obsessed nelly queen. Kelly insinuates as well that gay men who "trill" like queens should be ashamed, too, or at least ashamed enough not to trill in mixed company. And I think this chagrin is at work in almost every discussion of *Queer Eye*. As Michael Warner asks, "Can it be very surprising if those who are most concerned with winning respect"—whether queers themselves or heterosexuals concerned on their behalf—"might find themselves wishing that their peers in shame would be a little less queer, a little more decent?" (50).

Perhaps it is this feeling of shame that deters critics from citing specific examples of the show's sexual humor. Checking on Tom Kaden in a dressing cubicle, Carson exclaims, "Oh dear God, it's huge ... the belt" ("Make Room for Lisa"). In many, but not all, of the episodes, Carson is likely to address the straight man with some version of the following: "If at any time today, you want to make out with me, just let me know" ("Make Room"). Carson may not be flirting in earnest, but his jokes hardly shy away from the specifics of gay male desire. When Kyan and Carson accompany Adam Zalta to a day spa, Carson goes over the man's back with an exfoliating brush, observing, "It's just like currying my pony. My Pretty Pony"; when Kyan asks, "Does that feel good?" Carson adds, "Wait till I brush your *ass*" ("A Great Mess in Great Neck"). Standing back to see how an outfit looks on another man, James M., Carson remarks, "God, you're so hot. If I didn't know you, I'd try to lure you to a roadside rest area" ("Training Day"). Whether referencing anal sex or queer public sex culture, Carson obfuscates the nonthreatening atmosphere which he also sincerely fosters.

While Carson may be the most sexually verbal (for which he has received the brunt of criticism), none of the Fab Five refrains from physical contact with the straight men. Even though the touching is never predatory, whether it occurs in conjunction with a compliment or not, this physical contact seems to produce most unease in critics and viewers.[10] Goldstein, in a passage quoted earlier, observes the "playful slap [from the straight man] when homo hands stray below the belt" (par. 7). The incident to which he is referring has occurred only once in the series, when, in the first show aired, Brian Schepel jokes about keeping a tally of how many times Carson tries to help him tuck in his shirt; but even then it is a playful slap. To understand the degree of Goldstein's discomfort, one needs to review the entire sentence from which this comes: "Aside from a requisite hug when the work is done (and a playful slap when homo hands stray below the belt), the attended one never touches his attendants." Given the fact that this is just not true (the Fab Five touch each week's guest repeatedly), we can only speculate: is the mere fact of physical contact so embarrassing that it must be denied?[11] Or is it the mixed signals of the Fab Five — sexual innuendo and flirtation side by side with matter-of-fact conversation and neutral physical contract — which have to be misstated rather than discussed openly? I cannot know which is the case with Goldstein, but if it were the latter, he would at least have fathomed the show's method even if he regarded it as madness. Carson, for example, is both embodying a stereotype (as if to say, "you expect this of me, the loud nelly queen") and also camping his own performance ("you don't know that I am like this"); in short, fulfilling and lampooning our expectations, holding both the cartoon and its possible reality in ambivalent tension. What few seem to consider (or perhaps, refuse to consider) is that Carson is genuinely like that, even if (and this is the mind blower for many heterosexuals and some queers) he is not always like that. Likewise, by telling a man he has dressed, "you're hot," Carson is, on the one hand, simply admiring his own aesthetic creation. On the other hand, "you're hot" stands as an index of the constantly lurking prospect of gay desire for the male (in this case, heterosexual) body. Never fully acknowledged or dismissed, this erotic potentiality is constitutive of gay male experience, a constant possibility of pleasure and/or fear which the far-from-neutered *Queer Eye* reminds us is inescapable whenever gay and straight worlds meet.

Queer Eye succeeds because it is more than a PR campaign, periodically re-marking the differences between gay and straight culture as it paves over others. Admirers have at times hastened to gloss over the show's subversive embrace of the queen and the sexualized gay man. Kanner writes, "In each episode there's a flirtation and a sexually provocative scene, usually launched by Carson and understood to be playful and harmless when taken in context" (37). The flirtation on *Queer Eye* is playful, and perhaps harmless in the sense of not being a real sexual advance (though notice how many critics single out Carson, the most unapologetic about his mannerisms or desires). As Ben Patrick Johnson perceptively notes, the show's producers

> approach their audience on multiple levels. They put on a noisy big-top show while engaging the pathos of both sides of what has long been a broad cultural divide. In the process, *Queer Eye* runs a certain risk perpetuating stereotypes — the lisping gay man, the predator, the mincing, bitter, cultural aesthete. But the show's title includes a former gay slur, queer, which has been appropriated by the gay political movement as a term of prideful self-identification. Not surprisingly, the show, like its title, speaks from a position of empowerment [par. 12].

Johnson skirts the show's real daring, underplaying sexualized queeniness in an attempt, once again, not to alienate readers for whom "queer" or "queen" is unthinkable as a "term of prideful self-identification."

As Bruce Steele points out, the purpose is in fact to resurrect stereotypes, to flaunt gay sexuality and celebrate the erotic charge of the male body: "They even effortlessly refute the canard of the predatory gay man...: They slap and tickle, and everyone gets the joke. Flirting is just good fun, not a sexual assault. In a way that must drive [Supreme Court Justice Antonin] Scalia crazy, the Fab 5 are both aggressively sexual *and* nonthreatening" (43). I would suggest, however, that *Queer Eye* succeeds precisely because it punctures mutual, unspoken tensions between gays and straights and promotes merchandising, which is the show's financially obligatory window dressing.[12] It is gay men's fear of being sexual, being whole people, around straight men, that maintains the distance between the two. The same fear, as stigmaphobia, keeps gay men constantly monitoring the language and mannerisms of themselves and others and creates the impulse to distance themselves from anyone who fails to behave appropriately (read, queens) in front of the heterosexuals. Yet the straying "homo hands" to which a panicked Goldstein refers are reaching for a prize more complex than empowerment, a state of actualization and exchange which is less static. The show's sensibility refuses to sugarcoat the still appreciable gap between two cultures (or rather, between two different concepts of dignity and normality).

The Fab Five's camp humor and active sexualization (of themselves and straight men), coupled with their sincerity and objective advice, is their bravest, most subversive and thus politically effective, act.[13] This is unapologetic camping: their flirting is not innocuous; flirting with straight men is sexualizing them, at once dismissing and embracing the stereotype of the predatory queen. For admitting that straight men have bodies and that gay men are attracted to men is both to reject the notion that gay men lust after every straight man they meet and also to admit, that, given the fact that straight men have the bodies to which queers are physically attracted, this is not always necessarily untrue. The bravura of this dangerous move lies in its innovation: camping not in the safety of a gay bar or the privacy of a circle of friends, but in front of straight men and straight viewers; and (again in contrast to minstrelsy) camping not for the amusement of others at one's own expense or the expense one's community, but for the edification of others. Aggressive camping, including flirtation, means bringing to the fore what potentially may embarrass both the camping queen and his audience, saying not just "this is who we are" (which smacks of entreaty), but also "this is who we can be." This ambiguity liberates because it threatens, extending a friendly hand on the basis of the common ground shared by gays and straights while, with the other hand, retaining a firm grasp on what will always, for better and for worse, set us apart. As Kressley is quoted in an *Advocate* interview, "'We're not cartoonish, and we're not pretending to be supergay or superstraight or whatever. We're just being ourselves. I'm not going to make any excuses for who I am, and I don't think any of these guys are either'" (44). Being afraid of nelling out or letting slip a "she" in reference to a man defeats the purpose of being out in the first place. The Fab Five are welcome if rare counterevidence to Michael Warner's statement that "homosexuals were and still are afraid to be seen as queer" (65).

The risk is that some viewers, particularly some straight men, will not be disarmed by "good-natured bitchiness," much less willing to believe that the show's premise is "sincere rather than ironic" (Kanner 35).[14] It would be naive to forget that, despite pronounced shifts in cultural attitudes, some people will always be offended by queers, and this is not limited to those who will always hate them as well. Heteronormativity is profoundly deep-seated, inscribed too indelibly to be overcome, whether in a moment, a television show, or a movement. Even among the liberal and gay-friendly, some will inevitably be put off by this gesture or that joke. Moments such as these jar us all out of thinking we are fundamentally the same, reminding us that not every jagged anomaly can be subsumed in a sea of bland uniformity, for that seems deadly to a polity framed in checks and balances, sustained by friction and conflict. Genuine tolerance brings passions and aversions into sharp relief and requires us to navigate them, not blithely countenance them. Self-editing by queers does heterosexuals a disservice by implying that in their heart of hearts queers just want to be normal, and does queers themselves a disservice by suggesting, not so much that they can be normal but, contrary to a long communal tradition of critiquing the "natural," that anyone can.

Vociferous reactions to *Queer Eye*, negative or positive, confirm the clarity with which the show delivers truths that many viewers, acclimated to a normalizing gay and lesbian movement, find unacceptable and regressive. Those truths are that gay men are not straight; that norms are invidious; that gay men, according to the best insights of a collective past predicated on "resist[ing] normalization," are not normal; and that alliances which are possible between straight and gay culture do not eradicate those alliances which are not (Warner 143). *Queer Eye* is an antidote to a notion targeted by Michael Warner in *The Trouble with Normal* and all too evident in the responses to *Queer Eye*: namely, that "the way to overcome stigma is to win acceptance by the dominant culture, rather than to change the self-understanding of that culture," to question the "desire for a conformity that ... can never be fully achieved," to resist a "betrayal of the abject and the queer in favor of banalized respectability" (Warner 50, 43, 66).[15] I am not lauding a sort of victim pathology, espousing opposition for its own sake, and I am not saying *Queer Eye* does so, either. On the contrary, I believe *Queer Eye* teaches us the value of retaining a sense of what is absurd, fabulous, unifying, alienating, non-normative, disruptive, and even banal about our lives and desires, gay or straight.

Notes

Early talks with Karl Woelz helped me delineate in a fresh context the core issues of an old debate. His voice in those conversations lingers here and there. Karl, along with Kim van Alkemade, Martha Wickelhaus, and Dev Hathaway, generously read progressive drafts, and their careful questions and advice provoked numerous improvements. Thanks also to Merry Perry, who encouraged me to present part of an earlier version of the essay at the 2004 PCA/ACA Conference in San Antonio, and to Gerald Mulderig, who moderated the panel in which I was fortunate enough to participate.

1. Not all response has been negative, obviously. The show's pilot episode garnered Bravo its second highest ratings ever, and NBC, which had recently acquired Bravo, was quickly running thirty-minute-formatted episodes after summer repeats of its own highly rated show *Will & Grace*, creating the first network gay programming block. In December 2003 the American Film Institute supplemented its annual ten-best lists in TV and film with a list of nine "moments of significance": *Queer Eye* was number two.

2. While some of the *Queer Eye* commentary dealt with comes from the academy or from industrial media organs such as *The Advocate*, a number of responses come from internet-based publications such as *PopMatters* or *PopPolitics.com* or discussion threads on sites such as *Snarkfest*— what I would argue are, comparatively, "everyday" viewers; that is, the latter voices, borne on the medium of the internet, are more democratic, whether they are freelance professionals or amateurs.

3. One notable exception is Christopher Kelly, writing in August 2003: "In the summer when a conservative Supreme Court has struck down Texas' anti-sodomy laws — surely the most momentous step forward for gay civil rights in this country — here is a show that portrays straight people and gay people as one happy community, bonding over foie gras, Lucky Brands Jeans and the virtues of eyebrow waxing" (par. 5).

4. Warner prefers the term "normalizing" to "assimilationist" (52). Semantics aside, the same "hierarchy of respectability" that Warner delineates in the history of American gay and lesbian politics can be seen at work in discussions of *Queer Eye*, both in gay and mixed forums — discussions which, as this essay shows, are "built on embarrassment" (49). As Warner observes, negotiations of the last ten years for gay rights have, on the national level certainly, involved a quest for "respectability," "bargain[ing] for a debased psuedodignity, the kind that is awarded as a bribe for disavowing the indignity of sex and the double indignity of a politics built around sex" — and by extension, of a politics built around queers as sexualized beings (78, 66). I would connect much of the negative response to *Queer Eye* to the impulse, felt and acted on by the most well-meaning politically aware queers and straights alike, to hold at arm's length those more embarrassing members of queer culture, individuals whom it is too easy — and yet incorrect, inauthentic, and impoverishing — to dismiss as stereotypes. "The others, the queers who have sex in public toilets" (or at least joke about it as Carson does), "the boys who flaunt it as pansies or as leathermen," those "whose gender deviance makes them unassimilable to the menu of sexual orientations, the clones in the so-called gay ghetto ... — all these flaming creatures are told that their great moment of liberation will come later ... when we get to be about 'more than sexuality.'..." (Warner 66).

5. As Chasin notes, however, the DINK myth was soon exploded by new studies revealing the skewed sample on which the original marketing reports had been based — largely, white, affluent males (see Chasin 33–40). The studies to which Chasin refers can be found in Gluckman and Reed.

6. The negative reactions to the 1960s television show *Julia* illustrate the way in which even apparently progressive images are doomed to be labeled as damaging stereotypes. Yet as Ben Patrick Johnson, writing online for *Kiosque*, observes, using either Diahann Carroll or the Fab Five as benchmarks of inauthenticity is unfair and illogical: "Collectively, [the Fab Five] don't represent gay men as a whole any more than Diahann Carroll represented black women when her fictional character Julia appeared ... in 1968. No one TV program can demonstrate the breadth of a culture [or subculture].... Thankfully, *Queer Eye* knows better than to pretend to such importance — to do so would be absurd..." (par. 12).

7. The one gripe about representation with partial validity comes from Hemal Jhaveri, according to whom *Queer Eye* observes what seems to be "the rule for gay men on TV: cute, white, charming, and totally asexual" (par. 9). Aside from failing to explain how Jai Rodriguez and Thom Filicia qualify as "white," Jhaveri is correct about the generally overbearing whiteness of pop culture representation. And yet the same charge can be levied at straight shows (*Friends*) as well as gay ones (*Will & Grace*). For another invocation of minstrelsy, see Sawyer pars. 1 and 12.

8. Andrew Sullivan is quite right to point out that the airing of *Queer Eye* hardly equals the legalization of marriage. On the other hand, Sullivan's advocacy of gay marriage (see *Same-Sex Marriage: Pro and Con* [New York: Vintage, 1997]) is driven — in a way that perceptive analysts like Michael Warner find particularly troubling — by a quest more to be seen as normal than to secure equity under the law. In this context, Sullivan's reading of the show's invidious dynamic is simply another (albeit, more Foucaultian) version of Kelly's minstrelsy analogy or Sawyer's and

Kanner's "body servant" trope: "It seems as if heterosexuals are willing to tolerate homosexuals, but only from a position of power.... [A]rguing that [a] lesbian couple is morally indistinguishable from a straight couple is where many draw the line" (35). Sullivan could not be more on target in unmasking the unspoken homophobia and entitlement that makes even the most tolerant citizens, or those who admit the rational basis of queer claims to legal parity, balk at the line in the sand that is gay marriage. Yet as an analyst of *Queer Eye*, Sullivan conflates its appropriation of the heterosexual narrative (get the girl) with an endorsement of heteronormativity as the natural order from which the Fab Five accept their exclusion. My discussion of the realities of stereotyping and camp humor in *Queer Eye* demonstrate, I hope, that the latter is not the case.

9. The Fab Five's stereotypical occupations, along with their camping and frank sexual humor, render them threatening — and, to borrow Christopher Kelly's word, "execrable"— enough to a gay movement which has spent the last decade courting the mainstream in media and politics to justify the sort of attacks we see here. Michael Warner locates this sort of "identity ambivalence" at the heart of the contemporary national gay and lesbian movement (43). Garnering political representation and mainstream cultural presence for gays and lesbians in 1990s was accompanied by (and Warner argues, dependent upon) a shift toward "stigmaphobia," a quest for queer dignity apart from sex that is both grounded in and generative of shame about the "apparent indignity" of queer sex (74). (The term "stigmaphobia," along with the corollary "stigmaphilia," derives from Erving Goffman's *Stigma: Notes on the Management of a Spoiled Identity* [1963; New York: Touchstone, 1986].)

10. In a workshop I conducted in April 2004 for undergraduates involved in college and university GLBT activism and education, a number of participants (student and adult) voiced their discomfort with Carson's physical contact with the straight men, stating that Carson was "going too far" or that they, as viewers, "could tell [the man] was uncomfortable."

11. Not only do the straight men routinely allow themselves to be touched and flirted with, some of them even respond in kind. While shopping for tableware with Thom at Pier 1, Tom Kaden says, "Next thing you know, I'll have a boyfriend" ("Make Room"). Kaden, later referencing Carson's flirting while helping previous guests get dressed, offers to help Carson with *his* fly.

12. I would further question such a portrayal of consumer culture's absolute deadening power. If those who criticize *Queer Eye* are not turned into mindless shopping drones, why should it follow that viewers who enjoy the show *are?*

13. Gay men flirting with straight men is radical and subversive when some see this as reason enough to kill: on trial for the 1999 murder of Matthew Shepard, Aaron McKinney and Russell Henderson claimed "homosexual panic" as their defense. The legal failure of this tactic does not diminish the fact that it was, even to the perpetrators, a credible and intuitive defense.

14. To Kanner, "Carson Kressley's wit is sharp and quick ... delivered in a style that's undoubtedly too flamboyant for many straight viewers and too stereotypical for many gay ones" (35). And to judge from a series of postings on *Snarkfest.com*, she may be right. Jason, who initiates the discussion thread after reading the Terry Sawyer piece cited above, complains that "the presumption of the Fab Five and the

largely female audience watching is that there is something majorly wrong with straight men ... based completely on the way that they dress up and accessorize their lives" ("Few Straight Guys Watching Queer Eye" par. 4). Isn't what's really threatening not a makeover per se (after all, the ultracasual, just-rolled-out-of-bed look now in vogue was itself tweaked if not created by the industry) but a makeover *explicitly* at the hands of gay men? If what lurks unverbalized in the comments on *Snarkfest* is not the clichéd fear of "catching it" then it is a deeply ingrained, if unconscious, distaste for the company of openly gay men — which amounts to the same thing: according to Erin, the Fab Five "are a bunch of wannabe women, judging straight guys on their apprence [sic].... [H]ere we have 5 gay guys walking into a male hetero-sexual's [sic] life, verbally bashing it, and taking away any last bit of manhood he had left.... What kind of hetero-sexual man, in his right mind, would allow another gay man to judge him...??" (par. 25). Queer sexuality has made the gay man eligible for membership in that most repulsive of categories — the castrating bitch.

At the same time that these comments reemphasize how much work there is still do in terms of overcoming homophobia and opening channels of communication, the comments' vehemence attests to *Queer Eye*'s popularity with straight women, whose whetted desire for a well-groomed boyfriend emerges as terrifyingly palpable: "A friend said to me that when she watches the show she is in total agreeance with everything the fab five says. She can see everything that's wrong about the guy and that they are all things that women complain about all the time. They are the things that every woman wants to change about her man" (par. 9). The greatest threat may be not be a haircut or a coffee table; it may be conciliation, change, or even the contemplation of changing anything within the male perimeter. What emerges from the postings most clearly — and is perhaps most disheartening in terms of overcoming rigid conceptions of gender and sexuality — is an almost divine feeling of (or desire to feel) imperviousness to change:

> [I]f [one] checked on these guys 6 months later she would find them in their overalls and jeans, probably with bushy eyebrows and unkempt facial hair. They may still have the clothes and the shoes ... but they probably haven't done any more.... [I]f it wasn't already part of their general routine, they would not be adding trips to the upscale shop to buy new shirts.... They are making these changes to make someone else happy and not themselves [pars. 12–13].

15. *Queer Eye* is not ashamed to ally itself with what Warner describes as the "stigmaphile space ... where we find a commonality with those who suffer from stigma, and in this alternative realm learn to value the very things the rest of the world despises — not just because the world despises them, but because the world's pseudomorality is a phobic and inauthentic way of life" (43).

Works Cited

"AFI's Top Film, TV, Moments of 2003." *HollywoodReporter.com*. 16 Dec. 2003. 16 Dec. 2003. http://www.hollywoodreporter.com/thr/film/article_display.jsp?vnu_content_id=2-52526.

"A Great Mess in Great Neck." *Queer Eye for the Straight Guy.* Bravo-TV. Episode 102. 15 July 2003.

Chasin, Alexandra. *Selling Out: The Gay and Lesbian Movement Goes to Market.* New York: Palgrave, 2000.

Duralde, Alonso. "Tunes Queer for the Straight Ear." *The Advocate.* 30 March 2003: 61.

"Few Straight Guys Watching Queer Eye." Online posting. 30 July–30 Nov. 2003. 3 Dec. 2003. http://www.snarkfest.com/reruns/000337.php

Giltz, Michael. "Queer Eye Confidential." *The Advocate.* 2 Sept. 2003: 40–44.

Gluckman, Amy, and Betsy Reed. *Homo Economics: Capitalism, Community, and Lesbian and Gay Life.* New York: Routledge, 1997.

Goldstein, Richard. "What Queer Eye?: Are the Fab Five a Breakthrough or a Stereotype?" *The Village Voice.* 23–29 July 2003. 3 Dec. 2003. http://www.villagevoice.com/issues/0330/goldstein.php.

"Hair Today, Art Tomorrow." *Queer Eye for the Straight Guy.* Bravo-TV. Episode 101. 15 July 2003.

Jhaveri, Hemal. "Searching for a Gay Man." *PopPolitics.com.* 16 Nov. 2003. 3 Dec. 2003. http://www.poppolitics.com/articles/2003-10-22-gaytv.shtmhl.

Johnson, Ben Patrick. "A Queer Eye on Stereotypes and Ad Revenue: How Gay TV Breaks Ground on Main Street and Madison Avenue." *Kiosque.* 3 Dec. 2003. 4 Dec. 2003. http://www.culturekiosque.com/nouvelle/tele/queereye.html.

Kanner, Melinda. "Questions for *Queer Eye.*" *The Gay and Lesbian Review Worldwide* 9.2 (March-April 2004): 35–37.

Kelly, Christopher. "Gay TV Making Great Strides in Exactly the Wrong Direction." *MiamiHerald.com.* 26 Aug. 2003. 15 March 2004. http://www.miami.com/mld/miamiherald/entertainment/6618804.htm.

Leavitt, David. "The Marble Quilt." *The Marble Quilt.* New York: Houghon Mifflin, 2001. Rpt. in *Collected Stories.* New York: Bloomsbury, 2003. 489–525.

"Make Room for Lisa." *Queer Eye for the Straight Guy.* Bravo-TV. Epsiode 103. 22 July 2003.

Potts, Leanne. "Queer Eye Makes Over View of Homosexuals." *ABQJournal.* 12 Aug. 2003. 3 Dec. 2003. http://www.abqjournal.co/shock/72103personalties08-12-03.htm.

"Queer Eye for the Skate Guy." *Queer Eye for the Straight Guy.* Episode 123. Bravo-TV. 9 March 2004.

Steele, Bruce C. "The Gay Rights Makeover." *The Advocate.* 2 Sept. 2003: 42–43.

Sawyer, Terry. "Blind Leading the Bland." *PopMatters.* 22 July 2003. 3 Dec. 2003. http://www.popmatters.com/tv/reviews/q/queer-eye-for-the-straigt-guy.shtml.

Sullivan, Andrew. "Beware the Straight Backlash." *Time.* 11 Aug. 2003: 35.

"Training Day." *Queer Eye for the Straight Guy.* Episode 123. Bravo-TV. 23 March 2004.

Warner, Michael. *The Trouble with Normal: Sex, Politics, and the Ethics of Queer Life.* Cambridge: Harvard University Press, 1999.

Embattled Sex: Rise of the Right and Victory of the Queer in *Queer as Folk*

Rebecca Clare Beirne

A central tenet of much of gay and lesbian political thought is visibility. Television in particular has been widely fetishized as the ultimate conferrer of visibility, with the potential to "permanently [tear] the closet door off its hinges" (Judell). It is thus one of the most hotly contested cultural media, for while the importance of gay and lesbian visibility in the wider culture is almost universally agreed upon, a consensus regarding who is to be made visible, to represent us, is much more difficult to achieve. There is disagreement between those within the gay and lesbian community who want to control or modify behavior to promote conformity and, therefore, moral equivalency with the heterosexual mainstream, and those who revel in their difference and insist that society itself must be diversified (and sexualized). Many of the characters in the Showtime series *Queer as Folk* voice pro-assimilationist views, and the narrative impulse of the text is toward the "responsibility" and "marriage-like relationship[s]" (Seidman 133) favoured within assimilationist politics. The rhetorical conflict is presented as a war of images and capital between those who try to integrate homosexuals into the mainstream (via "normalizing" and desexualizing their practices) and those who intervene in, sexualize, and "queer" the mainstream.

Although several of the characters in the series are portrayed as assimilationist (Ted, Lindsey, Melanie, and sometimes Michael), *Queer as Folk* ultimately positions itself as anti-assimilationist (at least as far as sex is concerned), with the most direct and explicitly political intervention into this debate being situated in episode 203, which constructs (hyperbolic) fictional proponents of assimilationist views in order to deconstruct them. The confrontational images of sexual and sexually "deviant" homosexuals attempt to construct a counterdiscourse to the desexualized representations of gay men often found in television and much of mainstream cinema. These images constitute an attempt to rejuvenate a sexual politics reminiscent of Queer Nation,[1] which is given a broader audience through Brian's commodification of gayness in his advertising campaigns, and by implication, through the existence of *Queer as Folk* itself. The condemnation of exclusionary and desexualizing practices is, however, undermined in *Queer as Folk* through similar practices within the series where queerness is inaccessible terrain to all but a handful of gay white men.

The effort to erase sex from the public image of homosexuality is most explicitly attacked in episode 203, where a gay television show (*Gay as Blazes*), a gay conservative writer, and a gay and lesbian center represent the (gay) conservative attack on the centrality of sex to homosexual identity. The episode suggests that these arguments are potentially very convincing, but fatally flawed, and thus it provides a critique of arguments against public representations of gay sexuality. These devices also constitute a rebuttal to criticism that the first season was socially irresponsible. As Ausiello has noted, "not every critic is convinced that [*Queer as Folk*] doesn't engage its own form of backhanded gaybashing," and the series as well has been "condemned [for] ... playing into the stereotype that gay male life is an endless round of drug-riddled, indiscriminate couplings" (McFadden). In the effort to determine effective political strategies against homophobia and heterosexism, the representation of sex has been the central flashpoint. The positive manner in which sex is presented in episode 203 echoes the general sense of affirmation in the series: as Michael proclaims in the first scene of the first episode, gay life is "all about sex." In episode three of the second season, those who attempt to obfuscate images of gays as sex-centered[2] are exposed as hypocrites and liars, or as moral cowards unwilling to take any position that could harm their financial status, thereby jeopardizing their privileged social position. The audience is further persuaded against the sex-conservative rhetoric as it forms the basis of an attack on a number of the main characters to which the narrative is sympathetic.

It is worthwhile to examine in close detail the three instances in which the sexdebate is presented in this episode. Let us first look at *Gay as Blazes*—a satire of the type of television program that the critics of *Queer as Folk* might like to see. *Gay as Blazes* is an idealized gay world, devoid of tawdry connections to promiscuous sex and populated by a racially diverse group of upper-class, responsible citizens. The title *Gay as Blazes* is significant in its use of the term "gay" as opposed to "queer." The former term here (and in much of the contemporary U.S. movement) is mobilized to signify the normalized, desexualized homosexual, while the latter term alludes to the unapologetic, hypersexual homosexual (though at other points in the narrative the two adjectives are used fairly interchangeably).

Gay as Blazes includes a musical score reminiscent of a daytime soap opera, a requisite (Austen-esque) disapproval of the dancing, drug taking, and illicit sex at Club Sodom, and a castigation of those who allow themselves to "become a stereotype, instead of a role model for the community" (*QAF* 203). *Gay as Blazes* is resolutely not about sex, and yet in each of the two scenes depicted, the dialogue focuses wholly upon sex, albeit upon a rebuke of the same. Even Michael's statement regarding *Queer as Folk*—"it's all about sex" (101)—is inverted in this episode when he says: "the whole point of *G.A.B.* is it's not all about sex. There's more to gay life than that!"

While the latter is depicted as a valid point, the episode undercuts the characters in *Gay as Blazes*, characterizing their denial of sex as unrealistic and potentially untrue. Brian's response to the assertion, "it's important that the straight world sees realistic portrayals of us," is to call into question whether the respectable gays in *Gay as Blazes* are in fact more realistic, and also to ask "who gives a flying fuck what straight people think?" His interrogatives are intended to problematize two of the main assumptions upon which the politics of assimilation operate: firstly that "the stereotype" is not the truth, and secondly that gay culture should attempt to define and modify its behaviour in response to the potentially negative perceptions of heterosexuals.

Queer as Folk's critique of *Gay as Blazes* as a symbol of assimilationist discourse contains two main assumptions: the first is that conservative assertions of this type deny the basis of sexual identity and closet the "reality" of gay life in an effort to make homosexuality acceptable to the dominant culture; the second assumption is that attacks upon sexual diversity within the community promote the idea that "[i]ndividuals who do not conform to ... social norms may be considered deviant and inferior and will not necessarily merit respect and integration" (Seidman 150). Moreover, this assimilationist assumption implies that civil rights are not rights but "reward[s] [granted] by society for good behaviour" (Vaid 182).

Michael Warner discusses the distinction between stigma, in which a person is permanently tainted by their disgrace, a "social identity which befalls one like fate" (28), and ordinary shame that is related to deviant conduct. This distinction between stigma and shame illuminates the attempt to divorce gay identity from the sexual acts and desires implicit in that identity. *Gay as Blazes*' characters share with Warner's conservative gays a common perception of gay identity and its relation to shame. Both

> ... will have you know that their dignity is founded on being gay, which in their view has nothing to do with sex. If others are having sex — or too much sex or sex that is too deviant — then those people have every reason to be ashamed.... [they] challenge the stigma on identity, but only by reinforcing the shame of sex [31].

The characters in *Gay as Blazes* frequently reiterate their hyperbolic views on the inevitable equation of sex to shame, perhaps most interestingly demonstrated when they shame one of their own number for knowing a little too much about Club Sodom. When one of their company adds "and have sex" to the list of scandalous activities engaged in at Club Sodom, the remainder of the group look at each other and then at him in a pointed manner. A few horrified and withering glances are all that is needed to compel him to clarify, "so I've heard." Their denial of a relationship between gay identity and homosexual sex reinforces the perception that homosexual acts are perverse and shameful. If such an approach were indeed to be successful, the most it could achieve would be to bring about a state of virtual or conditional equality (to use Vaid's terms).

The vigorous critique of antisex assimilationist rhetoric in the episode is continued through the undermining of "the gay social conscience of Pittsburgh"—Howard Bellweather, who is emblematic of prominent gay conservative writers such as Bruce Bawer, Andrew Sullivan, and William Eskridge[3] and their renunciation of the sexual nature and the irresponsibility of the type of gay club culture depicted in *Queer as Folk*. Their argument rests on the view that there is a "rest of us"—a large culture of moral, respectable gays—who are given a bad name by a few deviants. Bellweather criticizes the presentation of Brian Kinney with a heroism award (for saving his lover Justin's life after a gaybashing), arguing that "Mr. Kinney is a miserable example of a modern gay stereotype—totally promiscuous, completely vain ... he can be found nightly in backrooms and sex clubs." Bellweather, citing Brian's sexual relationship with his "eighteen year old teenage lover," Justin, calls him a "pedophile deserving of not our honour but our contempt." Both the rhetoric and the content of Bellweather's attack upon Brian are reminiscent of the religious right's accusations of promiscuity, narcissism, and pedophilia against the gay community. The narrative implies that it is only through the denigration of others that the "gay conservative" identity can be formed, and that such an identity is ethically flawed and manifests an internalized homophobia and self-loathing.

Bellweather's acceptance speech for his "most outstanding gay advocate award" from the Gay and Lesbian Center contains both a civilizing impulse and a claim that gays perpetuate, if not cause, homophobia through their own irresponsible behaviour:

> How can we complain of being stereotyped, of being marginalized, when it is often members of our own community who, through their irresponsible behaviour, perpetuate such treatment. We are our own worst enemy, and so we must raise ourselves up by our [cut to].... In conclusion, it is up to us to change the misperception that gay life is all about sex. This is the gauntlet I throw down to you, to prove we are the concerned, committed citizens [that] we in truth are. Thank you.

The repeated usage of "we" in this speech is strange, as the speech concurrently unifies the gay community and posits a clear divide within it, placing responsibility to clean up their behavior not only on those who are irresponsible, but also on those who are "concerned, committed citizens." Bellweather's attempt to control the sexuality of others in order to render his own more respectable, can be seen as a further product of sexual shame: "On top of having ordinary sexual shame, and on top of having shame for being gay, the dignified homosexual also feels ashamed of every queer who flaunts his sex and his faggotry, making the dignified homosexual's stigma all the more justifiable in the eyes of straights" (Warner 32). This discourse thereby consents to the persecution of those whose sex is stigmatized by the dominant morality and ignores the liberal humanist notion that all human beings are worthy of respect — the same notion invoked by all those who demand gay and lesbian rights, including gay conservatives.

Bellweather's position and persona are primarily undermined by his attendance at a sex party for "barebackers" (practitioners of unsafe sex). This outing positions him as both irresponsible and sexually deviant, rendering his attack on Brian hypocritical. Despite the fact that no attempt is made to out him within the series, the same is nevertheless achieved through the audience of *Queer as Folk*, who are the same public that the producers are attempting to influence. Symbolically, it demonstrates the potential harm Bellweather can do to the gay community with his own irresponsible behavior, potentially spreading AIDS as well as a divisive and damaging message about the gay community. There is thus an explicit contrast drawn between those who are labelled irresponsible on the basis of a subjective moral principle and those who are irresponsible in practice, their behavior putting themselves and others at risk. His refusal to protect himself from a potentially fatal disease may reveal a subconscious wish to be punished for his homosexuality.

Toward the end of episode 203, Ted remarks, "[I] still believe in what he says, even if I don't believe in him." It is significant that the support for Bellweather comes from Ted, not because he is more conservative than the rest of the group (although we do find out later that he is a registered republican), but because in this episode, he has been engaged in a pornography and masturbation binge that has cost him his job, and the audience is aware that unlike the other *Queer as Folk* characters, he has had unprotected sex (111). That the future owner of "jerkatwork.com" whose fantasy is to be Brian Kinney, should be so interested in distancing gay identity from gay sex is curious, and it is just this ambiguity that *Queer as Folk* uses to underline the contradictions, tensions, and potential hypocrisy accompanying such beliefs. Ted's statement, however, also undermines the manner in which the characters of *Queer as Folk* take on Bellweather, suggesting that attacking ideas on the basis of their proponent's behaviour is ineffective. This method avoids engaging directly with ideas and ethics associated with sex and sexual shaming, and so can never really articulate a convincing counterargument. Instead, it undermines Bellweather's ideas through the same method that Bellweather uses, characterizing the subject under attack as more deviant and more dangerous than the individual who offers the criticism.

While Bellweather and *Gay as Blazes* seek to gain political currency by dissociating themselves from sex, Brian directly engages in queer sex as well as the aesthetic and style of the gay stereotype, and this is portrayed as perhaps the most effective political strategy within *Queer as Folk*. Visibility is achieved both in and through the text by selling gayness — both as a means of marketing to the straight population through the "sexiness quotient" and as a lucrative consumer market that can be tapped into by businesses. Due to Brian's position as an advertising executive, the text has frequent opportunity to raise the issue of the "pink dollar" and show the rigidly individualist Brian challenging the homophobia of wealthy capitalists via an appeal to their individual fiscal interests.

Various characters argue against this notion, most prominently Lindsey and Debbie, who advocate the boycott strategies common to left wing political causes. Lindsey accuses Brian of colluding with someone who "hates us" (episode 204), suggesting that he may indeed be a sellout or traitor. In these instances, however, his strategies generally gain success for himself as well as positive outcomes for gays and lesbians, and are thereby portrayed as having more wide-reaching cultural effects than the more traditional political methods of lobbying or demonstrations. A cynical, individualist and profit-focused society requires cynical, individually targeted and profit-based political strategies, and in this context, idealism and principles are not going to cut it. The wealthy homophobes in question initially express concern or outrage at his proposals, but are forced to (symbolically as opposed to ideologically) give way to their pragmatic self-interest.

This is overtly successful when Brian effectively rebrands the failing beverage "Poolside" to "Poolboy" over the course of Pride weekend (episode 204) and invites the infamously homophobic owner (Pool) to a gay bar festooned with rainbows. When Pool rejects the idea, Brian responds by saying "tell that to your shareholders Monday. That you turned your back on a consumer market with an annual disposable income of hundreds of billions of dollars" and offers to "deliver" said consumers to Pool after he shows his "community support by a nice big contribution to say, the Gay Marriage Initiative" (although Brian is in principle against gay marriage himself). Although the narrative does not include the implementation of Brian's strategy, the audience does see him take a large gulp of the "gay" drink, demonstrating that Brian has symbolically won him over by appealing to his capitalist priorities.

Instead of limiting his choices, it is his obsession with sex that gives Brian his success; indeed his gay male aesthetic is an asset. Sally Munt's observation that "[i]t is 'new gayness' that makes Stuart [from the British *Queer as Folk*] rich, not productive labour" (539) appears to be just as true of Brian, Stuart's American counterpart. Perhaps the most telling example of such profitability is revealed when Brian, having been unable to formulate a campaign slogan for a chain of steak restaurants, goes to the backroom of Babylon and overhears a leather daddy telling his trick to "eat the meat," which Brian then turns into the slogan for his advertising campaign (episode 218). The deviance and difference of homosexual culture should not be hidden or repressed because it has the power to titillate if not transform the mainstream audience and can consequently produce commercial profits. Through such moves, "Gayness has been formulaically rebranded as attractive and aspirational, it has acquired cultural and symbolic capital, it has, through commodification, become *respectable*" (Munt 539).

Homosexuality is portrayed as a commodity, whether as an advertising strategy, a potential market, or an exotic product. Moreover, it is a commodity that confers political visibility and indeed agency. This is further complicated by the position of *Queer as Folk* itself as a creation of which Brian himself would be proud — both a product sold through in-your-face gay sex and as a means for a (heterosexual) cable channel to target a niche and potentially lucrative market, "capitaliz[ing] on gay identity as a desirable (no longer shamed) commodity" (Munt 533). The early 1990s Queer Nation slogan "queer as fuck" (Healey 182) is here repackaged as a glamorous and filtered version of the politics of queer, via the mainstream discourse of advertising. *Queer as Folk* neglects to portray the problematic elements of commodification, such as co-optation, exploitation, and potential misrepresentation, viewing it principally as a positive development.[4]

The third series appears to shift direction as Brian's financial self-interests conflict with his sexual freedom. The perception that he has gone too far in his collusion and greed is not only espoused by the other characters, but also by the audience. He closets his trademark "no apologies, no regrets" queerness while assisting the mayoral campaign of Republican chief of police Jim Stockwell, who strikes at the very heart of queer sexual freedom and sexual expression in his campaign to "create a safe, clean, morally upstanding city" (episode 310). It is only through a grand gesture of "sacrificing everything" to challenge homophobia (instead of his usual system of dual financial benefit to himself and his client) that he is redeemed. Brian, in this case, has finally "fucked [himself] out of" instead of into "a job" (episode 311). As with the undermining of Bellweather, Brian destroys Stockwell's campaign by exposing conduct unbecoming — in this case the concealment of the murder of a teenaged male sex worker by Stockwell's ex-partner in the police force. The amateur detective work that discovered these circumstances, however, is insufficient alone, and it is ultimately only through Brian spending $100,000 on an advertising campaign to promulgate his findings, that Stockwell is defeated. The character who is generally portrayed as simultaneously exploiting and empowering gay consumers, buys back the freedom of those very consumers with his own pink dollars, bankrupting himself in the process.

Although money is portrayed as essential to the political process, the co-chairs of Pittsburgh's Gay and Lesbian Center, Phillip and Janice, are, nevertheless, critiqued in episode 203 for their focus on money. Although they do indeed support Bellweather's stance on sex and the gay community, they defend their capitulation to his moral agenda by arguing that "the scent of a scandal could send [our benefactors] packing, along with their clutchpurses." The political views of representative organizations are controlled by funding considerations, and those who administer these organizations are portrayed as overly image conscious and elitist.[5] That the Gay and Lesbian Center later issues a statement of support for the homophobic Stockwell, praising "his efforts to close down sexual establishments that have been a blight on the image of our community" (episode 310), further implicates them in the effort to police the sexual morality of the community. Thusly they attempt to distance themselves from the bad sexual citizens, thereby maintaining their image as respectable and, therefore, acceptable to the straight community and their benefactors.

While a corresponding critique of Brian's focus upon his financial interests is also offered in the series, it is portrayed less negatively than that of the Gay and Lesbian Center. This is perhaps due to the contrast between his ability to manipulate capital into an uncloseted, positive commodification, thus articulating his political beliefs through his actions, and the Gay and Lesbian Center's tendency to follow political trends and, hence, donors without reference to a broader social vision.

When the Co-Chairs of the GLC enter episode 203, they interrupt Melanie and Lindsay having sex, and this is intercut with scenes of Brian penetrating a handcuffed cop with his own nightstick. But while Brian remains sexually uninterrupted by the demands of others (in the form of the persistently ringing phone), as he puts pleasure first, the women are not only stopped, but are ashamed of the fact that they were having sex at all, but particularly for their use of a vibrator; this in spite of the fact that over twenty years after the sex wars began, the use of vibrators is fairly widely acceptable within the lesbian community.[6] Janice's generalized horror at sex and her attempt to disparage the two women by calling them "femmes" later in the episode position her as a common stereotype of the presex wars lesbian, and these qualities, together with the presentation of her as less feminine and attractive (according to conventional ideals of beauty) than the main female characters, are calculated to negatively impact the audience's perception of her within the narrative.[7] The use of style and mainstream sexiness to denigrate others creates a distinction between insiders and outsiders similar to that evident within assimilationist discourses.

Episode 203 concludes with the viewing of a second segment of *Gay as Blazes*. In this scenario, Emmett, sitting on the couch, offers the directive to "blaze this" (a repetition of Brian's statement when he turned off *Gay as Blazes* to howls of protest) and switches off the television; the screen flips to black at the sound of a gunshot. This concludes Emmett's transition from an avid fan at the beginning of the episode, to a critic who kills the transmission. This transition has been directly influenced by the representation of Blair and Blaine (his employers) as the "real" *Gay as Blazes* characters, and their subsequent exposure as hypocrites. Blair and Blaine make much of their respectable long-term monogamy and their efforts to uplift members of their community, at the same time they have sex with their maid and, surprisingly, do not consider this as breach of monogamy, but simply and euphemistically "a little help around the house."

In the *Gay as Blazes* scene, the characters, for whom Emmett's employers are analogues, offer to take in a young man off the streets. The young man says, "I didn't know gay people like you existed," to which his hosts respond, "we're not all sexual predators." The dramatic irony is of course that they are indeed sexual predators, but that is omitted on a series like *Gay as Blazes*. Previously we heard Emmett's rejoinder to his employers, "I may be a slut, but at least I'm an honest slut," which highlights the perception in *Queer as Folk* (as in Warne 34), that "everyone's a slut," but that only some are willing to admit it. This vision of honesty about the centrality and importance of sex captures the ethics of *Queer as Folk*'s queer culture, which has more to offer the wider culture than a mimicry of straight society's morality. *Queer as Folk*'s cynical presentation of assimilationist television programming, journalism, and organizational timidity suggests the perverse ethical vision articulated by Warner; one that arises from "those circles where queerness has been most cultivated" in which "the ground rule is that one doesn't pretend to be *above* the indignity of sex" (35). This vision of sexual ethics acts as a counter to the hypocrisy and closetedness of normalized gays and is perhaps most clearly seen in the manner in which the series defines and constructs the "queer."

"Queer" is utilized in the title and throughout *Queer as Folk* as a declarative "othering," associated with radical visibility politics; an "other" to both heterosexuality and the desexualized depictions and definitions of gay that have arisen in the popular discourse. Unfortunately, the usage of queer in *Queer as Folk* also dismisses the politics of multiplicity and coalition-building associated with the usage of the term, through the evacuation of multiple subject positions or identities; and the manner in which it signifies is so associated with exclusions that it diminishes possibilities of radicalism. Queer is reduced to a signification for gay white men, not only through the absences frequently espied in its representations in popular culture, but also through a vigorous and explicit exclusionary practice.

Critiquing the exclusions inherent in and defining assimilationist discourse of "the good gay" is thereby undermined in *Queer as Folk* through its construction of an opposition that is itself informed by exclusion. The resolute focus upon sex in both the dialogue of *Gay as Blazes* and the subsequent discussion among the characters of *Queer as Folk* diminishes the import of other issues of representation that arise visually and narratively through the segment. The cast of *Gay as Blazes*, for example, is much more racially diverse than that of *Queer as Folk*, and it also includes a disabled character. This difference is never addressed by the cast of *Queer as Folk* in their dialogue about *Gay as Blazes*. Instead, their focus is primarily on the issue of sex with more subtle references to class, but the issue of racial diversity is an absent presence: the viewer is so completely unused to seeing people of color in *Queer as Folk*, that this becomes immediately noticeable. The failure to mention the more diverse cast in *Gay as Blazes* may be either a tacit acknowledgement of *Queer as Folk*'s overwhelming whiteness, or a jab at the political correctness of those who insist upon the inclusion of people of color in all media broadcasts. No matter what the intent, however, the exclusions within the assimilationist discourse that *Queer as Folk* critiques draw attention to the program's own exclusionary representations.

Lesbians are present in the text, but they are routinely situated as the converse of queer and are subjected to a great deal of misogynist and lesbiphobic dialogue. Lesbians are also barred from the sexual economy of "queer" (with the exception of Leda, who is not a continuing character). Their desire for weddings and babies is antithetical to the definition of queer that Brian offers:

> ... but don't get the idea that we are some kind of married couple because we're not. We're not like fucking straight people, we're not like your parents, and we're not a pair of dykes marching down the aisle in matching Vera Wangs; we're queers, and if we're together its because we wanna be, not because there's locks on our doors... [206].

Considering that the sexual practices have been the key signifier of queer within the text, the exclusion of the same in the representation of women further codes them as not queer.

Women, both lesbian and heterosexual, are not figured as sexual beings, but rather as nurturers or caretakers (whether as friend or mother). Ironically, these women share similarities to the desexualized gay man often seen in mainstream film or television, whose sexual or even romantic entanglements are tangential to the text, if they are present at all. In this way, *Queer as Folk* emulates the very sanitized politics of the antiqueer that it criticizes, simply displacing the restriction onto another marginalized group — the same group that is also historically represented as either frigid or licentious. Men in the series can desire serious relationships, but they are not relegated to this position in the same way that women are.

In the final episode of the third season, the only color in the imagery emanates from the rainbow flag in an allusion to the camp classic *The Wizard of Oz*. The use of the rainbow spectrum as an icon of diversity, however, has its limitations considering the restrictive definition operative in the series. Ultimately, both the queerness of *Queer as Folk* and the politics of assimilation that it explicitly counters perform a similar process of exclusion, discriminating on the basis of either too much sex or too little. However, the importance of opposing sexual repression in gay and lesbian politics is persuasively highlighted by *Queer as Folk* through its critique of assimilation. The manipulation of sex panic in order to gain legitimation for homosexuality in the mainstream is presented as a problematic, and ultimately damaging, political strategy. With the restoration of color to the previously monochrome screen, the final scene of season three symbolically registers the victory of queerness over those forces that oppose it. Victory is gained over all those who seek to confine sexual freedom, hetero or homosexual alike.

Notes

1. In the sense of providing images of queers as sexual beings through such strategies as "kiss-ins," as opposed to the more common association of outing associated with Queer Nation, though forms of outing are also encountered in *Queer as Folk*.

2. There seems to be a clear divide in reviews of *QAF*— it is by turns praised for being un-stereotypical in its depictions of gay men as sexual beings, or criticized for being stereotypical in its depictions. This disagreement over what exactly the stereotype seems to be is determined by context, i.e., whether one is examining representation on film and television, where the desexualised gay, at least from the mid–1990s onwards (Seidman 13–4) is the norm, or more general perceptions (as well as some mainstreamed representations) that see the homosexual as defined by their sexual perversions.

3. Gay conservative Christian Bawer's treatise *A Place at the Table* boasts on its back cover of its "stunningly frank critique of an unrepresentative but highly visible gay subculture that falsely equates homosexuality with promiscuity, hedonism and political correctness. ... debunk[ing] the myth of a monolithic "gay lifestyle," showing that homosexuals' politics, tastes, beliefs, and sexual tendencies are as diverse — and their values as mainstream — as those of heterosexuals." A writer for *The New Republic*, *The Advocate* and author of *Virtually Normal*, Sullivan is well known for his polemics on the subject of sex, marriage, and the supposedly pathological promiscuity of homosexuals who need to embrace maturity and responsibility through marriage. Eskridge is a law professor and advocate of gay marriage and its potentially "civilizing influence" on irresponsible gay men.

4. For an analysis of the impacts of commodifying homosexuality, please refer to Chasin, pages 235–272 of Walters *All the Rage*, and Clark.

5. See "Looking for Mr. Geffen" (238–273) in Vaid for a thorough analysis of the systemic orientation of the major gay and lesbian organizations in America (such as the National Gay and Lesbian Task Force or the Human Rights Campaign) towards politically pandering to those who are potentially large-scale donors.

6. See Healey (especially "Of Quims and Queers" 181–202), or any contemporary lesbian magazine.

7. See Walters "From Here to Queer" for a critique of the demonization of lesbian feminism in, and evacuation of gender from, queer discourse.

Works Cited

Ausiello, Michael. "Queer Execs to Critics: Folk Off!" *TV Guide Online*. 04 Jan. 2002. TV Guide Magazine Group. 01 Jul. 2004 http://www.tvguide.com/news/insider/article.asp?articleID=60530&articleOrder=60530&articleNum=0&flag=progid&keyword=iProgramID%3D2769771.

Bawer, Bruce. *A Place at the Table: The Gay Individual in American Society*. New York: Touchstone, 1994. 2nd ed.

Chasin, Alexandra. *Selling Out: The Gay and Lesbian Movement Goes to Market.* New York: Palgrave, 2000.
Clark, Danae. "Commodity Lesbianism." *Camera Obscura* 25–26 (1991): 180–201. Rpt. in *The Lesbian and Gay Studies Reader.* Henry Abelove, Michele Aina Barale and David M. Halperin, eds. New York: Routledge, 1993. 186–201.
Cowen, Ron, Daniel Lipman, and Tony Jonas. (Executive Producers). *Queer as Folk: The Complete First Season.* Showtime Entertainment, 2001. Running time 1,205 minutes
_____. "Episode 1." Russell Mulcahy (dir.), Ron Cowen and Daniel Lipman (Writing).
_____. *Queer as Folk: The Complete Second Season.* Showtime Entertainment, 2003. Running time 956 minutes.
_____. "Episode 3." Michael DeCarlo (dir.), Ron Cowen, Daniel Lipman and Karen Walton (Writing).
_____. "Episode 4." Michael MacLennan (dir.), Ron Cowen, Daniel Lipman and Michael MacLennan (Writing).
_____. "Episode 6." Bruce McDonald (dir.), Ron Cowen, Daniel Lipman, Matt Pyken and Michael Berns (Writing).
_____. "Episode 18." Alex Chapple (dir.), Ron Cowen, Daniel Lipman, Matt Pyken and Michael Berns (Writing).
_____. *Queer as Folk: The Complete Third Season.* Showtime Entertainment, 2003. Running time 673 minutes.
_____. "Episode 10." Kevin Inch (dir.), Ron Cowen, Daniel Lipman and Shawn Postoff (Writing).
_____. "Episode 11." Chris Grismer (dir.), Ron Cowen, Daniel Lipman and Brad Fraser (Writing).
_____. "Episode 14." Kelly Makin (dir.), Ron Cowen and Daniel Lipman (Writing).
Eskridge, William. *The Case for Same-Sex Marriage: From Sexual Liberty to Civilized Commitment.* New York: Free Press, 1996.
Healey, Emma. *Lesbian Sex Wars.* London: Virago, 1996.
Judell, Brandon. "QAFolk Is as Queer as Can Be." *PlanetOut.* Dec. 2000. PlanetOut Partners USA, Inc. 01 Jul. 2004 http://www.planetout.com/popcornq/db/getfilm.html?63647.
McFadden, Kay. "It's Here, Its 'Queer.' It Doesn't Make Us Cheer." *Seattle Union Record.* 01 Dec. 2000. Pacific Northwest Newspaper Guild. 01 Jul. 2004 http://www.unionrecord.com/arts/display.php?ID=478.
Munt, Sally. "Shame/Pride Dichotomies in Queer as Folk." *Textual Practice* 14.3 (2000): 531–546.
Seidman, Steven. *Beyond the Closet: The Transformation of Gay and Lesbian Life.* New York: Routledge, 2002.
Sullivan, Andrew. *Virtually Normal: An Argument About Homosexuality.* London: Picador, 1995.

Vaid, Urvashi. *Virtual Equality: The Mainstreaming of Gay and Lesbian Liberation.* New York: Anchor, 1995.
Walters, Suzanna Danuta. "From Here to Queer: Radical Feminism, Postmodernism and the Lesbian Menace." *Signs* 21.4 (1996): 830–869.
_____. *All the Rage: The Story of Gay Visibility in America.* Chicago: University of Chicago Press, 2001.
Warner, Michael. "The Trouble with Normal: Sex, Politics, and the Ethics of Queer Life." Cambridge: Harvard University Press, 1999.

Queering the Straight World: The Politics of Resignification in *Queer as Folk*

Esther Peeren

What happens when two versions of a series revolving entirely around the lives of queer characters enter the straight television landscapes of Great Britain and the United States? I want to explore how the British drama *Queer as Folk* and its United States counterparts practice of linguistic resignification challenges the dominant politics of representation in their respective national contexts. The original *Queer as Folk* was broadcast in eight episodes on Channel Four in 1999 with a two-hour special following in 2000. Since Channel Four is a public television channel, the series was programmed late at night because of its explicit sexual content. The American remake first appeared in December 2000 on Showtime, a subscription cable channel known for its progressive programming.[1]

Through its transnational but intralingual transplantation, *Queer as Folk* raises important questions concerning the functioning of minority discourses, both in terms of their opposition to the mainstream and in terms of cultural, temporal, and spatial differences. Already in its title, *Queer as Folk* positions itself as the bearer of a discourse that is contrary. Originally, the Yorkshire proverb "there's nought as queer as folk" referred to the strangeness of people in general. Using it as the title for a series that celebrates homosexual life and sexuality invests it with a supplementary meaning that not only changes the sense of the proverb, but also recuperates the word queer from its common derogatory usage. The title then comes to signify something like the following: homosexuals as people in general, as no longer incontrovertibly other, but as ordinary folk. However, this is not the end of its possible resignification. The linking term "as" works both ways: it can indicate that queer is like folk and/or that folk is like queer. The latter reading (supported by the original meaning of the proverb) would entail a blending of people in general — a generality implicitly understood as straight — into queer rather than the other way around. What the title achieves is a blurring between the categories of other and self, so that the references of these terms are no longer immediately clear: in the relation between queer and folk, who is the other and who is the self? Who is strange and who ordinary? Who the minority and who the mainstream?

The way the title of the series works to destabilize both signifiers (queer and folk) and refigure their interrelationship constitutes an instance of Mikhail Bakhtin's "linguistic stratification." For him, it is only through being associated with a particular social group's worldview that a word acquires living meaning, one that is not fixed, but open to restratification or reaccenting by other social groups. Bakhtin writes:

> Various tendencies [...] are all capable of stratifying language, in proportion to their social significance; they are capable of attracting its words and forms into their orbit by means of their own characteristic intentions and accents, and in so doing to a certain extent alienating these words from other tendencies, parties, artistic works and persons ... create slogan-words, curse-words, praise-words and so on ["Discourse" 290].

In the title *Queer as Folk*, the word "queer" travels through three such stratifications: in the original proverb, it meant simply strange; later, it became a derogatory term for homosexual; and now, in the title of the television series (as in "queer activism"), it is reaccented as a positive term. In Bakhtin's terms, the word is alienated from its meaning as a curse word and turned into a word of praise or pride. Significantly, this latter inversion is achieved by way of its previous proverbial meaning of a generalized strangeness, evoking what Judith Butler, in a discussion of queer politics, calls "the temporality of the term" (*Bodies* 223). It is by uniting the generality of the original noninjurious meaning of queer with the specificity of the group designated by its derogatory incarnation that a resignification occurs; the word "queer" is pulled into another orbit, where it no longer signifies the incontrovertible other, but rather the other or different in all of us. While this otherness is overtly figured as homosexuality, it is a homosexuality celebrated rather than abjected, construed as ordinary rather than problematic and conflicted, conceived as different, but no stranger than other so-called normal sexualities.

What is constructed in *Queer as Folk*, by means of its title, its content, and its position within the television landscape, is not just a stratification of the single word "queer," but what could be called a queer "speech genre." Bakhtin defines speech genres as "generic styles for certain spheres of human activity and communication" ("Speech Genres" 60): as concrete manifestations of the eternal stratification of language. A speech genre is what binds a social group together — a means by which it establishes a world of its own. Significantly, both versions of *Queer as Folk* are framed as journeys into another world, into the world of the other. This is already apparent in their respective opening scenes.

In the British version, the first episode begins with a monologue spoken by Vince, one of the main characters. He is shown in medium close-up against a bright yellow background, thus evoking the mode of the documentary, which is traditionally used to provide insight into the other — the criminal, the insane, the racial other, the sexual other. The genre features a series of representative others, mingled with so-called experts, all framed in a decontextualized manner and asked to comment on the difference between the representative group and the norm. Vince does precisely this:

> Now sometimes you're halfway through a shag and you just get bored with it. So you wank him off in the doorway and move straight on. 'Cause you keep on looking. That's why you keep going out. There's always some new bloke, some better bloke, just waiting around the corner.

The inclusive use of "you" instead of "I" presents an attempt to draw the viewer (whether homo- or heterosexual) into the orbit of the queer speech genre.

In the American remake, the monologue is spoken in voice-over by Vince's equivalent, Michael, as the camera surveys a gay club:

> The thing you need to know is: it's all about sex. It's true. In fact, they say men think about sex every twenty-eight seconds. Of course, that's straight men. With gay men it's every nine. You can be at the supermarket or the laundromat or buying a fabulous shirt when suddenly you find yourself checking out some hot guy. Hotter than the one you saw last weekend or went home with the night before. Which explains why we're all at Babylon at one in the morning instead of at home in bed. But who wants to be at home in bed? Especially alone, when you can be here, knowing that at any moment you might see HIM, the most beautiful man who ever lived. That is, until tomorrow night.

This statement sets out what the viewer needs to know to enter the queer world of the characters. The transition from straight men to gay men simultaneously establishes a parallel and distance between the two groups. Gay men are placed in the position of other, but the viewer is also invited to share this role. This is again achieved through the strategic use of the pronoun "you." At first, this "you" is clearly someone other than the speaker. Michael — at this point still a disembodied voice — is initiating the viewer into the particular gay mindset construed in the series. Later on, however, the "you" becomes inclusive of both Michael and the viewer: "You can be at the supermarket.... "The locations referred to here are familiar (even ordinary) to the American viewer and so is the question "who wants to be alone in bed?"

The monologue thus oscillates between the affirmation of differences and the stipulation of parallels between queers and straights. The use of the generalized "you" (inclining to "one" or "everyone") instead of "I" is interrupted only by a short shift to "we" when Michael refers to himself and his friends inside the narrative. But again, this "we" potentially includes the viewer, who, by watching, to some extent participates in the narrative events. Michael's opening monologue fulfills the promise of the title's doubled meanings: the queer experience is at once universalized (by relating it to the experience of all those looking for a hot man or woman), and particularized (by letting there be no mistake that this is a man speaking about sexually desiring other men).

The viewer's sense of being pulled into another orbit, of entering another world, is further strengthened by the fact that both series link the queer lifestyle to a bounded queer universe. In the British original, this is Manchester's Canal Street, and in the American adaptation it is Pittsburgh's Liberty Avenue. These locations have a well-defined margin separating them from the straight world, an alien realm whose incursions into the queer universe are perceived as threatening. An alien world that does, however, offer opportunities for strategic forays across the border. Both series feature the queering of straight spaces in episodes that place gay sensuality, gay sex, and gay pornography in the workplace and the school. Like the reappropriation of the word queer, this process resignifies these presumably straight spaces into potential extensions of the queer world that can then no longer be seen as strictly and safely separated, but as intermingled, crossing and blurring the lines between apparently antithetical universes.

Daniel Lipman, co-writer and co-producer of the American *Queer as Folk*, has said, "lots of shows have gay characters and that helps get people used to the fact that this is part of the tapestry of the world. But when you see a show like this in which all the characters are gay — there are very few straight characters, and they all live in a gay world — that is very important" (qtd. in *Ledger*). This reference to a gay world not only signals the construction of a queer universe on the narrative level, but also hints that the series as a whole sought to achieve a restructuring of the television tapestry by creating an exclusive space for queer representations within the traditionally straight spectrum of television. At this metalevel, the series becomes part of a larger queer speech genre, which is an overtly political discourse that places itself in the cultural dialogue as an instrument of identity politics. Within its narrative, *Queer as Folk* may present the gay world as the inside or standard, but on the metalevel of television programming and cultural dialogue, the gay lifestyle still functions as the subject of the straight hegemony.

This marginalized status of the gay lifestyle in the cultural context can be approached through Hamid Naficy's concept of accent as defined in *An Accented Cinema: Exilic and Diasporic Filmmaking*. Following on Naficy, I want to position *Queer as Folk* and its American remake as accented television.[2] Like the exilic and diasporic filmmaking Naficy explores, *Queer as Folk* is accented on multiple levels.

First, both versions are accented on the "intradiegetic level" of the characters' speech. The characters employ a host of "sociolects": queer speech, homophobic speech, and various professional speeches can be distinguished. In the British version, these sociolects are also accented in the more traditional sense of the word. With the series set in Manchester, all characters speak with a distinct Northern inflection. Hence, their speech is doubly accented, both with regard to their pronunciation and their selection of vocabulary and speech style. At this first level, the accent thus refers both to localized pronunciation and to differences in intonation, style, and semantics.

Second, both series are accented on the level of narrative structure. The presentation of gays and lesbians as protagonists is in itself nonstandard. Few gay or lesbian characters appear on mainstream television, particularly in prominent roles, and if they do, they tend to be stereotyped, desexualized, or presented from a straight perspective. *Queer as Folk* challenges this pattern by presenting queer characters as regular people rather than exotic curiosities, by explicitly depicting queer sexuality, and by establishing a queer focalization (the narrative is consistently presented through queer eyes)[3]. At this second level, the accent is no longer only about linguistic accentuations, but envelops constructed and perceived social differentiations.

Finally, *Queer as Folk* exhibits accented modes of production, distribution, and reception. The writers of both series, as well as the producers of the American show, are gay men, and both versions were marketed mainly — though not exclusively — to a gay audience. In terms of its reception, the debate within the gay community reflected the same paradoxical stance identified by Naficy in the audience of accented cinema: a simultaneous demand for positive portrayals and for the full representation of difference within the community.[4] However, where Naficy's accented cinema is characterized by its "collective reception" (63) on the part of homogeneous exilic or diasporic audiences, both versions of *Queer as Folk* have unexpectedly become popular with heterosexual audiences. This opens the way for a consideration of the dialogue that accented television can establish both within and beyond the represented community. Moreover, the way the heterosexual audience has responded to the queer accent indicates how accents never remain the exclusive property of a particular social group, but, as Bakhtin intimates, may be drawn into widely divergent discursive orbits.

Consequently, it becomes essential not only to explore how accented media are accented, in the manner of Naficy, but also to determine the effect of their accentedness. Unlike the exilic accent, the queer accent — being, speaking and "doing" (in its performative sense) queer — does not originate outside a national language, but within it. It is, to speak with Judith Butler, an abjected accent. As the mark of a constitutive outside that is nevertheless within, it flags that unlivable place in the margin or on the border that enables the dominant language to constitute itself as neutral, as unaccented. However, because the standard can define itself only against the nonstandard, the accent, far from being unilaterally defined by the standard, also defines the norm. Consequently, the accent is potentially capable of redefining the standard, of reaccenting it by restoring it to its prenaturalized status of one accent among others. In line with Derrida's metaphor of fantasy on translation, all languages can be conceived of as mere accents of the mythical pre–Babelian tongue (99). Hence, any so-called standard is already confused — riddled with contradictions and ambiguities — from the start.

Queer as Folk comes some way in achieving a reaccenting or reconfusion of mainstream television and a simultaneous deaccenting or demarginalization of queerness, not by rigidly separating itself from the norm — as most of the accented films discussed by Naficy seem to do — but by colonizing a space at the center from where it becomes possible to question both the presumed naturalness of dominant television and the abjection of the queer accent. Separating the accent from the standard ignores the fact that the two are embroiled in a process of constant renegotiation. It reconfirms and perpetuates their hierarchical relationship. Exploring their mutual dependency, on the contrary, raises questions about the standard itself: How did it come to represent itself as the standard? What power relations are involved in its continuous naturalization and perpetuation of itself as the standard? And what is at stake in its marginalization of all other accents?

Focusing on the relation between accent and standard reveals the means by which an accent actively challenges its own marginalized status. By appropriating aspects of the mainstream, the accent emerges as no longer incontrovertibly opposed to the standard: the terms of the opposition become infectious and blurred rather than mutually exclusive. Of course, this type of appropriation works both ways, and there is always a danger that the mainstream will incorporate the accent so as to render it harmless. The American sitcom *Will & Grace* is a good example. Here the queer accent is neutralized by removing all evidence of gay sexuality, reducing queerness to wordplay and jokes, and privileging a heterosexual woman as focalizer. In *Queer as Folk*, on the contrary, the queer accent retains its edge (it features gay and lesbian sex, portrays the gay characters as full human beings, and presents everything from their point of view), doing so, moreover, without placing itself completely outside the parameters of mainstream television. While *Queer as Folk* is certainly polysemic in that it allows various sections of the audience to construct alternative meanings, it does not permit any of its viewers to avoid seeing sexuality as part of being queer or to simply equate gay sexualities to straight sexualities.

Herman Gray, writing about the representation of blacks on American television, distinguishes three ways minority accents can enter into standard representation: assimilation (where blackness is made invisible, a nonissue), pluralism (where black culture is separate from white culture, but equal to it), and multiculturalism (where there is diversity and difference). *Will & Grace* is a typical example of an assimilationist adoption of the queer accent, whereas *Queer as Folk* offers a combination of pluralism (its world is almost exclusively gay, and it conveys a clear message that gays are in many ways regular folks) and multiculturalism (gay relationships and gay sex are emphatically represented as different from heterosexual relationships and sex). This combination preempts both the resistive response, "they're just freaks," and the neutralizing conclusion, "queers are really just like heterosexuals."

Of course, mainstream acceptance inevitably requires certain concessions to the so-called standard, and *Queer as Folk* is not all accented. In both the British and the American version, the queer accent is framed by a familiar television format: in Britain, the frame is that of the comedy/drama about a group of friends and their relationships (in the mode of the successful BBC series *This Life*); in America, it is the (melo)dramatic continuing serial with ensemble cast, which Jane Feuer describes as one of the dominant narrative forms in American television (111) and of which *Thirtysomething* and *Sisters* (the latter, incidentally, made by the same team of writers/producers as *Queer as Folk*) are prime examples. The filmic styles of both series are also unaccented: in Britain, *Queer as Folk* is filmed in the highly realistic "gritty" manner common to British television drama, while in the United States it has the glossy, polished look of American television, also known as the "advertising aesthetic" (Grindstaff 150). I want to posit that it is precisely this use of familiar modes of framing and filming that enables *Queer as Folk* to achieve a (partial) reaccenting of both the queer and the dominant television language.

Most immediately, the queering of the gritty drama and (melo)dramatic serial genres undermines the prevalent pathologization and medicalization of televised homosexuality, where "coming out" is represented as a severe psychological struggle or homosexuality is reduced to the story of AIDS (Gross 412). The two *Queer as Folk*s undermine this association in different ways and to different degrees: the American version retains the theme of AIDS, but relegates it to minor characters and storylines, while the British version almost completely banishes the disease (as well as gay activism) from its storylines. Both versions, furthermore, explicitly sexualize the representation of queer life without presenting gay sexuality as problematic.

Such internal departures from the common television portrayal of homosexuality, however, require the support of a familiar frame; had both series been unfamiliar in format too, this might have led to their dismissal by the mainstream audience. As Gayatri Spivak has argued, before minorities can speak up for themselves, there has to be a willingness to listen to them: "'The subaltern cannot speak' means that even when the subaltern makes an effort to the death to speak, she is not able to be heard, and speaking and hearing complete the speech act" (292). One cannot speak if nobody listens, particularly when one's speech is accented. For a long time, the queer accent was inaudible and invisible on television. A series like *Queer as Folk* represents an instance of what Spivak calls "subaltern insurgency," which is "an effort to involve oneself in representation, not according to the lines laid down by the official institutional structures of representation. Most often it does not catch" (306).

The main reason *Queer as Folk* did catch is because of its co-optation of a familiar frame for an unfamiliar content: the mixing of the official institutional structures of representation with subaltern elements is what rendered it audible and visible. If the standard is to be resignified, the margin needs to pervade it, blurring the line between standard and accent, rather than functioning as its constitutive outside, which, as Butler points out, inevitably ends up acting as the norm's tacit support.

Thus, whereas the accent as Naficy employs it appears diametrically opposed to the standard, *Queer as Folk* suggests a more flexible relation between the two terms that is perhaps more aptly theorized through Bakhtin's notion of the speech genre. Speech genres have vastly different scopes, ranging from the language of a whole culture to the language of the day, and they continually cross each other's paths: "Languages do not exclude each other, but rather intersect with each other in many different ways.... It might even seem that the very word 'language' loses all meaning in this process — for apparently there is no single plane on which all these 'languages' might be juxtaposed to one another" ("Discourse" 291). The way language refers not to a unified entity, but to any distinctive accentuation of linguistic signs immediately challenges any straightforward or permanent division of languages into standards and accents.

Whereas the accent is a subordinated term with pejorative connotations, implying the existence of a neutral dominant language, speech genres become hierarchical only through their entanglement with social power relations, and any hierarchy is provisional. A dominant genre may become marginalized and vice versa. In this way, speech genres expose hierarchies of linguistic accents as cultural, sociohistoric constructions, presenting the mainstream not as an accent-free language, but as a speech genre naturalized to the point of appearing to be without inflection: the standard is a homogenizing, centralizing, interested genre that seeks to perpetuate its dominance by confining all other genres to the inferior status of accent.

This does not mean I want to discard the accent completely. The value of the accent lies in the way it conveys the constructed, perceived, and experienced marginality of certain speech genres within the sociocultural context. This marginality may be a construct, but it nevertheless has very real material effects. The lack of queer television representation is one, and so is the way the queer accent itself tends to privilege the male gay accent over the lesbian one (this tendency is also apparent in *Queer as Folk*, particularly in the British original). The accent is a manifestation of a constructed hierarchy that may not be absolute, but that nevertheless governs relations between social groups and works to confine minorities to their proper place at the margins.

While it is important to realize that any hierarchy of speech genres is constructed and subject to reaccentuation, it is equally important to acknowledge that not all accents have the same clout: some are heard, some are indistinct, and others are actively silenced. Using the term speech genre for anything ranging from a professional jargon to an ethnic or sexual minority accent obliterates the vital distinction between a chosen, partial inflection that can be put on at will and the enforced, non-relinquishable accent of an actively abjected minority. As Butler notes, there is no "I" before the accent, no "I" before "queer." We are marked by certain identity categories, and these marks cannot simply be wiped off. We have no choice but to work with the terms that already occupy our orbit. To avoid both the leveling generality of Bakhtin's speech genres and an overly rigid opposition of standard and accent, I want to examine the two terms through each other and distinguish between accented and standardized speech genres.

The complexities of reaccenting a word, of drawing it into a new orbit, particularly if it is part of an accented speech genre, is borne out by a scene in *Queer as Folk* that centers on the term queer. This term is difficult to resignify because it is part of a standardized, authoritative speech genre and burdened with a history of negative associations and injury that is present in each enunciation. As Butler puts it: "[I]t is always an imaginative chorus that taunts 'queer'!" (*Bodies* 226). A word like queer functions as a test for what Pierre Bourdieu calls "semantic elasticity." Like an elastic band, the meaning of a certain word can be stretched to a point, after which it might snap back to its old form: "*l'élasticité sémantique n'est jamais infinie*" (212). This indicates that the word is always contingent and can never be brought under full control of either a standardized or an accented speech genre.

The scene I want to analyze occurs in the first episode of both the

British and the American *Queer as Folk*. Vince/Michael is awoken by a car alarm, goes outside, and catches some children in the process of vandalizing the car he has on loan from his friend Stuart/Brian. Vince/Michael chases the children away and is shocked when he looks at the side of the car (which remains invisible to the viewer). Later, we will learn that the word QUEERS has been sprayed in red all over the side of the car. In the American version, the word is FAGGOT, and the color is a more symbolic pink.

Vince/Michael then takes the car to the apartment of Stuart/Brian, who has just spent the night having sex with an underage boy (Nathan/Justin). Stuart/Brian looks at the car and decides to take the boy to school in it. In the British version, Vince insists they drop Nathan a safe distance from the school ("they'll see the car"), but Stuart is adamant and speeds up the driveway, honking. As he pulls up in front of the school, the writing on the car is displayed to all (including, for the first time, to the viewer). The other pupils point, laugh, and make kissing sounds in the car's direction, and one boy comments: "come on, boys, give us a kiss!" Stuart replies, threateningly, "I'll give you a good fuck, you tight little virgin. You won't be laughing then!" Then, Stuart and Vince drive off, leaving Nathan to deal with the continuing taunts. When the car reappears in the next episode, Stuart has had it repainted.

Although a degree of resignification takes place in this scene, predominantly through the sheer brazenness with which Stuart presents the car and through his humiliation of the taunting boy, the reappropriation of the term queer is limited spatially and temporally, confined to the school grounds (Nathan's space) and complete the moment the car drives away. Lacking Stuart's cockiness, confidence, and age, Nathan has no reply for the additional abuse to which he is subjected after being labeled queer. Although he does not deny the appropriateness of the label (privately, he prides himself on his successful initiation into gay sexuality), Nathan is not able to achieve sustained control over its usage. In Bakhtin's terms, Nathan lacks the social significance to sustain Stuart's defiant reappropriation of the insult; instead, the word is drawn back into the orbit of his taunting schoolmates. In this particular scene and throughout the British series as a whole, the resignification of queer is neither lasting nor authoritative. On Canal Street, it may function as an unequivocal term of gay pride, but outside that space it continues to reappear as a term of violence that is not as easily painted over as Stuart's car.

The American remake problematizes resignification more explicitly and features a more sustained reaccenting of the term "faggot." The school scene remains virtually identical, but instead of staying with the schoolboy, the camera tracks Brian's car as it drives off, holding the word FAGGOT center screen. People on the sidewalk turn their heads and point at the car, and then the camera moves in closer and records the following discussion:

BRIAN: "I'll drop you by the store"
MICHAEL: "The hell you will. You'd better get this thing repainted before you go into the office"
BRIAN: "I'm not having it repainted."
MICHAEL: "What?"
BRIAN: "I like it this way."
MICHAEL: "Are you crazy?"
BRIAN: "No, they are. Well, I say, fuck them! They can write it in neon across the sky. (shouting into the air) FAGGOT!!!"

They both laugh, and the episode ends with a long shot of the car driving into the city, triumphantly honking its horn. In the next episode, it turns out that Brian has had the car repainted after all. Again, it appears that the defiant reappropriation of the injurious term as a pride word cannot be sustained, not even by a character as openly and provocatively gay as Brian, who also possesses social standing. The sequence of events — the insult, the queering of the insult, and the final erasure of both — signals the difficulty of resignification, particularly if resignification is to occur not just within a limited space, but in the world at large. As Bakhtin notes,

> Not all words for just anyone submit equally easily to this appropriation, to this seizure and transformation into private property: many words stubbornly resist, others remain alien, sound foreign in the mouth of the one who appropriated them and who now speaks them; they cannot be assimilated into his context and fall out of it; it is as if they put themselves in quotation marks against the will of the speaker.

> Language is not a neutral medium that passes freely and easily into the private property of the speaker's intentions; it is populated — overpopulated — with the intentions of others. Expropriating it, forcing it to submit to one's own intentions and accents, is a difficult and complicated process [*Imagination* 294].

The car scene unites two speech genres that assign contradictory meanings to the words queer and faggot, and makes them come head to head. On the level of the narrative, there is no resolution as the word moves between the vandalizing children, the gay characters, the schoolchildren, and the people watching the car. Each group pulls the term into its orbit, but rather than belonging completely to either group, the term oscillates between them, sometimes edging this way and then the other.

Resignification is an issue not only on the diegetic level of *Queer as Folk*, but for the series as a whole through its positioning in the straight television landscape. The series itself is designed as a resignification of the media representation of queer sexuality, both in Britain and in the United States. Thus, when we see Brian shouting "FAGGOT!" into the air, his word is also aimed at the extradiegetic audience, at the television world, at the entire cultural system of stereotypical representations. Far from rendering itself newly invisible — in the manner of the repainted car — the series claims to cross the television landscape as the car crosses Pittsburgh: loud and proud, not hiding anything.

Even on the extradiegetic level, however, this claim is not wholly validated, especially with regard to the American version. There were hostile reactions in the American media, problems attracting advertisers, issues of censorship, and prohibitions against broadcasting on a public television channel. Moreover, it was a great problem finding actors willing to play gay characters. Whereas the British version features actors previously and since seen on other mainstream television shows, the cast of the American *Queer as Folk* is comprised largely of unknown actors. More troubling is the fact that several of these actors were originally advised against participating on the grounds that playing a gay character could ruin their careers. As a consequence of this, some of the actors felt compelled to aggressively assert their real-life heterosexuality, often in disturbingly bigoted terms. The following comment by Hal Sparks (Michael) on having to engage in male-to-male kissing is indicative:

I get a lot of crap for saying this, but it's a little bit like kissing a dog, because you don't have any emotional, internal stuff that you would have when you actually want to be with someone. So, as an actor, it's a unique challenge because you've got to bring it from someplace, make it convincing. And I think if I've done that, then that's invaluable [Ausiello].

The appearance of this comment in an article entitled "Sparks: Straight as Folk" constitutes a reverse resignification of the *Queer as Folk* title: once more, being ordinary is linked to being straight and homosexuality becomes an aberration, something that one has to work at to make convincing. For Sparks, the "invaluable" achievement appears to lie in making it believable that two men might actually want to be with each other, and that between them, there might be "emotional, internal stuff."

In the end, what we encounter both on the intradiegetic and on the extradiegetic level of *Queer as Folk* is the limit of resignification, when it involves not just any speech genre, but one that is accented and abjected in a particular sociocultural context. This does not mean that resignification is necessarily doomed to failure, but it does mean that it is never a straightforward practice that can be kept completely under control.

Notes

1. For an extensive selection of reviews, news articles and interviews on both series, see the *Queer as Folk* archive: *www.queerarchive.com*
2. Naficy, who sees television as characterized by "distracted vision and glance" (29) rather than by the directed gaze of film spectatorship, points to television's suitability as an accented medium — singling out cable television, which can accommodate the sensitive and demanding subject matter excluded from public television — as particularly effective.
3. In its very title, *Queer as Folk* takes up Larry Gross' complaint that "hardly ever shown in the media are just plain gay folks, used in roles which do not center on their deviance as a threat to the moral order which must be countered through ridicule or physical violence" (2001: 412).
4. Naficy writes: "[d]efensiveness and the desire for counterhegemonic representations often create communal pressure for each film to contain all of the best that the 'original' or the 'authentic' culture is perceived to possess *and* to represent as fully as possible the diaspora community" (65).

Works Cited

Ausiello, Michael. "Sparks: Straight as Folk." *TV Guide Online*. 17 Oct. 2000, http://qaf.mskiteonline.com/article.php?page=article22

Bakhtin, Mikhail. "The Problem of Speech Genres." *M. M. Bakhtin: Speech Genres and Other Late Essays*. Caryl Emerson and Michael Holquist, eds. Austin: University of Texas Press, 1986. 60–102.

———. "Discourse in the Novel." Caryl Emerson and Michael Holquist, trans. *The Dialogic.*

———. *Imagination: Four Essays by M. M. Bakhtin*. 1981. Michael Holquist, ed. Austin: University of Texas Press, 1996. 259–422.

Bourdieu, Pierre. *Choses Dites*. Paris: Les Éditions de Minuit, 1987.

Butler, Judith. *Bodies That Matter: On the Discursive Limits of "Sex."* New York & London: Routledge, 1993.

———. *Excitable Speech: A Politics of the Performative*. New York and London: Routledge, 1997.

Cowen, Ron, and David Lipman. *Queer as Folk: The Complete First Season*. DVD. Showtime Entertainment, New York, 2001.

Davies, Russell T. *Queer as Folk*. VHS. Channel 4 Television Limited, London, 1999.

Derrida, Jacques. "Roundtable on Translation." Peggy Kamuf, trans. *The Ear of the Other: Texts and Discussions with Jacques Derrida*. Christie McDonald, ed. Lincoln and London: University of Nebraska Press, 1985. 93–162.

Feuer, Jane. "Narrative Form in American Network Television." *High Theory/Low Culture: Analysing Popular Television and Film*. Colin MacCabe, ed. Manchester: Manchester University Press, 1986. 101–14.

Gray, Herman. "The Politics of Representation in Network Television." *Media and Cultural Studies: Keyworks*. 1995. Meenakshi Gigi Durham and Douglas M. Kellner, eds. Oxford: Blackwell, 2001. 439–61.

Grindstaff, Laura. "A Pygmalion Tale Retold: Remaking *La Femme Nikita*." *Camera Obscura* 16.2 (2001): 133–75.

Gross, Larry. "Out of the Mainstream: Sexual Minorities and the Mass Media." *Media and Cultural Studies: Keyworks*. 1995. Meenakshi Gigi Durham and Douglas M. Kellner, eds. Oxford: Blackwell, 2001. 405–23.

Ledger, Brent. "Free Trade: Queer as Canuck Limey Yanks." *XTRA!* 11 Jan. 2001, n. pag. http://www.xtra.ca/site/toronto2/arch/body731.shtm

Naficy, Hamid. *An Accented Cinema: Exile and Diasporic Filmmaking*. Princeton and Oxford: Princeton University Press, 2001.

Spivak, Gayatri Chakravorty. "Subaltern Talk: Interview with the Editors." *The Spivak Reader*. Donna Landry and Gerald Maclean, eds. New York & London: Routledge, 1996. 287–308.

A Trip to the Queer Circus: Reimagined Masculinities in *Will & Grace*

Richard J. Conway

In this text, I intend to investigate whether traditional masculinity is being reimagined and restructured within the peripheralized (anti)space opened up by modern situation comedy and to question whether normative masculinity can be reimagined in comedy precisely because this genre exists as a space of the unreal. In doing this, I also wish to explore the idea that modern comedy in its reimagining of normativity provides an (anti)space comparable to that of the carnivalesque espoused by Mikhail Bakhtin. Bakhtin's carnival is defined as a "laughter of all the people" (*Rabelais* 12). In its hyperreal (anti)state, the audience participates in the carnival and then retreats from it to become "real" again. However, the characters in the carnival can never leave because "they stand on the borderline between life and art in a peculiar midzone as it were" (198), creating an inside/outside dichotomy (Eaton 33). Thus, I further wish to examine whether the fluid, reimagined states of masculinity become temporarily acceptable within the Bakhtinian carnival because these virtual "othered" males are so queered as to be humorous and so disempowered as to be disabled. Not only are these "othered" states unable to produce real consequences within the narrative of comedy, but their disempowerment prevents them from re-creating and renegotiating masculinity and its relations outside the (non)delineations of the carnival.

NBC's *Will & Grace* is one of television's first situation comedies to position a gay man as central to its narrative. Before this syndication, the issue of homosexuality was rarely dealt with explicitly in situation comedy, but was merely implicit or intimated (such as in the BBC's *Are You Being Served?*). This renegotiation of normative masculinity away from the realm of the straight, white, upper middle class, Anglo-Saxon protestant male, as Neale and Krutnik propose, reveals the need for situation comedy as a genre "to address and incorporate changing cultural standards and a sense of its own 'development' as a medium" (236). These newly incorporated standards should reflect the changing cultural milieu, and in this framework, one ought to see situation comedies reflecting the reality of contemporary social contexts. This reflection could be seen in the representation of the domestic issues centered around the growth and maturity of the nuclear family in *Father Knows Best* of the 1950s or, as Neale and Krutnik outline, the positive reflection and inclusion of black culture in *The Cosby Show* (244) in the 1980s. Through its reflection and incorporation of the societal values, situation comedy allows its audience to both recognise its particular social framework and simultaneously distance itself from those same standards. As such, the laughter of the carnival becomes both laughter at the characters in comic situations and laughter with the characters as we recognize the framework in which we exist and participate.

However, in his work, Bakhtin explicitly denies that the laughter of the carnival is a "reaction to some isolated comic event" (*Rabelais* 12), but rather it is laughter that is "universal in scope" (12). He insists that the carnival, by definition, is void of "footlights"(12), as these would remove the nature of the carnival by distinguishing between spectator and actor. In this vein, it would seem that the situation comedy is simply rendered a modern manifestation of what Bakhtin called the discourse of "spectacle"(12). However, in the role of spectator, the audience identifies with the pseudoreality of the comedic discourse, buying into its verisimilitude, and so the lines between reality and the comic hyperreality become blurred. Thus, the audience becomes part of a carnival from which the modern televisual medium allows them to leave at any time they wish. The audience is both spectator and actor, and as such, it inhabits the same narrative space as the carnivalesque characters while it is simultaneously distanced from them.

This concurrent incorporation and expulsion of the spectator allows normative masculinity to reinvestigate itself while ensuring that any altered or queered state can be easily vacated. Within this context, the audience confronts the reimagined states of masculinity presented by Will and Jack in *Will & Grace*, a program which presents us with two alternatives to naturalized heterosexual masculinity: Will, the "straight" gay man, and Jack, the "camp" gay man. These two roles are marginalized forms of masculinity, and their prioritization as central characters marks a move away from the centrality of heterosexual masculinity that predominated within the domestic environment of earlier situation comedies.

The first episode in series one of *Will & Grace* entitled simply "Pilot" opens with a telephone conversation between Will Truman and Grace Adler. The scene consists of intercuts between two locations which we assume to be at a distance sufficient to warrant a telephone conversation. The camera documents statements and responses between the two characters, whose intimacy is immediately evident. However, this emphasis on closeness is both complimented and contradicted by the sense of physical distance implicit within the phone call format. Thus, the set and the dialogue of the opening scene immediately introduces Will and Grace's familiarity/distance dichotomy and preempts Will's nonsexual heterosexuality. The initial exchanges within the opening conversation imply that Will is propositioning Grace sexually. The flippant familiarity of "Come on, Grace you know you want to" invites the audience to believe that Will and Grace are a heterosexual couple. However, this implicit romance is rendered an explicit friendship when Will reveals that he is talking about watching the television series *ER*.

From the outset of the series, we are presented with a reimagined form of masculinity: the straight man who happens to be gay. Will Truman is presented as a normal guy who has a normal job and lives in a normal apartment. The familiarity in which Will is inscribed is resolutely heterosexual and westernized. For all intents and purposes, Will is a regular Manhattanite. The attributes of his life are heteronormative: he works within the legal profession; he lives with and loves a straight woman; and his recreation time is spent drinking beer and playing cards with his buddies. His behavior belies his homosexuality, as he is ascribed the trappings of normative masculinity; he is constructed as a traditional or "real" man. However, this characterization of Will as "just like everyone else but gay" is threatening to established masculinity because Will carries with him a radically deconstructive characteristic: his homosexuality. This sexual proclivity becomes dangerous when it is attributable to a man bearing all of the traits of heterosexual masculinity. It threatens to deconstruct the binary structure of gender roles. Will's heteronormative characteristics destabilize the carnival's suspension of hierarchy. Thus, Will's masculinity is rendered pseudoheterosexual and his homosexuality transformed into a nominal joke. He can be just like everyone else and still be labeled homosexual. His sexuality becomes a harmless foible, a quirky characteristic that lands him in humorous situations, his sexual eccentricity a comedic analogue to Karen's postmaterialist superficiality or Grace's neurotic competitiveness.

Thus, Will's queer sexuality is neutered and tamed. The comedic discourse is not a safe enough realm to reimagine Will in this way, and as such, his libido is suspended, becoming entirely rhetorical, merely an impetus for humorous dialogue. His heterosociality is rendered nonsexual heterosexuality. The few times that Will is allowed to kiss another person, the recipient is invariably Grace, such as in the episode "He's Come Undone" where he dreams of having sex with her. Here the audience is presented with a virtual reality occurring within the virtual reality of the situation comedy carnival. Will dreams of kissing Grace, and as such his missing attribute (heterosexuality) is rehabilitated by his constant and recurrent infringements into virtual-virtual heterosexuality. Will may be homosexual in name, but the narrative always reminds us that his gayness has always already crossed the line to become quasi-heterosexuality. Jack derides him for his ostensibly heteronormative relations with Grace: "You flinched, flinchy. Wifey tried to give you a smooch, and you flinched. What's the matter, flinchy? Trouble in paradise?" Will's relationship with Grace is recognized as a form of marriage. Jack calls her "wifey" and asks Will if there is trouble in "paradise." Thus, Will is rendered paradoxical; he becomes a married pseudoheterosexual who is nominally homosexual as well as a virtual homosexual who is a castrated heterosexual. These contradictions reimagine Will as the embodiment of an absolutely safe masculinity.

Will is a character in the carnival from the outset; he is part of an unreal and virtual realm. His heterosexuality lacks heterosexuality, and his queer otherness is recuperated by his ostensibly heteronormative marriage. Thus, Will's homosexuality must necessarily be trivialized to render its deconstructive power void. The safeguard protects masculinity while the humorous situations in the carnival remove any threat that Will's homosexuality will ever become real. Thus, Will's sexual relationships with men are either in the distant past or made homosocial in the present. These relationships are rendered homosocial in order to further nominalize his gayness. His boyfriends exist as distant memories of real people (Michael), as embarrassing pseudorelationships (Scott), or as closeted pseudoheterosexuals (Matt). Will's relationship with Matt in particular is coded homosocial as they play sports together despite Wills lack of interest in the activity. If his partners are in practice his friends, his homosexuality is merely a humorous distortion of homosociality, and Will is merely a latent, yet castrated heterosexual. Thus, Will's homosexuality does little to undermine normative masculinity as he becomes trapped between binary oppositions of straight and gay, castrated and sexual, married and single. His homosexuality cannot significantly alter masculinity because Will does not in effect exist; he is trapped between binaries in a "peculiar midzone" (Bakhtin 12) and his lack of actuality renders his queered masculinity a fleeting joke and his virtual existence carnivalesque. Thus, normative standards are upheld but manipulated. Situation comedy's apparent renegotiation of the boundaries of naturalized masculinity are in fact conservative of its traditional demarcations. Homosexuality is unacceptable within its framework, and despite the all-inclusive acceptability of the carnival, gayness can only ever be a burlesque.

This virtual joke is further manifest in the character of Jack McFarland, who exists as a preimagined (anti)masculinity. Jack is the camp queen. His form of masculinity is so far removed from the standards of normativity as to be rendered ridiculous. His conformity to already established (anti)frameworks render him queer. He is the jester who exists in an eternal realm of performance. Jack is safe because he embodies the carnival; he is allowed to exist in this virtual realm because he has been acceptably peripheralized. He does not need to be neutered or tamed because his behavior affirms the normality of established masculinity. He does not possess any of the reality signifiers that are attributed to Will; he has no fixed abode and no fixed job; he in effect does nothing. Jack, in Bakhtin's terminology, is one of the

> [C]lowns and fools ... the constant, accredited representatives of the carnival spirit in everyday life out of the carnival season. Like Triboulet at the time of Francis I, they were not actors playing their parts on a stage [...] but remained fools and clowns always and wherever they made their appearance [12].

Thus, Jack never stops being carnivalized; he is radically excluded queer and as such, he "signifies [constant] performance rather than existence" (Babuscio 44). Jack is virtual, existing at a further distance from the actual than Will. The unreality of his character poses little threat to masculinity; the more camp Jack is, the less camp normative masculinity is. This allows him to explore "the [virtual] limits to which one's character might attain" (Babuscio 43) and so Jack is able to possess a libido. Unlike Will, Jack is constantly man-hungry and sexual. This sexual drive only seeks to emphasize his own deviance as Jack is rendered too laughable to be threatening and too carnivalesque to be real.

In his essay *Television Situation Comedy*, Mick Eaton identifies the presence of an "inside/outside dichotomy in sit-com [*sic*] which operates across the levels of characters, stock sets [and] use of film footage" (33). He proposes that

> [e]vents from the outside can be allowed to enter the situation to provide for weekly narrative development, but these events/characters have to be dealt with in such a way that the parameters of the situation are ultimately unaffected by either their entry or expulsion so that the situation can be maintained and taken up again the following week [33].

This in/out dichotomy structures the narrative device in which characters move temporarily from outside the narrative to the center of its action, interacting with the stock or set characters to affect transitory consequences. These ramifications are necessarily false because "nothing that has happened in the narrative of ... [this] week must destroy or even complicate the way the situation [will continue to be] grounded [the next week]" (33). Situation comedy becomes a nonepisodic and yet episodic discourse as each week's story becomes unaffected by, and yet a repeat of, the previous weeks narrative. No external character produces a consequence that would interfere with the "continuous internal 'mythology' and hermeneutic [of] the series as a whole" (Drummond qtd. in Neale and Krutnick 235). This internal hermeneutic of constant renewal carnivalizes the situation comedy as a genre. The very structure of the type becomes an antistructure of the fleeting and the transient. This is reflected by the genre's erasure of the narrative's future and past; a practice that preserves the present and simultaneously removes time. Events from the outside cannot alter the framework of the inside and vice versa, thus carnivalizing the sitcom characters who (de)exist in the constant yet transient present. As such, each episode becomes a repetition of a formula which itself is based in a constant yet fleeting present. Comedy remains within Eaton's "timeless *nowness* of television situations" (Eaton 34). Since situation comedy exists in the present and yet never proceeds to the future, it is both and neither. The future in situation comedy becomes suspended as time stagnates and stalls, and yet it is constantly renewed and revitalised in the transient moments of the present comedic situation. The constant renewal of the present and deferral of narrative closure renders linear consequentiality void, as this nonconsequential temporality neuters real causality within the situation comedy. Neale and Krutnik observe:

> [w]hereas in the feature film narrative closure is marked by establishing an equilibrium which differs from that disrupted at the start, in the sitcom the end of the episode represents a *return* to the initial situation [234].

Hence, the timelessness of the situation in situation comedy becomes a mask of verisimilitude that hides this virtual nontemporality by disguising it as actual temporality. As such, we find this situation funny because it looks real, yet it is obviously unreal. This quasi realism enables the virtual world to mimic situations produced in reality, but to escape any permanent consequences that necessarily follow. Thus, in NBC's *Friends*, Rachel is able to keep up her job as a waitress even though she consistently makes mistakes and is regularly told she is dreadful; in Fox's *Grounded for Life*, Lily can take a taxi home alone and angrily expect someone else to pay when she arrives, and yet the incident is forgotten by the next episode. Likewise, in *Will & Grace,* we see that Karen can drink alcohol and read catalogues at work while maintaining her position throughout the series. The return to initial parameters in situation comedy is manifest in the episode of *Will & Grace* entitled "Head Case." This narrative involves Grace's attempt to redecorate what has recently become both her and Will's apartment. In the process of renovations, Grace knocks two large holes in the wall separating the two bathrooms. This hole, in any realistic situation, would take weeks to repair, yet in this instance, we can see that the damaged structure becomes a microcosm of the nonlinear consequentiality present in the situation comedy. The structural damage that Grace inflicts is repaired through their dialogue; merely saying that she will repair the wall is sufficient to rebuild the structure. The flaw is a manifestation of Neale and Krutnik's "return to the initial situation" (234) hidden behind a veil of realism. People do knock down bathroom walls. However, within the parameters of situation comedy, the wall does not need to be rebuilt physically because the structure of returning to the initial will be adhered to whether its actual repair takes place or not.

This carnivalized antistructure, as well as the nonlinear causality within, hermetically seals situation comedy in a segregated world of the virtual. From this, one can see that the inside/outside dichotomy changes from a mere narrative structure to an undefined, yet always present boundary that distinguishes the unreality of situation comedy as a genre from the causal realism of its relatives — the serial and the soap opera. In these, as Jane Feuer has proposed, "both situations and characters grow organically" (107). This lack of organic growth within the narrative and structure of situation comedy renders it a world apart from the realisms of the related genres, and through its (mis)appropriation and (ab)use of standard temporality, the norms of acceptability are altered. Thus, normative masculinity is allowed to "see [a new] reality with the eyes of the genre" (Bakhtin "The Formal Method in Literary Scholarship" 134), and as such, this reality becomes temporarily unreal and provisionally reimagined.

Situation comedy allows its audience to entertain a discourse that would not be acceptable in reality. As such, normative masculinity can be reimagined because no matter how radically marginalized its representation is, it will be acceptable and yet laughable precisely to the extent that the renegotiated masculinities cannot affect reality. The situations cited earlier become temporarily acceptable in the (anti)structure; Karen is able to keep her job as Grace's assistant precisely because it is not actually a job in any real sense, it is simply a device, a mask of verisimilitude that allows her to return each week. Her actions as a bad assistant become acceptable because the genre prioritizes the laughable over the actual or probable, the virtual over the real. Thus, realism becomes deferred as characters live in the constant and yet fleeting present. They become renewed and yet overused as "the formal necessities of the [situation comedy] as a whole provides [an] existential circle from which the characters cannot escape" (Eaton 37). Thus, the situation comedy becomes a virtual realm where consequences are void. This lack of consequence renders time neutral, and yet this deconstruction of the boundaries of linear time are contained so that it is radically conservative in its inability to extend this deconstruction beyond itself. It literally conserves the non-linearity within its own boundaries, and while situation comedy alters normal states and restructures normative consequentiality, it does not renegotiate them for a reality outside itself. From this, the consequences affected within the situation comedy become carnivalized and unreal. We laugh at the situations that characters find themselves in because the unreality of the causality that led them there is humorous. Thus, they become part of the modern day carnival where the established order is suspended, and thus, the characters that affect these pseudoconsequences become virtual others precisely because the footlights demark them as separate from reality. Here, we see a move away from Bakhtin's real carnival whereby the deconstruction takes place on all levels, as all become consumed within "the suspension of all hierarchical precedence" (*Rabelais* 13). In this carnival, the spectator can leave and remain separate from the mayhem while laughing at and with the unreal reality it presents.

Works Cited

Babuscio, Jack. "Camp and the Gay Sensibility." *Gays and Film*. Ed. Richard Dyer. London: BFI, 1977. 40–55.

Bakhtin, Mikhail. *Rabelais and His World.* H. Iswolsky, trans. Bloomington: Indiana University Press, 1984.

_____. *The Formal Method in Literary Scholarship: A Critical Introduction to Sociological Poetics.* Baltimore: John S. Hopkins University Press, 1978.

"Bud the Snob." William D. Russell. *Father Knows Best.* NBC. 16 Jan. 1955.

Eaton, Mick. "Television and Situation Comedy." *Popular Television and Film.* Tony Bennett, ed., et al. London: BFI/ The Open University Press, 1981. 26–52.

Feuer, Jane. "Narrative Form in American Network Television." *High Theory/Low Culture: Analysing Popular Television and Film.* Colin McCabe, ed. Manchester: Manchester University Press, 1986. 101–114.

"Head Case." Eric McCormack. *Will & Grace.* NBC. 05 Oct. 1998.

"He's Come Undone." Eric McCormack. *Will & Grace.* 08 Feb. 2000.

Neale, Steve, and Frank Krutnik. *Popular Film and Television Comedy.* London/ New York: Routledge, 1995.

"Pilot." Eric McCormack. *Will & Grace.* NBC. 21 Sept. 1998.

Straight and Crazy? Bisexual and Easy? Or Drunken Floozy? The Queer Politics of Karen Walker

Danielle Mitchell

> The sentimental designation of the nuclear family as a haven, a refuge from the cold and cruel world, has become harder to maintain when social movements such as feminism and child advocacy have brought to light the very real exploitative and abusive behavior within some families.... Indeed, ultimately such revelations about family practices call into question the whole concept of the nuclear family as a legally privileged unit that is entitled to special status....
> — Martha Fineman, *The Neutered Mother, the Sexual Family*

One almost has to be hiding under a rock or secreting oneself in a cave to miss it. The social contestation over sexuality has hit center stage, played out in real and metaphorical theaters from Broadway to *The Enquirer*, stockholder to church meetings, and suburban block parties to television. The discourse on sexuality that works to construct subjectivity is being manufactured at breakneck speed, proliferating throughout the machines of state and culture. Pronouncements about same-sex marriage, for instance, are being pumped over the airwaves for morning, afternoon, evening, and late-night editions of the news. Related stories appear with frequency in both the *New York Times* and small town newsletters. And the tickers on CNN and Fox currently run updates throughout the day, alerting the public to the legal battles and ceremonies taking place in San Francisco.

The extensive media coverage is not all about marriage, of course. The idea of family remains a key area of dispute in the contemporary contest over the inclusion of LGBT persons in mainstream cultural institutions and practices. Although much of the dispute is framed within pro and con camps, such binary logic is ineffectual for understanding the contestation over sexualities and family politics in a cultural milieu dominated by contradictions. Homophobic violence coexists with a broad social appreciation for Melissa Etheridge, *Will & Grace*, and *Queer Eye for the Straight Guy*, each achieving iconic status. And restrictive social codes coexist beside expanded opportunities in a number of states for LGBT couples to become legal co-parents. The battles over sexuality and social policy are as intense and divisive within LGBT organizations (that many assume represent unified fronts and political values) as they are in the general population. Factors such as race, sex, class, gender, and even appropriate understandings of sexuality reveal the existence of multiple LGBT communities, each politically interested, often politically opposed, and frequently invested in political change harmful to the needs of others. The discourses of sexuality and family, then, are complicated and often contradictory, simultaneously produced by an array of forces privileging values that range from liberal tolerance to conservative exclusion to social transformation. Consequently, the fact that representations of LGBT cultures and families are fraught with social significance and discrepant interpretations should come as no surprise.

This paper will focus on one site of such representation, *Will & Grace*, in order to discuss another — same-sex marriage. Competing interpretations of the sociopolitical and ideological effects of the show render problematic any simplistic understandings of its cultural power. But given its prominent inclusion of gay characters as well as the popularity of its first-run and syndicated episodes, *Will & Grace* plays a significant role in the production of sexuality. However, I want to shift the analytical focus from the often discussed gay characters (Will and Jack) to Karen Walker, played by Megan Mullally, because I believe she symbolizes the program's most progressive political work. In short, by challenging the binary construction of sexuality and working to queer marriage, Karen constructs a framework through which to recontextualize current social debates over the state of the family. Hence, her ability to make space within popular culture to understand marriage as a conflicted political site that includes privilege and normalization, progressive benefits and conservative regulatory effects has important implications for LGBT politics. In this paper, I will discuss her both as a fictional character and as a social figure who challenges the same-sex marriage movement to produce counterdiscourses that depart from hegemonic nuclear family structures.

Who's Who and What's What? Contextualizing Karen

Part of NBC's Thursday night "must see TV" lineup, the popular, Emmy-winning *Will & Grace* presents a main ensemble of four characters: straight interior designer Grace (played by Debra Messing); two gay men, the attorney Will (Eric McCormack) and the chronically underemployed Jack (Sean Hayes); and the feisty, often drunk socialite Karen, whose performativity is all but stably heterosexual. Until recently, it was the only primetime program aired on network television to present gay life (however problematic its depictions) as a legitimate programmatic context. Other shows certainly have had story lines about same-sex attraction and/or have included regular gay characters; *NYPD Blue*, *Spin City*, *Dawson's Creek*, *Melrose Place*, *Dynasty*, and *Soap* each included a gay man in the cast, as have countless other programs. And *All My Children*, *Roseanne*, and *Buffy the Vampire Slayer*, among others, have included lesbian characters. But *Will & Grace* does something different. Rendering gayness so central to the logic of the program that to be straight becomes a marker of difference, the program constructs a homosocial context as its norm in a medium where the Gay and Lesbian Alliance Against Defamation (GLAAD) asserts that only "2% of the 540 lead or supporting" characters on TV are gay (Shister, qtd. in Walters *All* 103).

However, the show's medium itself— comedy — relies on heterosexism as its currency, capitalizing on homophobic humor to ensure its broad market appeal. Mullally asserts as much in "Girl Talk": "The gay bashing is built into the show," she says; "the characters gay bash each other" (O'Donnell 3, 73). And as my students recently reminded me, were it not for that fact, they would be sickened rather than entertained by watching the program. The jokes thus reinforce difference and homophobia because gay men remain stereotypical figures of ridicule. In other words, rather than creating a subversive identification between heterosexual viewers and gay characters, the humor enables many viewers to interact figuratively with and be entertained by gays while also remaining firmly planted within heterosexist logic. The playful entertaining banter that rhetorically finesses a broad viewing audience to watch the gay-inclusive program, then, also provides a venue in which "the [homophobic] feelings liberals have taught themselves to deny are fully exercised. [Moreover,] whatever guilt might attend that release is defused by the queer [character] who attests to [the] harmlessness" of the gay-bashing humor (Goldstein 4). Factors such as these have led critics such as Melinda Kanner and Suzanna Walters to argue that *Will & Grace* is actually a "gay-but-normalized text" that produces the "new homophobia on TV" under the guise of a progressive appearance (34; *All* 113).

While such criticism is important, particularly in terms of establishing how Jack, Will, and the show's humor work to (re)produce the discourse on sexuality and its dominant stereotypes, I want to turn the lens of analysis to Karen Walker. One of the four ensemble characters, now a widow, and a woman whose "pet peeves [according to Will] are sobriety and kindness," her character may have as much — if not more — relevance for queer politics as either of the gay male characters. Specifically, she suggests a queer sexuality and constructs an economic understanding of marriage that can be used to queer notions of the family.

If Not Hetero or Homo, Then What? Karen and Queer Theory

Like the 1960s adoption of the term gay by liberationists who abandoned the clinical term homosexual and "redeploy[ed] a nineteenth-century slang term," the re-signification of queer is a strategic attempt to alter how we understand the subject — both the person and the area of knowledge we call sexuality (Jagose 72). Although a common enough occurrence, queer should not be operationally defined as "a quality related to any expression that can be marked as contra-, non-, or anti-straight" (Doty xv); this conflation would misinterpret the theoretical import of the term. As Annamarie Jagose explains, queer as a term and theoretical stance includes a political intent to "question conventional understandings of sexual identity by deconstructing the categories, oppositions and equations that sustain them" (97). And on a broader scale, it can be used to deconstruct whatever relations of power, identities, and social structures are considered normal. Thus, the point of queer theory is to destabilize structures of power and subjectivities, as well as the systems of logic through which we understand and regulate them. Karen creates a rhetorical and ideological space for such destabilization. Redefining the means by which sexuality and marriage are understood, she makes room for the production of counterdiscourses — those that challenge dominant social images and practices and destabilize myths to produce alternative conditions and possibilities.

Although not a title character, Karen is responsible for much of the program's electricity; her drug-induced cutting sarcasm that flies in the face of politically correct — and even anti-homophobic — discourse is often the spark required to ignite audience laughter. While Karen and Jack routinely play off of each other in order to entertain the audience, sharing campy jokes, rubbing bellies, caressing butts, squeezing breasts, and generally creating a dynamic of teasing, touching, and verbal sparring, Andrew Holleran notes that her "cynical, bleak, and nihilistic" commentary often upstages the flippant Jack, making her the show's central farcical figure of heartless humor (3). Consider her frequent targeting of Will as an example. She taps into his insecurities about gender-appropriate performance by deploying signifiers such as "Wilma," "she," and "wife" to resex him rhetorically. Such moves not only make fun of him, but also appeal to and perpetuate the dominant social conflation of gayness with femininity in order to generate laughter. This is, in fact, one of the central comedic and rhetorical strategies of the program, occurring 283 times in its first three seasons alone (Linneman). Will's character does attempt to challenge stereotypes of gayness, but Karen's witty repartee and the discourse of gender it relies upon work to reverse the challenge by (re)securing masculinity within the domain of male heterosexuality. This is an important conservative feature of her character and the program in general, yet it is Karen's performance of sexuality that I am most interested in here, especially its relationship to a less conservative ideological agenda.

Essentially, Karen's desire cannot be contained within a heterosexual framework or a normalized gay discourse. Take, for instance, the fact that her marriage did not define her as stably heterosexual. While her multiple bath-sharing scenes with Grace and Rosario (her maid) make her more quirky than queer, her character does explicitly identify a history of same-sex attractions and physical encounters. And in the last couple of seasons, there are moments when she is almost predatory in her pursuit of the female flirt. Thus, being neither a wife nor a widowed woman interested in heterosexual intimacies strictly delimits Karen's sexuality. In fact, when it comes to flirtation, attraction, and sex, she appears to have a policy of equal opportunity: whether Karen is married or not, she flirts with gay men, straight men, married and unmarried men as well as lesbians, straight women, married and unmarried women. Karen thereby rejects the dominant paradigm of binary sexuality and disrupts the rules of monogamy that tend to restrict the range of people with whom one is able to flirt. As a result, she challenges images of the wife and performs sexuality outside the parameters of the binary system in which a subject is either hetero or homo.

Whereas Grace, Jack, and Will (and many members of the viewing audience) understand their sexuality as firmly sex object-oriented, Karen "move[s] along the perimeters" of dominant subject formations rather than reside in any one location (Kanner 35). That is to say that she plays by a different set of rules when it comes to sexuality — rules that adopt a queer posture by denying the legitimacy of either/or understandings of sexuality. Consequently, her performance of desire and attraction call into question the delimitations associated with the prevailing paradigm of sexuality. But interpreting her character as a poster queer has troubling contradictions that must be taken into account before accepting her as a catalyst in the move toward transformative politics.

The program's narrative tempers Karen's ideological potential, rendering more complicated her relationship to the transgression of sociosexual expectations. As previously discussed, her jokes often appeal to conservative assumptions; and as a character who revels in excess, whether through her use of hyperbole, prescription medication, or alcohol, Karen's actions can be interpreted as the deeds of an eccentric — someone out of touch with reality who should not to be taken seriously. With the persona of an overmedicated jokester whose best friends, according to Will, are vodka and gin, Karen is a figure of drunken impertinence designed to create laughter through outrageous and often rude behavior. Were we to interpret her character as a mere figure of entertainment free of ideological import, however, we would miss the social commentary under the giggly yet sharply medicated surface. For instance, we might be persuaded to dismiss the implications of her behavior with Jack, choosing to interpret her only as his drunken playmate and benefactor. The narrative supports this reading of their interactions because, in addition to spending much of her time under the influence, it is quite clear that Jack has no desire to engage physically any woman beyond the level of flirtation. After all, even in procreation Jack has no actual sexual contact with women; his son is the product of a sperm bank. Furthermore, Karen is a caricature of the wealthy socialite, a persona that has serious implications for readings of her character because her performance is enabled by her privilege.

Her position as a wealthy white woman enables her to disrupt social expectations in ways that most of us cannot, as our subjectivities are produced and delimited by different material realities. Once the wife but now the widow of a wealthy businessman, Karen is free from both the domestic responsibilities (such as childcare and home maintenance) and the pressure of work. While she does have a job, it consists largely of misfiling papers, ignoring telephone calls, thumbing through magazines, and ridiculing her boss (Grace). Yet she need not fear the consequences of ignoring the capitalist dictates of efficiency and productivity. Monetary investments in the interior design firm secure her position, as her (husband's) financial portfolio secures her social privilege. This position of power is further reinforced through the repeated dehumanization of her domestic help; she frequently refers to her servants by function (Driver, Cook), for example, and treats Rosario as a possession, asserting that she owns her. Granted, Karen does call Rosario her friend. And the show's humor suggests that Rosario and Karen are equals, especially when Rosario ridicules her: "Have you looked up your ass you drunken fool?" But their sarcastic quipping creates only a mirage of equality; the rhetorical construction of equality cannot hide real material disparities in power. These factors construct Karen as a contradictory queer figure, rendering safe her taboo-breaking behavior, because rather than attempt a transformation, they reproduce the ideologies of social relations — ideologies that oppress many and continue to divide LGBT organizations and communities.

Given Karen's complicated relationship to structures of power, Julia Parnaby would resist interpreting Karen (or anything else, for that matter) as queer. In "Queer Straits" she objects to popular deployments of the term and the larger field of queer theory because they often fail to account for material realities and work to reproduce conservative ideas. That is, while appearing to further a progressive agenda, the deployments actually reinforce social inequity by eliding their own production of dominant ideology. Such points are well taken. Karen's actions cannot be understood outside the context of her socioeconomic power. She plays with mores because she can; she consumes her "party mix [of] uppers, downers, and candy corn" without being stigmatized because she can; she disregards conventions of etiquette because she can; her privilege enables her to do so.

But Karen is not simply a drunk to be ignored. Nor is she a wealthy fag hag who merely voyeurs gay culture. And she is far from being straight, crazy, or a floozy. A more appropriate approach is to read Karen as a bisexual figure, exhibiting attraction outside the either/or binary privileged by dominant constructs of sexuality. But she can also be read as a queer figure, not because she elides the material issues that concern Parnaby, but because she makes them so obvious. By repeatedly demonstrating how racial and financial privilege enables her performance and by openly characterizing marriage as an economic institution, Karen makes overt the material dynamics that produce the prevailing system of intimacy and creates a rhetorical space for a critique of human relations that can, in turn, be used to destabilize structures of power.

Making Marriage Strange(r)? Destabilizing Dominant Frames of Reference

If, even in light of Karen's questioning of binary sexuality and her flirtatious behavior with persons other than her husband, viewers are inclined to ignore larger discussions of marriage, the program's narrative makes it almost impossible to do so. Karen simply raises the issue of marriage too many times for it to be treated as a nonissue. More importantly, it is through these discussions that she recontextualizes the social construct of marriage; she makes it strange by relocating it within a logic of economics. This relocation subsequently enables a queering of bourgeois images of romantic marriage.

As previously suggested, Karen tends to see people in relation to the value they have for her. When it comes to her staff, for instance, she often fixates on their labor-based function and their usefulness to her. While it may be overstating to assert that this rubric explains all of her relationships, textual evidence suggests that the value of some previous intimacies can be understood in similar terms; they were important insofar as they were materially (and, consequently, socially) useful in her efforts to secure and sustain privilege. Their value was based not on their productive labor, but on the means by which they worked to enhance her cultural and economic capital. When we first meet Karen's mother, for example, we learn that the women share a dubious history of tag-teaming for dollars; they would target and then establish relationships with wealthy men in order to acquire money. Even though Karen puts much distance between herself and her mother, as well as their antics, the pattern of financially assessing men for what they have to offer her remains a line of inquiry pertinent to her marriage. Before Stan's death, for example, she often referred to him as her cash cow, regarding him as a necessary evil that had to be dealt with in order to protect the wealth and social privilege that accompanied being his wife. Understanding this aspect of Karen's character is not so easy as merely calling her a gold digger, however.

By making clearer the relationship between marriage and economics and by deemphasizing marriage as the locus of passion and family as the site of emotional fulfillment, Karen performs the disparity between mythical and actual relationships, between dominant and idealized cultural images and material realities. Her work in this regard echoes Frederick Engels' efforts to call into question socially naturalized concepts of marriage, love, and family. In *The Origin of the Family, Private Property and the State*, he discusses monogamous marriage as "the first form of family to be based not on natural but on economic conditions" (128). Rather than being the product of "individual sex-love," compulsory marriage is the precondition for the emergence of that form of love. In this reversal of hegemonic logic, the concept of romantic, freely chosen marriage based on interpersonal chemistry is a means to elide or ideologically conceal the compulsory nature of marriage. There is more freedom to choose a spouse. There are more opportunities for people to establish financial independence and to remain unmarried. Yet the social and financial pressures to and privileges for marrying compel participation. And as Laura Kipnis notes in *Against Love*, the economic rationality once responsible for the "pre-assignment" of spouses remains the dominant logic for the newly enabled norm of partner "selection." The once external imperative to rank "mates for material and social assets is now incorporated into the psychology of love and unconscious structures of desire," internalized such that individuals "fall in love with mates who are also — coincidentally — good investments" (63). Regardless of the efforts of dominant social ideology and cultural myth to construct marriage as a love connection, the institutions of love and marriage remain as intimately linked to economics as they ever were. Consequently, while marriage is a choice, it is one that subjects are expected to make and to make wisely and in accordance with businesslike logic, as marriage is a strategy for negotiating sociohistorical material conditions.

Karen understands marriage in this way. To her, it is less about privileging a male/female love dyad than it is about pragmatism and survival, constructing a relationship that works to fulfill needs and create privilege. None of this is to say that Karen lacks affection for Stan, that she fails to perform any of the emotional work necessary to sustain a marriage, or that her relocation of marriage and sexuality within different frames of reference render her completely outside dominant ideologies and performances of marriage and intimacy. Certainly Karen peels away layers of cultural myth through her apparent boredom with motherhood and marriage, her frequent discussions of marriage as a means to secure social privilege, her consistent reliance on mind-altering substances, and her fluid understanding of sexuality. And her concern with money and position as well as her sharp-tongued wit may create the appearance of a cold, manipulative woman with little regard for the feelings of those around her, including her husband. They are never really seen together, after all. Whether he is out of the country, in another room, in prison, or dead, Stan is/was a character invoked rather than embodied, and invoked most often as a target of ridicule. Yet Karen does display concern for him. She mentions to others that she loves him, squeals "Out! Out damn spot!" after considering an extramarital affair, and becomes hurt and outraged when Stan actually does have an affair. But her response to this last example is particularly important because it leads back to her construction of marriage as an institution of exchange.

In short, Karen's response to Stan's affair is based on more than her sense of betrayal. Not only does she feel hurt, but she also feels cheated, as if a possession has been stolen — her rights of ownership threatened. Karen provides context for her response on multiple occasions, clearly articulating the link between marriage and property. When considering the possibility of filing for divorce, for example, she tells Will that she owns Stan. And in discussion with Beverly Lesley, both characters understand themselves as the property of their respective spouses, commodities produced and acquired through the legal contract of marriage. Karen thusly reiterates marriage as a means to establish financial comfort, social privilege, and ownership. And by further contextualizing the institution outside the ideology of heterosexual romance, outside the myth of individual sex/love, and within a more material rhetoric, she renders problematic dominant ideologies of marriage and participates in the current sociopolitical (re)construction of that institution. Take, for instance, how Karen's stance on marriage suggests a financially based logic central to the political efforts of mainstream LGBT advocacy groups.

Since the first modern attempt to secure gay marriage (circa 1970), one of the main arguments deployed by the LGBT movement focused squarely on the relationship between dollars and sense: if marriage is an institution responsible for creating personal, familial, and national stability via its economic and emotional effects, then it only makes sense to reinforce and further extend that stability. Excluding LGBT persons and their children could only perpetuate instability. Battles for legalization in Hawaii, Alaska, Massachusetts, and Vermont, as well as the current national debate, draw upon this logic to link marriage and financial security, protection, and privilege. As The Human Rights Campaign explains, marriage ensures for its participants "more than 1,000 federal protections and responsibilities" (online). Social security benefits can be collected only by married persons and biological or legally adopted children, for example. Since same-sex marriage is not legal and third-party adoptions are not nationally available either, "a typical LGBT couple could lose over $10,000 per year" in the event that a partner or parent dies (Lambda 1). Furthermore, same-sex partners would also be levied an inheritance tax that hetero spouses do not incur, creating additional financial burden. Such practical economic benefits that would result from the recognition of LGBT partnerships are virtually incalculable, as they range from the major issues of taxes and health insurance costs to everyday benefits such as the discounts offered by car rental companies who consider and charge spouses as if they are one driver. And access to marriage would surely provide such economic (as well as an extensive array of social) benefits to lesbians and gays who marry, as well as to their children.

If Karen Walker symbolizes an effort to queer social structures — sexuality, marriage, even expectations of sobriety and appropriate behavior — she also suggests the need to call them into question. So while her rhetoric lends itself well to current political efforts to legalize same-sex marriage by constructing sexuality as a fluid system and by highlighting the economic aspects of marital relationships, it can also be used as a lens for analyzing such efforts. Following on her lead, then, perhaps the question that should be asked is not why lesbian and gay couples are excluded from the privileges associated with marriage, but how their inclusion might serve to perpetuate that very system of privilege that is based on economic rewards (or punishment) and the normalization of desire.

If we value the queer directionality suggested by Karen's recontextualization of marriage and sexuality, we must move beyond the practical, financial benefits of marriage to also consider how it works in less positive ways. We must consider the ways that "same-sex marriages [fail to] present a *fundamental* challenge to the institution of marriage..."

(Walters "Take" 135). Additionally, we must ask how legalization would perpetuate systemic inequity by perpetuating the privatization of social resources. As Judith Stacey asserts, for instance, the fight for same-sex marriage has gained its momentum from its compatibility with the values and practices of capitalist hegemony. If this is true, another risk posed by the marriage contest is that particular privileges, once accorded only married heterosexuals, will be spread to a wider group of persons but not actually destroyed. If marriage is used as a means to solve material inequities, for instance, then it will do so for only a segment of the overall population because it privileges a privatized system for the distribution of resources and a privatized solution to systemic problems.

One's willingness to comply with state-privileged, sociosexual, familial arrangements should not be the basis for economic, personal, or social well-being. Rather than seeking access to the institutions that function to sustain an inequitable privatized social order, a counterdiscourse capable of producing transformative relations would envision universally equitable social relations as the goal. And eliminating the social and material, that is, the ideological compulsion to marry would enable the emergence of more equitable social formations.

Karen may not articulate this conclusion herself, yet her questioning of what it means to be a wife, mother, woman, and sexual being suggests a queer politics that does lead us to question what structures, values, and ideological stances ought to be used as the foundation for social privilege and family. While Will might tell us that "You don't get relationship advice from Karen; you get [instead] what wine goes with mood stabilizers," and while she may certainly have a good understanding of how to mix drug cocktails, she also has something valuable to add to the current debates over family and social change — debates that often advocate for inclusion into privilege rather than for universally equitable treatment.

Works Cited

Doty, Alexander. *Making Things Perfectly Queer: Interpreting Mass Culture*. Minneapolis: University of Minnesota Press, 1993.

Engels, Frederick. *The Origin of the Family, Private Property and the State.* 1972. New York: International, 1993.
Fineman, Martha. *The Neutered Mother, the Sexual Family and Other Twentieth Century Tragedies.* New York: Routledge, 1995.
Goldstein, Richard. *The Attack Queers: Liberal Society and the Gay Right.* New York: Verso, 2002.
Holleran, Andrew. "The Alpha Queen." *The Gay and Lesbian Review* 7.1 (Summer 2000): 65. online. InfoTrac. 17 Jan. 2002.
Human Rights Campaign Fund. "The State of the Family: Laws and Legislation Affecting Gay, Lesbian, Bisexual and Transgender Families." Washington, D.C. 2002. online. www.hrc.org
Jagose, Annamarie. *Queer Theory.* New York: New York University Press, 1996.
Kanner, Melinda. "Can *Will & Grace* be 'Queered'?" *The Gay and Lesbian Review* 10.4 (July-Aug 3003): 34–35.
Kipnis, Laura. *Against Love: A Polemic.* New York: Pantheon, 2003.
Lambda Legal Defense and Education Fund. "Denying Access to Marriage Harms Families: Social Security." 17 July 2002. online. http://www.lambdalegal.org. 15 August 2002. 3 pages.
Linneman, Thomas. "The Intersection of Male Homosexuality and Femininity on *Will & Grace*." *Current Representations of LGBT People in Entertainment Television: The Case of* Will & Grace. GLAAD Center for the Study of Media and Society. ed. Van M. Cagle. online: GLAAD, 2001.
O'Donnell, Rosie. "Girl Talk." *Rosie* 129.5 (March 2002): 68–74.
Parnaby, Julia. "Queer Straits." *All The Rage: Reasserting Radical Lesbian Feminism.* Lynne Harne and Elaine Miller, ed. New York: Teachers College, 1996. 3–10.
Stacey, Judith. "Married to the Market: The Haves and Have Nots of Contemporary Conjugal Politics." 5 Feb. 2004. Duquesne University.
Walters, Suzanna. *All the Rage: The Story of Gay Visibility in America.* Chicago: University of Chicago Press, 2001.
———. "Take My Domestic Partner, Please: Gays and Marriage in the Era of the Visible." *Queer Families, Queer Politics: Challenging Culture and the State.* Mary Bernstein and Renate Reimann, eds. New York: Columbia University Press, 2001. 338–57.
Will & Grace. Max Mutchnick and David Kohan, Creators and Producers. National Broadcasting Company.

Desire and the "Big Black Sex Cop": Race and the Politics of Sexual Intimacy in HBO's *Six Feet Under*

Guy Mark Foster

CLAIRE: What do you see in him?
KEITH: He's just David, you know.
CLAIRE: (Laughing) I know. That's why I was asking.
KEITH: He is smart. He's kind. He's funny. I know he can be a little uptight. Underneath that he's such a little boy. Innocent. And I like that. Most of the men I meet — Well, they just kind of want me to be just one thing.
CLAIRE: What? Like 'Big Black Sex Cop'? (Impersonating a type of gay man:) "Sorry I was speeding, Officer. I guess you have to punish me now."
KEITH: (Smiling) Yeah. And I don't wanna be that. (Beat.) Rent a video. (Claire laughs.) David, he gets me. When someone sees you as you really are, and wants to be with you, that's powerful.

This tantalizing exchange between Claire Fisher (Lauren Ambrose) and Keith Charles (Mathew St. Patrick), two of the main characters from the critically acclaimed HBO television series *Six Feet Under*, takes place after dark in a vacant lot in downtown Pasadena. Earlier, Claire, the precocious teenage daughter of the proprietors of a local funeral home, had arrived to search for the remains of a human foot a former boyfriend had tossed from his car window after Claire had angrily stuffed it inside his locker in retaliation for his having bragged to classmates about their fetishistic sexual tryst. Keith, an LAPD police officer, who is a black gay man who just happens to be dating Claire's closeted brother David (Michael C. Hall), shows up separately to fulfill a promise he had made to David that he would try to locate the severed appendage before Claire got into any more trouble. Claire's delightfully knowing comment, anticipating Keith's description of the type of men he had dated before meeting David, makes spectacularly vivid the kinds of psychic risks to which many contemporary blacks are vulnerable in a white-dominated society that claims to be color-blind with respect to race, but which in reality is far from it. Claire surmises that those men wanted Keith to play the archetypal role of the hypersexual black stud of their fantasies and nothing more — a role that, we are to presume, David does not want him to play (at least not full-time).

Notably, Keith does not explicitly mention the racial identities of the men he dated prior to David. Claire simply assumes these men are white; either that, or she assumes that whatever these men's racial or ethnic identities happen to be they have already internalized dominant (i.e. white) cultural beliefs about the way black bodies signify in an antiblack culture like the U.S. After all, Claire's "Big Black Sex Cop" remark can only make sense to viewers, as indeed it can only make sense to Keith (who confirms its accuracy), if we are willing to acknowledge all that we know of the mythologized discourse that has surrounded the black body over time within colonial and U.S. racial regimes.

This unlikely conversation between and David's younger sister and Keith asks viewers to consider that Claire, and by extension *Six Feet Under*, offers Keith a progressive white vantage point for a critique of "color blindness." It is a matter of common knowledge that color blindness has been the dominant public understanding of race in the U.S. since the end of the Second World War, replacing centuries of the ideology of color-consciousness, which held that whites were superior in every way to other races, especially blacks. And while *Six Feet Under*, especially in those scenes with Keith, initially appears to offer viewers a trenchant critique of this present ideology, I will argue that the show's representational politics has not completely departed from this dominant postwar strategy for dealing with race. While *Six Feet Under* would like us to believe that David is different from most of the other men Keith has dated, I want to argue that the show actually offers its viewers no concrete evidence in support of this claim.

As scholars have argued, one of the principal drawbacks of color blindness as a strategy for reconciling ourselves with an overly race-conscious past is that it represses rather than confronts and resolves racial tension, and the repressed always returns in less palatable ways. Because *Six Feet Under*, with few exceptions, suppresses verbal references to race while fully exploiting race's presence in the form of black/white visual differences, it allows race's unspoken absence to resurface in unexpected, even troubling, ways. Thus the narrative is engaging in a self-conscious effort to manage or contain otherwise problematic discourse about race that might prove disruptive to the specific brand of color blindness that underwrites its portrayal of Keith and David's relationship. This representational approach has led *Six Feet Under* to depict Keith and David reductively as a gay male couple rather than, what they appear to some viewers to be — a gay male interracial couple.

Taking Black Folks' Issues Seriously

Since its premiere on June 3, 2001, *Six Feet Under* has enjoyed both critical and popular acclaim. The mainstream press and the lesbian and gay media have consistently praised the series for its sensitive and progressive treatment of lesbian and gay concerns, and the show has garnered many nominations and awards. Yet the show has not been recognized by the NAACP Image Awards, which has overlooked the series in general and overlooked its lone black actor, Mathew St. Patrick, in particular. Perhaps this has more to do with the type of character St. Patrick portrays than with his acting ability, as homosexuality and black/white intimacy have long been controversial within black communities. The NAACP's failure to endorse of *Six Feet Under* in general and St. Patrick in particular could easily be attributed to both homophobia and mixophobia.

While this could quite easily be the case, I would like to suggest there might be a more productive way to read the organization's actions: as a calculated response to color blindness' demand for Americans, white and nonwhite alike, to suppress all race discourse in the interests of overcoming racism. Put simply, the NAACP's refusal to sanction the show could be seen as the organization's way of thumbing its nose at such discourse altogether, thus ignoring and rejecting the typical mainstream television portrayal of black characters in multiracial casts.

The cultural critic Herman Gray uses the term "assimilationist" to characterize such portrayals. As he puts it, "the worlds [these programs] construct are distinguished by the complete elimination or, at best, marginalization of social and cultural difference in the interest of shared and universal similarity." Black characters, when they do appear, are incorporated within "hegemonic white worlds void of any hint of African American traditions, social struggle, racial conflicts, and cultural difference" (85). Although HBO is a cable station, Gray's characterization of mainstream network television could easily apply to the way *Six Feet Under* has portrayed Keith Charles. As a result, African American viewers who tune in expecting the show to engage with their fears and anxieties about black cultural identities in general and race mixing in particular are often disappointed.

Suppressing Race, Narrating Gender

Let's look closely at several scenes during season one of *Six Feet Under* that demonstrate the asymmetrical relationship between race and gender that I have been discussing. The first scene to consider is that in which David Fisher is first outed as a gay man. It opens with a flashback to David's older brother Nate (Peter Krause) as a young boy, entering the embalming room where his father (Richard Jenkins) is hard at work embalming a recently deceased, middle-aged man. The scene closes in the present day with Nate, his brother David, and Rico, a Fisher family employee, all adults, conversing uncomfortably in this same embalming room over the body of Nate and David's recently deceased father. Suddenly David's cell phone rings and, not wanting to have the conversation in front of Nate and Rico, he excuses himself into the hall. One of the central purposes of this scene is to convey important information about the Fisher brothers: namely, their essential conflict with one another, one the show will seek to resolve over the course of season one. As evidenced by his reticence to talk to his lover in front of Nate, David is clearly struggling with his sexuality, a struggle with which the viewers are asked to sympathize. "Not only has David just been outed to us, the viewers," writes Samuel Chambers, "but when he returns to the embalming room [after his conversation with Keith], we feel (and fear) *with him* that perhaps the closet door has been left ajar" (28). Nate and Rico may know his secret.

But a far more complex model of sexuality circulates within the show's sociopolitical imaginary than the author is willing to acknowledge, given his exclusive fixation on the revelation of homosexuality. For who precisely is the "we" that, as Chambers describes it, "feels" and "fears" along with David that his secret identity as a gay man has just been revealed? For Chambers, as well as for much contemporary lesbian and gay/queer theory overall, the "we," the "world" that most matters is a universalist one in which the concept of heteronormativity stands apart, untouched and carefree, from other forms of subjectification. It is, as Chambers puts it, "*the* structuring norm," and it is therefore unmediated by other forms of difference. What is equally important, however, and more often ignored, is that this scene also outs David racially as white. It does this in part because the caller on the other end of the line, David's lover Keith, is not white, but black. To quote Stuart Hall, with only a slight adjustment from his original emphasis, "*we* know what 'white' means not because there is some essence of 'whiteness' but because *we* can contrast it with its opposite — 'black.'" "Meaning," in other words, Hall tells us, "is relational. It is the 'difference' between 'white' and 'black' which signifies, which carries meaning" (328).

While the "we" in Hall's utterance recalls the "we" in Chambers, there is a crucial distinction between the two. The latter resists claims to a universalist social reality in favor of an awareness of the ways in which U.S. social formation is constituted more generally by racial history. For the former this history is ancillary, and therefore not worthy of mention. And precisely because of the history of the U.S. as a racially segregated nation, the meanings that Americans attach to the sight of black and white bodies in close, intimate proximity to one another becomes weighted with sexual significance. As Siobhan Somerville has argued, "the figure of the color line itself instantiate[s] desire," regardless of gender (36).

It is incumbent upon viewers as well to recognize that David's outing not only reveals him as a gay man, but that it also reveals him as a particular kind of gay man — specifically, a "dinge queen," a pejorative term for a white gay man who is either primarily or only sometimes attracted to men of color — in this case, black men. Remarkably, this insight is one which critics like Chambers appear all too willing to overlook, perhaps because of the distasteful associations such terms, and others like it, often conjure. While this reticence is certainly understandable, such thinking, and the labeling it inspires, is nonetheless a central part of gay male culture, one that disproportionately affects gay men of color. Hence, refusing to challenge the underlying beliefs of such labeling only allows the troubling assumptions imbedded within them to remain conceptually intact, and therefore laden with enduring cultural meaning and power. Because the representational strategies of *Six Feet Under* interpolate the ideal viewers as white, middle-class, and heterosexual, the audience is only invited to think of David and Keith as a gay male couple and not as both a gay male couple and an interracial couple. This limited way in which viewers are directed to think of Keith and David is reinforced throughout the first season by other scenes in which race and gender are semantically opposed.

In Episode Four, for example, Keith chases down and verbally lashes out at a white male motorist who calls David and him "fucking fags" for taking too long to pull out of the space in which they are parked. Walking back to Keith's SUV, David tries to downplay the man's homophobic remark by saying to Keith: "I don't think he meant anything by it." Incredulous at David's lack of outrage, Keith fires back: "You hate yourself that much?" Later in the episode, David meets up with Keith at the lesbian and gay church they have been attending together and apologizes for their disagreement in the parking lot. David then asks if Keith thinks he really hates himself. At this point, Keith, in a tone that is reassuring, but nonetheless firm, asserts that he knows that David is emotionally regarding his struggle to accept his sexuality; after all, Keith has been there himself, but he, Keith, has no intention of "moving backwards for anybody," and this includes David. When David responds that he is not asking Keith to "move backwards" but only to "be patient" and "a little calmer," Keith makes the following reply:

> Do you have any idea what I put up with on my job everyday? How many times the word fag has been written on my locker? How many times I wonder going into a dangerous situation if I'm even gonna get backup? We were stepped on yesterday, David. And I did something about it because I am tired of it. When you get tired of it, you let me know.

It is obvious that David's struggle to accept his sexual identity is offered as the sole context from which viewers are to construct meaning to this heated exchange with Keith, one of several between the lovers during the show's first season. The fact that Keith is not only a gay man, but also African American is presented as irrelevant in terms of the show's verbal narrative. His response to David, therefore, can only be allowed to serve one purpose — as corroborating evidence of his identity as a gay man. If what Keith says is allowed to serve multiple purposes, it may cause the viewer to oscillate between the various options and subsequently to derail the effort the show is making to "fix" narrative meaning, to maintain its dichotomous structuring of race and gender, and therefore to analogize the two forms of oppression. For what this scene and numerous others strive over and over to demonstrate is that Keith is proud while David is ashamed of being gay.

But what about Keith's earlier rhetorical question, the one that implied that David's attempt to downplay the homophobic slur offered incontrovertible proof that David hates himself for being gay? Might there be another way to interpret this remark and thus situate it against my reading of the scene as one that privileges David and his single-issue identity struggles? For, as I have argued, strong criticism is often directed at blacks who couple interracially with whites in African American communities. Such men and women are not only accused by other blacks of turning against their own culture, but they are often also accused of hating their own black skin as well as hating the black skin of other African Americans. The cultural critic bell hooks captures this dilemma nicely when, in an interview with the black British filmmaker Isaac Julien, she asks: "[H]ow can we name the black desire of the white body without reinscribing the idea of black self-hatred or distaste for the black body?" (qtd in Julien and McCabe 127).

And yet at the level of the show's verbal narrative such concerns are suppressed. As viewers, we are not asked to consider how having a white boyfriend might create anxieties for Keith, whose loyalties may not lie exclusively with the largely white gay community, but also with black heterosexual culture. Why the black heterosexual community? Because most black gay men are vulnerable not only to homophobia but also to racism due to the visibility of their black skin — which for some men supercedes knowledge of their gayness — many choose to take refuge from time to time in the black community, which is overwhelmingly heterosexual. As Cathy Cohen states, "The prospect of facing continuous residential, occupational, and social exclusion as a manifestation of widespread racism, even in primarily white lesbian and gay communities, underscores the importance of [lesbians and gay men of color] securing, often at very high stakes, feelings of safety and familiarity" (93). These "high stakes" very often translate into black lesbians and gays having to endure forms of homophobia from relatives, friends, and acquaintances in the black community. The small consolation for such men and women is the knowledge that at least the homophobia one suffers is not doubled by racism.

Six Feet Under at times attempts to manage or contain racial discourse by displacing verbal references to race onto references to some other, often related, textual concern. We can see evidence of this occurring throughout several episodes, the most notable perhaps in Episode Five when David and Keith argue once again over David's struggles with being gay. This time the argument centers around David's apparent need to keep the two men's relationship a secret. Keith accuses David of taking one step forward when he finally comes out to his brother Nate, but then of taking "a giant leap backwards" when he refuses to allow Keith to accompany him to his family's church and risk being identified by the congregation and his family members as gay. Stung by what he perceives to be an unwarranted attack on the depth of his commitment to Keith, David's only response is to retaliate and wound his black boyfriend in what he imagines represents a comparable site of vulnerability for him, his racial identity. "So now I'm a Nazi collaborator?" David asks, smugly. "You know a lot of African Americans might say the same about you being a member of the LAPD."

On the one hand, David's allusion to the controversy generated by the 1991 Rodney King beatings in Los Angeles and the subsequent trials, coupled with the extermination camps of the Third Reich, helps to place his conflict with Keith in a historically and culturally specific context — after all, some African American police officers were made to question their personal and professional loyalties during this admittedly trying period, just as some Jews were vilified for their collusion with Nazi war criminals during World War II. On the other hand, David's attempt to equate these two scenarios with the tensions caused by his own ambition to be a deacon in the Episcopal church and his identity as a middle-class gay man is not only strained, but also arrogant and spineless. Keith's devastating reaction to David's cool logic is therefore entirely appropriate given the self-satisfied superiority his suddenly very white boyfriend has just exhibited. Hence, when Keith, after hearing this, leans in and shouts viciously into David's face, "You fucking coward!" and then jumps into his SUV and drives out of the parking lot, the viewer is invited to share vicariously in Keith's disappointment. But about what precisely is the audience supposed to be disappointed? Is it the fact that David is in such denial about his shame at being gay that he cannot begin to appreciate his boyfriend's efforts to help ease him through the process of coming out, or that his shame is so totalizing it leads him, opportunistically, to make two false analogies that expose his naivete about that which matters most to Keith, a gay man and a person of color?

It is at this point that I suggest the show exposes its displacement of verbal energy about race onto other concerns that stand in or act as a surrogate for its suppressed discourse about race. For when David suggests that Keith may be in bed with the enemy for being a black police officer, his comment attempts to manage and contain the meaning of race the show exploits for its own liberal ends. In so doing, it simultaneously reveals that its preferred concept of race is exclusively manufactured for the benefit of its ideal viewers, individuals who are white, middle-class, and heterosexual and do not care to be implicated as racists. Within

African American communities, however, being in bed with the enemy also refers to someone who betrays the racial collective by entering into sexual and romantic relationships with whites. Because *Six Feet Under* chooses to suppress this "other," group-specific meaning of the terms it deploys, the show exposes its own ideological investments in the central tenets of a belief in color blindness that refuses to acknowledge the importance of membership in cultural groups and the extent to which such ties can exert influence (welcome and unwelcome) on individual choices.

In an illuminating exploration of the interracial sexual dynamics of the Academy award-winning motion picture *Monster's Ball*, Jane Flax writes: "Subjects are inducted into the symbolic order of contemporary America, not only through the Father's no of the incest taboo and the phallic interjection of sexual difference, but also through the Law's demand for racial interpellation.... The race/gendered reading of my body thus provides a narrative of identity. It enables [bodily] organs to speak and tell me who I am" (60). Flax suggests that we do not arrive at gendered subjectivity apart from racialized subjectivity or vice-versa, but that the two come into existence simultaneously as part of a mutually informing as well as mutually transforming partnership. The same holds true for our sexuality. Indeed, the very intelligibility of a subject's sexuality is dependent upon the extent to which our gendered and racial identities satisfy or, as the case may be, fail to satisfy dominant and, for African Americans, marginalized cultural norms and expectations. Moreover, this is the case not only with David (who we see repeatedly attempting to conceal his sexuality as a gay man from his family, friends, and community), but also with Keith, whose multi-issue identity concerns repeatedly fall out of view. Where are the black community members in Keith's life, for instance, who may be less troubled by his homosexuality than by the fact that his boyfriend is white? The inclusion of a sister and parents for Keith in season two did little to answer this question since the fact that Keith is interracially coupled with someone white was never presented as a concern for these characters; only the fact that he is gay was relevant. So although *Six Feet Under* consistently narrativizes David and Keith as gay men, and therefore as a gay male couple, the show has failed to develop the two men as individuals or as a couple with a marked racial difference. In its unwillingness to even register Keith's racial identity, let alone to explore it in narrative terms, *Six Feet Under* stubbornly conveys the message that only gender matters, not race.

We are told repeatedly during the first season, for instance, that Keith is a "proud gay man." But if Keith is a "proud *gay* man," is he also a "proud *black* man"? Curiously, on this last point the series maintains a steely silence. The writers refuse, for instance, to even consider how a particular gay man's lifelong experience with, for instance, antiblack bigotry may or may not influence the extent to which he is willing or unwilling to endure homophobia. Not only that, but the dialogue between David and Keith that follows the heated confrontation in the parking lot seems to imply that the motorist's comment was inspired solely by his antipathy towards gay men and not also, or even primarily, by the fact that one of these men happens to be black and one white. For what was it precisely that convinced the motorist Keith and David were a gay couple in the first place? Neither man behaves in an especially flamboyant or swishy manner, two visual descriptors a heterosexist culture relies upon to maintain rigid distinctions between what it regards as stereotypical gay male behavior and the stereotypical behavior of the supposed straight male. But what if it was Keith's and David's racial difference that initially raised this man's suspicion?

At times, the color line becomes instrumental in making desire legible. Scholars have noted for some time that homosexual and interracial object choices have been conceptually linked in the dominant culture's visual economy as perverse deviations from more normative forms of sexual desire. As Siobhan Somerville has noted, "Racial difference performed an important visual function in ... turn of the century American culture," one that has allowed racial differences between paired individuals to bec[o]me a marker for the sexual nature" of that pairing (34–35). Somerville's astute analysis might likewise be applicable, with only slight modification, to Keith's and David's incident with the bigoted motorist. Writes Somerville, "In effect, the institution of racial segregation and its cultural fiction of 'black' and 'white' produced a framework in which [a too intimate relation between blacks and whites of the same gender] became legible as 'perverse'" (35). In other words, Keith's and David's own racial difference is conceivably the very thing that, in the motorist's eyes, marked their alliance as anomalous, so that they were subsequently identified or, to use Althusser's term, "hailed," as gay men. Because *Six Feet Under*'s script fails to acknowledge that (in some instances at least) antiblack and antigay biases might be mutually constitutive, the show is unable to offer an explanation for Keith and David's identification as fags when, in truth, there is nothing in their gendered behavior to convey this idea. In this instance, gender performance is decentered as the privileged lens through which to make visible a sexual identity that might otherwise go unnoticed.

But if such an identity can become visible, even if at times that visibility is a misrecognized one — after all, not all mixed-race pairings of black and white men are inflected by eroticism, just as not all mixed-gender pairings of same-race men and women are inflected this way — what language do we use to distinguish them from what they are not? In other words, does the language of color blindness foreclose such distinctions altogether, or can such a language be reconfigured to speak on behalf of such erotic entanglements, but in a way that acknowledges race rather than evades it? Moreover, by embracing a narrow understanding of color blindness and applying it in both institutional and interpersonal scenarios and suggesting that the best way to eradicate the challenges associated with race is to ignore them are we simply setting ourselves up for failure? Why not confront those challenges head-on and work to negotiate them ethically? In other words, why run from the very people we have made ourselves into?

The fact that *Six Feet Under* does not shy away from calling attention to Keith Charles' racial identity, even at the same time as it privileges his identity as a gay man, is not necessarily problematic on its face. After all, there are black Americans who choose to prioritize different aspects of their identities over race (see Conerly 1996; Scott 1994). What is a problem, however, is the show's tendency to isolate Keith from black institutions and individuals, as well as from black cultural references, in order to control and fix the meaning of blackness the show is willing to engage. Equally troubling is the show's occasional portrait of the unsettling impact Keith's very presence has on the numerous white characters with whom he interacts, including his boyfriend, David. Although some of this anxiety is intentional and therefore pleasurable for many viewers (present company included), much of this anxiety is certainly not intentional, and for this reason it is deeply revealing. This latter anxiety exposes the show's stubborn adherence to a public understanding of race and color blindness, which, in its present form, is inadequate to the task of resolving the crisis of difference that has long plagued our collective national life. One way out of this current impasse (but by no means the only way) is for the show's creator and his team of writers to give themselves collectively up to their own anxieties as racialized citizens of this troubled republic. Doing so would mean simply allowing the many abbreviated eruptions of verbal references to racial sameness and racial difference that structure the show to run their logical course rather than doing as they have done, repeatedly ducking their heads in and out of the depths of race as if testing their toes in frigid waters. After all, some of us are already in the water, swimming, or, as the case may be, trying to keep ourselves from drowning.

Acknowledgments

I am indebted to John Thurston for his comments on an earlier version of this article and to Joseph Skerrett for his wisdom, encouragement, and thoughtfulness.

Works Cited

Chambers, Samuel A. "Telepistemology of the Closet; or, The Queer Politics of *Six Feet Under.*" *The Journal of American Culture* 26.1 (March 2003): 24–41.

Cohen, Cathy J. *The Boundaries of Blackness: AIDS and the Breakdown of Black Politics.* Chicago: University of Chicago Press, 1999.

Conerly, Gregory. "The Politics of Black Lesbian, Gay, and Bisexual Identity." *Queer Studies: A Lesbian, Gay, Bisexual, and Transgender Anthology.* Brett Beemyn and Mickey Eliason, eds. New York: New York UP, 1996. 133–145.

Flax, Jane. "Monster's Ball: Representations of Race and Gender in the Contemporary United States." *Black Renaissance/Renaissance Noire* 5.1 (Spring 2003): 57–68.

Gray, Herman. *Watching Race: Television and the Struggle for "Blackness."* Minneapolis: University of Minnesota Press, 1995.

Hall, Stuart. "The Spectacle of the 'Other.'" *Discourse Theory and Practice: A*

Reader. Margaret Wetherell, ed., et al. London and Thousand Oaks: Sage, 2001. 324–344.
Julien, Isaac, and Colin McCabe. *Diary of a Young Soul Rebel.* London: British Film Institute, 1991.
Scott, Darieck. "Jungle Fever? Black Gay Identity Politics, White Dick, and the Utopian Bedroom." *GLQ: A Journal of Lesbian and Gay Studies* Vol. 1. No. 3. (1994): 299–321.
Somerville, Siobhan B. *Queering the Color Line: Race and the Invention of Homosexual in American Culture.* Durham: Duke University Press, 2000.

"We cannot afford to keep being so high-minded": Fighting the Religious Right on *The L Word*

Margaret McFadden

> One of the show's major themes is that cultural divide that we all are living on the brink of right now, the divide between biblical America and the rest of us. And I feel that we very much take that on, and we try to humanize those stories and make the case.
> —Ilene Chaiken, Executive Producer (Hensley 48)

In January 2004, Showtime premiered a new serial drama called *The L Word*, which focuses on the lives of a group of six lesbian and bisexual women and their friends, relatives, and lovers in upscale West Hollywood, California. At the center of this circle are Bette Porter (Jennifer Beals) and Tina Kennard (Laurel Holloman), who have been together for seven years and who are trying to conceive a child through artificial insemination. Their close friends, whom they meet regularly at a café called "The Planet," include Marina Ferrer (Karina Lombard), the café's owner; Shane McCutcheon (Katherine Moenning), a hairdresser with a very active sex life; Dana Fairbanks (Erin Daniels), a tennis pro who fears that coming out of the closet will harm her career; and Alice Pieszecki, a journalist at a local magazine who firmly insists that the others accept her bisexuality as a legitimate choice. Other major characters include Tim Haspel (Eric Mabius) and Jenny Schecter (Mia Kirschner), a young couple who live next door to Bette and Tina and whose relationship is thrown into crisis when Jenny has an affair with Marina, and Bette's sister Kit (Pam Grier), a musician who is struggling with alcoholism and trying to get her career back on track.

Over a thirteen-episode season, the show opened up a number of intersecting plot lines, but one of the most compelling subplots explored the very timely issue of the religious right's growing power and influence in contemporary American politics. This story line traces a right wing Christian group's attempt to prevent the showing of a controversial art exhibition at the California Arts Center (CAC), the museum directed by Bette. This is a thinly fictionalized version of real events of recent decades that raises awareness of the considerable political power of the religious right and makes a compelling argument that queers and progressives must fight against the religious right to preserve our liberties: most importantly, our rights to represent ourselves in the public sphere and to live our lives freely without assimilating to the values and morality of conservative cultures.

The L Word systematically constructs a sophisticated analysis of the strategies with which right wing, fundamentalist Christian activists organize against queerness and other forms of sexual liberation in mainstream American politics today and offers a pointed critique that operates on many levels. Further, the show effectively mobilizes viewers' sympathies in support of a progressive and progay position; fundamentalists are literally described as monsters and, as represented in the series, they are. While acknowledging the difficulty of the current conservative political climate, the show encourages progressives to take on the religious right. But the program also explores the moral and political question of whether or not the left wing should adopt the right's tactics within the struggle and argues for the careful maintenance of the moral norms of the show's lesbian world.

The creators' resolution of this dilemma is clear: queer people fighting to defend our lives in the public sphere may have to resort to the same questionable tactics that are used against us. Yet we are also encouraged to consider the dangers of doing so. If we respond to the religious right's strategies in kind, will we risk losing what is most important to defend about queer cultures, which is our refusal of conservative moralities and the sexual shame that undergirds them? In the end, the show provides a nuanced vision of what is at stake, suggesting that, while are fighting back, we cannot concede the conservatives' position that homoerotic art — or a gay and lesbian life — is shameful or indefensible. More specifically, we cannot simply respond to conservative attacks with appeals to the First Amendment right to free speech, which makes the content of the images irrelevant; we must defend their homoerotic content (and the lives they represent) as valuable and not at all shameful. More generally, we must affirm our right to sustain the alternative social and moral worlds that we have created for ourselves.

To understand how the show conveys this empowering message, one must be familiar with the basic outline of the story, which casts Bette in the central role. Characterized as a cerebral, Ivy League–educated, and highly ambitious museum professional, Bette takes considerable risks to achieve her goal of moving the CAC from the margins of the art world to the cutting edge. Over the objections of her conservative board and with the timely assistance of the eccentric wealthy art collector who has assembled the controversial art show, Bette arranges for "Provocations" to come to the CAC immediately after its New York opening.

As the CAC prepares to mount "Provocations," a right wing Christian group calling itself the Coalition of Concerned Citizens launches a campaign to keep the show from opening, describing its works as pornographic and/or blasphemous. The Coalition is led by Faye Buckley (Helen Shaver), who directs a well-organized group of activists as they use various grassroots political tactics to ensure that the works in the show are never seen by museum goers. After deciding that the controversy will not blow over, Bette challenges Buckley to a public debate in which the battle between civil liberties and censorship will be showcased for the public.

The televised debate is the climax of the show's political arguments, but the subplot continues, reminding us that more is at stake here than abstract intellectual arguments about obscenity and censorship. In episode twelve, Bette and supporters are arrested as they use abortion clinic defense tactics to keep protestors from blocking the delivery of the "Provocations" artworks to the CAC, an event that reminds us that these same conservatives would deny women reproductive freedom, as well as other equal rights, and that this conflict is part of a much broader national struggle.

The artworks are finally delivered and the show opens to great acclaim; in the season finale, we see that Bette has triumphed over the forces of repression. Yet the victory is somewhat ambiguous because, for all her brilliance in the public sphere, Bette has never fully understood the connection between the public and the private. In the midst of the controversy, she has allowed herself to lose track of her own moral center, her relationship with Tina, and her participation in the lesbian community, symbolized by The Planet and by Alice's chart of the sexual and emotional connections between the women of this community.

As a sign of having lost her moral compass, Bette, who has heretofore been an ardent and somewhat self-righteous defender of monogamy, allows herself to be drawn into a passionate affair with an attractive carpenter (Ion Overman) who is working at the museum. She fights the battle for the right to represent homoeroticism and gay and lesbian life in public without recognizing the toll this is taking on her own lesbian family in private. After the opening gala, Tina confronts Bette about the affair and the final episode ends with Tina leaving Bette, a development that draws our attention to the high personal costs queer people pay to defend their lives against ruthless opponents.

This plot line is developed over several episodes to provide viewers with a clear understanding of what is at issue and to create a detailed portrait of the fundamentalist character and intrigues. Further, the show does not take up a topic so complicated until well into the season, when regular viewers have become familiar with the cast. The narrative encourages the audience to identify with Bette by telling the story from her perspective and guides the sympathetic viewer towards a specific conclusion regarding the right wing threat to queer people and to free expression. So what vision of fundamentalists are we given?

First, the show represents these conservative Christian activists as sophisticated, well-organized, and effective and anatomizes the means by which they achieve their political goals. The Coalition's leader, Faye Buckley, is presented as highly intelligent, politically shrewd, and media savvy. When Bette says she wants to debate Buckley, the CAC's lawyer warns her, "The woman's a gladiator in the public arena. She's brilliant. She pretty much always wins." Bette is undaunted, but Buckley does indeed prove to be a formidable antagonist as she leads the campaign against the museum. She is the figure who most clearly articulates the Bible-based, "family values" ideologies that drive her group — ideologies premised on the view that nonreproductive sexuality of any kind is a threat to social order that must be eliminated, or at least hidden from public view. In this context, she asserts that homosexuality is immoral and depraved, a threat to the natural social order ordained by God, and that it is her duty to contest the supposed gay agenda that seeks to force society to acknowledge homosexuality as an acceptable choice. Further, she argues that any representation of homoeroticism is, by definition, obscene and pornographic, and designed to recruit more homosexuals by making the lifestyle seem like a normal option. Her goal is to define such representations as dangerous to anyone who might encounter them and thereby to justify their elimination from public discourse and visibility. These views constitute the familiar public policy advocated by the religious right in the United States over the last two decades, so the audience is encouraged to see the ensuing analysis as a political parable about our time (Berlant 55–81).

The L Word is quite specific in showing us how right wing activists work, and what we see is chilling. Bette's first indication that there will be trouble about "Provocations" occurs when her assistant, James, asks her to take a phone call he thinks she needs to hear. The anonymous caller snarls, "God will punish you for putting up that blasphemous filth in your museum.... You're all going to burn in hell," and the staff tells her that it is the fifth call that day. In episode nine, Bette returns to the CAC and finds its doors and windows covered with stickers and signs attacking the forthcoming exhibition. James tells her the Coalition is responsible, and that hate mail has been arriving for days, but that they had not taken it seriously enough to bother Bette with it.

The calls were only a prelude to the variety of clever tactics that the conservatives use in their crusade against the exhibition. In episode eight, Bette confronts activists who are asking passersby to sign a petition against the "sick and horrible material" in the show. The conservatives also use economic pressure in their effort. A member of the CAC's board quits after he receives a package full of his company's credit cards that have been cut in half and are accompanied by the message that the cardholders do not wish to do business with "blaspheming pornographers." Some of the conservatives' tactics are quite underhanded. In episode nine, Bette is accosted by an initially ingratiating Faye Buckley, who lures her into a conversation that Bette does not know is being videotaped. Episode ten reveals the distorted version of that conversation spliced together by the Coalition. Buckley's video has Bette saying that the world we live in is godless and that art reflects that condition. Further, in response to Buckley's question, "Do you think the fact that you're homosexual makes you morally bankrupt?" Bette is edited to say, "I am a pervert; only a pervert could show this work." When Bette protests that the conversation has been altered, that the edited tape twisted her statements, the CAC's lawyer explains, "That's what they do," and adds, ominously, "You can be sure this tape has been sent to every conservative congressman." Further, he warns that while the law is on the CAC's side, the political climate is not. These scenes situate the story line in a realistic and familiar context: well-organized conservative Christian activists have powerful friends in high places and have effectively moved the country to the right (Berlant 3–10).

Having learned from Tina's doctor that Tina has had a miscarriage, Bette returns home to comfort her distraught partner and hears a loud disturbance outside. Investigating, she discovers a man erecting a large sign on her lawn that accuses her of promoting "godless filth" and a woman filming her reaction with a video camera. She chases them off in an angry confrontation, asserting, "This is my home! This is my family! You have no right to come here, do you hear me?" The man replies, "You have no right to corrupt children!" As they run away, his female accomplice adds, lamely, "You're going to hell!"

These scenes do important work in the political analysis. They exemplify the crucial feminist insight that the personal and the political are intertwined; Bette's confrontations with the conservatives are intercut with endearing scenes in which she buys copies of her favorite children's books for the expectant mother and later comforts the sobbing Tina. The conservatives target her home and her personal life in order to achieve their political goals — the conflict in the public sphere inextricably bound to the private sphere of home, family, and children. Further, a contest between competing visions of human rights is being staged in this context. Bette asserts her right to live openly with her family without interference, a position the conservatives reject, arguing that both her real lesbian family and the representations of queer life in the artworks are inherently immoral, corrupting children and, by extension, the entire society.

In addition, the show suggests that the same conservative activists who are so self-righteous in their condemnations of others, are also hypocritical and dishonest, willing to use any tactic, however unscrupulous, to achieve their ends. *The L Word's* analysis of this hypocrisy is developed more fully when Tina urges Bette to come to the Headquarters for Social Justice, an organization at which Tina volunteers. There, Oscar Alvarez, a friend, introduces her to a colleague who is trying to fight a powerful businessman whose refinery is causing cancer in children in a poor neighborhood. The refiner is actually a televangelist. Oscar notes sardonically, "Some Christian, huh?" This scene questions whether conservative activists are really concerned about children; they struggle to protect children from pornography but not life-threatening carcinogens. And their supposed moral superiority is called into question by their greed and lack of concern for the rights of poor people of color.

Oscar also reveals what Bette's research into the Coalition had not discovered: that Faye Buckley's daughter ran away from home at fourteen because she was being abused by her father, and her mother did not or could not stop it. The daughter, Cora, now seventeen, works in porn films and prostitution, and Oscar shows Bette and Tina one of her films. He also has police and child services records and evidence that Buckley bribed a judge to expunge Cora's record. So she is not quite so righteous as she claims to be and, given her own family's history, her condemnation of other families is hypocritical.

We also see that Buckley is a dirty fighter and a subtle racist. When she and Bette are told before their TV debate that a staffer, Darla, will be by soon to take them both to makeup, Buckley remarks with menace thinly disguised as concern, "It must be hard for makeup people to find your color, it's so ... in-between. I guess Darla will have to mix." Since Bette is biracial, Buckley's jab unsettles her a bit.

This subplot also suggests that what underlies the hypocrisy of these activists is a deep cynicism and opportunism. Do they really believe the charges they are making, or do they simply regard the exhibition as an opportunity to raise their political profiles and gain more power and influence by mobilizing the power of sexual shame (Warner, 14)? After Buckley has accosted Bette outside the museum, she remarks smugly about an anonymous delivery that Bette had received earlier that day, "Oh, and I hope you liked the flowers. They're just my way of saying, 'Nothing personal.'" This is a key scene because, for Buckley, making vicious personal attacks to achieve public goals is just business as usual, but for Bette, the struggle is deeply personal, as well as political. The televised debate between Bette and Faye Buckley is the culmination of those scenes illustrating the power and effectiveness of the religious right. That debate affirms the need for queers to defend themselves against shrewd and ruthless political enemies. As Bette argues to her board, we cannot just sit "with our hands folded in our laps while they call us pornographers and pedophiles." If the other side uses vicious tactics, the museum board may have to do the same. For most progressives, this is a troubling prospect. However, Oscar reminds Bette that the scruples and principles of the left wing are self-defeating:

> Because people don't know how to play this game. The progressives, we are accused of being morally bankrupt, but they have so many fucking skeletons in their closets, and we don't touch them. We take the high road; we wind up in the ditch. We leave our dirty laundry hanging out all over the place because we're not so ashamed of it. They grab it and wave it around and make *us* look like perverts. We have to get into their closets. We cannot afford to keep being so high minded, because we're getting killed.

Bette seems unconvinced by this argument and is reluctant to use the porn video against Buckley in the debate, despite the encouragement of her lawyer and the museum board. Instead, she concentrates on the careful rehearsing of answers to any questions that her opponent may throw at her. Bette clearly does not want to sink to the tactics of personal attack, the same strategy that will be used against her, but she also will not deny that she is a lesbian (or apologize for it) in order to make her position more palatable to straight society.

An encounter between Bette and Tina as they enter the television studio illustrates Bette's motivation in the debate. While Tina is helping

Bette with a few last minute questions and reassuring her that she is completely prepared, Bette kisses her intensely and whispers conspiratorially, "Let's do this in front of Faye Buckley." Tina smiles in return and agrees, "I'm there!" Then they walk hand in hand toward and then past the camera. At this moment, the narrative emphasizes that the solidarity and support of their relationship is crucial to Bette's confidence in the debate and is the underlying reason she must continue the struggle; she is, in the end, defending their right to exist as a couple, to express their sexuality openly and without shame, and to be part of a lesbian community. Faye Buckley will try to make her ashamed, and she must resist.

The televised argument proceeds along predictable intellectual lines. It is a remarkably compressed version of the important national debate between the religious right and those who support civil liberties and sexual freedom. At rehearsal, Bette revealed that she would appropriate the standard liberal arguments about the First Amendment right to free expression of unpopular views: the Supreme Court's definition of obscenity, the ability of people to think critically about art, and the need to reject censorship in a free society. Buckley's response also proceeds predictably, deploying the standard rhetorical devices perfected by conservatives like Senator Jesse Helms. She tries to change the subject by blurring the boundaries between representation and reality and attacks the art for encouraging homosexuality. She argues that it is typical liberal bad faith to "promote an agenda" and then take no responsibility for "the immoral behavior it encourages." In response, Bette maintains that art does not advocate behavior and asks:

> If I were trying to convert people to my lifestyle, as you seem to be implying, Ms. Buckley, do you really think I'd do it with images of a man flaying himself and trussing up his testicles? That piece makes me so uncomfortable, I can barely look at it. I don't think it's going to make anyone want to become a lesbian.

Bette's response cleverly exposes the slippage in Buckley's argument and parries Buckley's attempt to move from an attack on provocative art to an attack on queer people's right to exist and be visible. She does not try to dodge discussing the difficult content; indeed, she brings it up. Carefully calculating, Buckley next combines two other standard conservative subjects: anti-intellectualism and personal attacks on artists or art professionals, both of which are designed to resonate with those who oppose the so-called cultural elite who conservatives argue are destroying American society:

> She thinks she's clever enough to trick the rest of us into believing that filth isn't filth, blasphemy isn't blasphemy, pornography is not pornography, but the stuff speaks for itself. And however hard she tries to defend it with her fancy language and her insulting logic, all it is sheer, disgusting, filthy, ugly pornography. She is a pornographer!

Recognizing Buckley's attempt both to discredit her and to elide the distinction between provocative art and pornography, Bette makes a difficult decision, which is to follow Oscar's advice and respond with a personal attack of her own. Placing on the table the video featuring Cora Buckley, she acknowledges the exploitation of young women by the porn industry, noting that the girls involved were often runaways from troubled homes. The camera cuts to Buckley's face, which registers shock and fear. Bette continues as the camera cuts to images from the porn film and to images of Cora soliciting men in cars: "Those children lacked love. They were abused. How awful it must be to come from a home life so desperate. There is a world of difference between complex, provocative art and the tragedy of the porn industry."

Clearly caught off guard, Buckley goes in for the kill, providing the ultimate example of using personal information to savage a political opponent and making it clear that conservative activists are utterly ruthless and without compassion. She says, with loathing:

> Faith makes seemingly complex things simple and obvious. The Bible condemns homosexuality. That's why God took your unborn child from your lesbian lover. And that was a blessing. That baby is with him now. So he doesn't have to suffer the degradation he would have been subject to had he been born into your depraved life.

Given the stress she has been under, it is no wonder that Bette finally gives in and sheds the tears she has repressed until now. Buckley's last lines are delivered in a way that suggests Faye is fighting back tears herself;

having delivered this devastating blow, she approaches Bette, who pushes her away fiercely and gasps, "Monster!"

This is a very complex and powerful scene, brilliantly played by the two actresses. While it obviously secures the audience's emotional investment against the Christian right, it also raises the moral question of whether or not progressives and queers should fight the conservatives with their own nasty tactics. On one hand, Oscar's strategy seems to have worked. Those viewers who might not have thought about such matters before must notice how mean-spirited the rhetoric of the religious right is and how devastating their attacks can be on queer people. Buckley's statement is so cruel that it is hard to imagine that she would not lose all credibility with any but the most rabid of her Coalition. Her actions are profoundly un–Christian and indeed monstrous. In the final episode of the season, "Provocations" does open to great acclaim, and Buckley's absence from the scene is noted by the press, so Bette seems to have won an important political victory.

On the other hand, the connection between the political and the personal turns out to be heartbreaking for Bette. While she triumphs in the public sphere, she ends up destroying her relationship with Tina, which has been shattered by Bette's infidelity, a development that is quite surprising given Bette's previously firm disapproval of partners who cheat. Perhaps the unfortunate consequences for Bette expose the high personal cost of doing this kind of political work. Moreover, when Bette alludes to the profession of Buckley's daughter during their debate, she may inadvertently embrace the religious right's unhealthy attitudes about sexuality and advocate the idea pornography and other representations of sexuality are shameful. If this is what she has done, she has affirmed the dominant culture's homophobic and sex-phobic norms, the same that seek to narrowly and exclusively define the composition of a normal family and the same would discredit and condemn Bette for her failure to live up to that social paradigm. When Bette plays by the rules of the straight world, she implicitly loses sight of the values that organize queer communities; indeed, she may have lost her own moral center — her relationship with Tina and the other women. This is a danger the show seems to warn us against.

To understand why these issues are so important for queers and progressives to consider, we must explore the parallels between this story line and real political events of recent decades. The plot of the "Provocations" episodes closely follows events of the late 1980s and early 1990s, when right wing Christian groups began an overt culture war on controversial art and artists as well as on the National Endowment for the Arts for allegedly funding such obscenities. The Rev. Donald Wildmon and his American Family Association launched the assault against the NEA, galvanizing the support of conservative members of Congress and various right wing ideologues like Patrick Buchanan, Pat Robertson, and Jerry Falwell to condemn works such as Andres Serrano's 1987 photograph, "Piss Christ," the photographs of Robert Mapplethorpe, and Marlon Riggs' film, *Tongues Untied*. The political effort to eliminate the NEA also led its chairman, John Frohnmayer, to try to appease critics by revoking fellowships granted in 1990 to four performance artists — Holly Hughes, John Fleck, Tim Miller, and Karen Finley — who became known as "The NEA Four" when they sued for (and eventually won) restoration of their grants. All four thematize sexuality in their work, which made them ideal targets for the right's wrath. Frohnmayer's decision did not appease the critics, nor did it protect the Endowment from a well-organized conservative campaign to insert a "decency clause" prohibiting the funding of artworks with specific kinds of content into the NEA's 1990 appropriations bill. Although Frohnmayer was vilified by civil libertarians and many in the arts community for caving in to the political pressure, his larger goal was to keep Congress from deauthorizing the NEA entirely; he was equally unpopular with those on the right for his defenses of artistic freedom and his refusal to accept their definitions of what was proper to support (Dubin 226–48).

These right wing Christian political leaders were obviously the models for *The L Word's* Faye Buckley, who uses their (highly effective) strategies: the vilification of individual artists, the misrepresentation of particular artworks, and the effort to collapse the boundaries between representation and reality and between art and obscenity. For example, Jesse Helms famously railed against "soaking the taxpayer to fund the homosexual pornography of Robert Mapplethorpe, who died of AIDS while spending the last years of his life promoting homosexuality" (Meyer 207). Recent histories of this period reveal that many conservative activists cynically exploited the issue of government funding for queer art or culture as a way to raise money and gain political power, and because these subjects were so lucrative as fundraising themes, the right wing demagogues were quite unconcerned about whether the claims they were making about the art, the artists, or the funding agencies were accurate. As Frohnmayer explained after describing an inflammatory and misleading full-page ad against the NEA that Pat Robertson placed in *USA Today*, he gradually realized that "We were dealing with ruthless streetfighters and we were getting the bejesus kicked out of us" (227, 274–75, 175–76). This is quite close to Oscar's argument about the self-defeating ethics of the political left.

More specifically, *The L Word*'s narrative provides a fictionalized version of what happened when Cincinnati's Contemporary Art Center booked a controversial retrospective exhibition of Mapplethorpe photographs in 1990. "The Perfect Moment" was slated to open in Cincinnati in April of that year, but conservative Christian activists mobilized to force Dennis Barrie, the Director of the CAC, to cancel the show. Many of the tactics used against Bette in *The L Word* were actually used against Barrie and his family. Barrie courageously resisted the pressure, and the show opened to large crowds, but that same day he was arrested and charged by county prosecutors with pandering obscenity and child pornography. These charges were based not on the entire array of 175 images, but on five photographs that depicted homoeroticism or sadomasochism and two portraits of naked children. Barrie was acquitted in September 1990 (Meyer, 206–18; Dubin, 170–90).

These events in Cincinnati are also chronicled in the 2000 film Dirty Pictures, which was written by *The L Word*'s executive producer, Ilene Chaiken. Chaiken's understanding of the complexities of these controversies is certainly reflected in the *L Word* episodes that take them up; Chaiken wrote two key episodes that focus on the art museum controversy and analyze the conflict in a very sophisticated way. Not surprisingly, the fictionalized *L Word* version of these events closely mirrors what happened in Cincinnati and offers an implicit critique of how Barrie and his lawyers evaded the charges that the works were obscene and pornographic.

Bette's strategy in the debate with Buckley largely follows the one

Barrie and his lawyers took, which was to make the argument in defense of the images on first amendment grounds and to try not to talk about the actual content of the images. Barrie's team also called expert witnesses from the art world who testified that the works in question had great value for formal and technical qualities such as lighting, composition, and printing and who either ignored the subject matter or situated it in relationship to works by other emotionally troubled (but canonical) artists like Van Gogh. As Richard Meyer has noted, however, "The trouble with such arguments, as both Carole Vance and Douglas Crimp have argued, is that they tacitly accept a view of homosexuality as degrading and unspeakable" (217). Vance contends, "If we are afraid to offer a public defense of sexual images, then even in our rebuttal we have granted the right wing its most basic premise: sexuality is shameful and discrediting" (qtd. in Meyer 218). The show's narrative suggests that Chaiken understands this danger and rejects this homophobic approach.

Bette does struggle to keep the debate focused on the legal issues, where her positions are strongest and perhaps most mainstream. But she is also willing to defend the content of the images and so avoids granting Buckley her premise that these artworks are depraved and perverse. Bette refuses to give in to the dominant culture's repressive desire to stigmatize homosexuality and tries to affirm the alternative ethos of the queer worlds that produced those challenging images, and viewers are encouraged to identify with this position.

Michael Warner recently argued that the right wing has attempted to impose a vision of normal (and thus privatized) sexuality onto queer communities and that that vision depends upon a notion of sexual shame that defines homosexuality as immoral and perverse, as something inherently deserving of repression and concealment. Against this pathologizing of queerness and visible queer communities, Warner contends that queers must defend their right to public sexual cultures, and the visibility of that sexuality is essential to their ability to imagine and thus express their desires and their identities. Further, he argues that queer communities operate with an alternative sexual ethic and alternative notions of family, community, and intimacy that must be defended, and he rejects normalizing queerness and assimilating to conservative notions of sexual moralism and privacy.

The L Word presents us with a representation of just such a strong queer community. Centered on The Planet, a café that is also the site of evening parties for the West Hollywood lesbian community, this alternative world has its own values, norms, knowledges, relationships (friendships and intimacies), notions of family, and sexual connections. Further, the intimate relationships that have connected the women in this world are made very explicit in the form of Alice's chart, which documents the lesbian sexual history of the community, and which, when she puts it on the internet, grows in three dimensions before their eyes. *The L Word* thus makes visible and celebrates the alternative lesbian world that these women have constructed together and does not attempt to repress or sanitize the centrality of sexuality to this world. It thus resists the pathologizing and stigmatizing of sexuality that the right wing attempts to impose upon the queer community; the show affirms lesbian sexuality in all its complexities. Further, it is clear that this world does have, as Warner argues, its own sexual ethics and visions of intimacy as well as its varied forms of relationships.

The central characters define themselves as a family, confirming anthropologist Kath Weston's argument that queer people have long constructed "families of choice" because more conventional family forms are either unavailable or unsuitable. The show is intent on defending these alternative forms as valid and healthy for the participants and presents the characters as able to rely on each other for vital emotional support and caring. So while the narrative affirms the need to fight the right with every tactic available, it does remind us not to lose sight of what we are really defending.

Ultimately, the show's political position is clear. The right wing attack on the museum's art exhibit is meant to embody the real world right wing attacks on queer lives and visibility that are so central a part of our national political discourse right now. Christian fundamentalist groups have clearly been the most active, powerful, and effective opponents of gay rights (and women's rights and civil rights) legislation and are currently the most vocal and vehement fighters against legalizing same-sex marriage. In this context, *The L Word* affirms Oscar's assertion that "We cannot afford to keep being so high minded, because we're getting killed," and presents us with a model of successfully fighting back against ruthless and unscrupulous conservatives who represent a real threat to the lives and freedoms of queer Americans. Because the program so effectively mobilizes its audiences' emotional investment in the characters and reveals the increasingly desperate means by which conservative activists work to promote discrimination, it has the potential to motivate its audience to join the struggle. Exposing the connections between the homophobia, the sexism, and the racism of the religious right, the show sounds a wake-up call to all those progressives and queers who believe they can just live their lives as they wish and remain outside the political fray as conservatives strive to enshrine their notions of family values in public policy.

In the end, the fundamentalists' attack on the art show also stands symbolically for the right wing attack on the increasing representation of queer lives in popular culture, so the battle against censorship of art is simultaneously a battle for the right of shows like *The L Word* and *Queer as Folk,* which provide representations of queer worlds from a queer perspective, to exist. Faye Buckley and her ilk are wrong when they argue that such representations somehow advocate for or recruit people to homosexuality. Instead, in this viciously homophobic and repressive cultural moment, these shows do serve the vitally important political function of making visible (and thus imaginable to those who may have such desires) appealing queer lives and communities.

Works Cited

Berlant, Lauren. *The Queen of America Goes to Washington City: Essays on Sex and Citizenship*. Durham: Duke University Press, 1997.
Dirty Pictures. Frank Pierson, dir. MGM, 2002.
Dubin, Steven C. *Arresting Images: Impolitic Art and Uncivil Actions*. New York: Routledge, 1992.
Frohnmayer, John. *Leaving Town Alive: Confessions of an Arts Warrior*. Boston: Houghton-Mifflin, 1993.
Hensley, Dennis. "L Is for Leisha." *The Advocate*. 17 February 2004: 41–48, 52–3.
Meyer, Richard. *Outlaw Representation: Censorship and Homosexuality in Twentieth-Century American Art*. Oxford: Oxford University Press, 2002.
The L Word. Ilene Chaiken, executive producer. Showtime, 2004.

Warner, Michael. *The Trouble with Normal: Sex, Politics, and the Ethics of Queer Life*. Cambridge, Harvard University Press, 1999.
Weston, Kath. *Families We Choose: Lesbians, Gays, Kinship*. New York: Columbia University Press, 1991.

Politics of the Sitcom Formula: *Friends*, *Mad About You*, and the Sapphic Second Banana

Kelly Kessler

The 1990s brought an onslaught of gay and lesbian characters to prime time network television. One genre in which these representations tended to cluster was the situation comedy. Programs such as *Friends, Mad About You, Roseanne, Spin City,* and *Will & Grace* showcased this new type of stock character and set the bar for gay and lesbian prime-time comic representation. In response, the mainstream media valorized these shows as a sign of a gay renaissance. Directly relating the visibility of gays and lesbians to an emerging sense of public awareness and acceptance, outlets such as *OUT* and *Entertainment Weekly* celebrated this new gay/lesbian visibility.[1] The issue that remains to be examined, however, is the political or progressive efficacy of the representations that were being produced throughout that decade. Though I refuse to believe that these representations were in *all* ways negative (as an overeducated, white lesbian in a long-term relationship, I found and find great satisfaction in seeing myself represented on the small screen), I do concede that many of these emerging representations lacked the breadth and political awareness needed to challenge the dominant system. Issues of class, race/ethnicity, beauty, and political oppression were often avoided in an effort to generalize privilege. Like "race" shows of the 1970s, such as *Good Times*, *What's Happening*, and *That's My Mama*, this proliferation of representations — along with continuing similar ones today — may have been serving as a ghettoizing agent through its limited scope and ineffective location in the sitcom genre.[2]

I will examine the representation of lesbians in two popular NBC comedies, *Friends* and *Mad About You*, and particularly, the relegation of these characters to the role of "second banana" and their interaction with the generic codes of the situation comedy. I will illustrate how the formula of the situation comedy, especially the role identified for the secondary character, inhibits significant progressive representations of marginalized groups, and inversely, in the spirit of a liberal pluralist democracy, neutralizes the difference, rendering the representations ineffective or destructive. By examining the generic formula, the shows themselves, and the theories related to lesbian visibility, I hope to reveal the potential negative ramifications of these lesbian characters.

Despite this influx of lesbian representation, surprisingly little has been published regarding the phenomenon. Critics such as Marguerite Moritz, Frank Bruni, Rose Collis, Stephen Tropiano, and Steven Capsuto have touched on the subject from various perspectives, identifying the progressive limitations of the then current representations. In the 1990s, both Collis and Moritz examined the impotence of television's lesbian representations, highlighting the lack of overt sexuality, recurring roles, personal agency, and positive narrative reinforcement. Recognizing the trend of "one time only" situation comedy lesbian appearances and the demonization or desexualization of dramatic lesbians, Moritz concludes that these representations protect the sensibilities of the ever-important hetero viewer/consumer. Similarly, Bruni ties the threat of the "gay kiss" (referring to shows such as *Roseanne*) to the dissolution of the viewing audience's ability to think of gays and lesbians in terms of abstraction. The gay kiss forces hetero audiences to confront homosexuality head-on, consequently compelling them to deal with uncomfortable social realities. Though these critics pinpoint problems with various types of representations, they appear to be skirting what may be the cause: the inherent limitations of the genre that produce many of these images — the situation comedy.

Sitcom: The Genre

A wealth of the current literature examining the situation comedy points to the genre's progressive shortcomings. Because of the centrality and stability of the characters, the potential for both narrative and political progress is limited. Horace Newcomb, in the canonical *TV: The Most Popular Art*, identifies confusion as the situation comedy's most effective comedic device. He states:

> At the center of the situation, complication, and confusion stand the characters of the situation comedy. They are cause and effect, creator and butt of joke, the audience's key to what the formula means. As we have seen, that formula allows for very little development, no exploration of idea or conflict; the stars merely do what they have always done and will continue to do [34].

Newcomb recognizes in the genre the predetermined solution within the complication. From the beginning of the episode, the audience knows that whatever complication arises, it will be solved, and the characters will be able to laugh at the situation (41). Consequently, inherent in the genre is a communal sense of security among the show's viewers.

Similarly, critics such as David Grote and Hal Himmelstein suggest that the situation comedy possesses certain safety measures that prevent the audience from experiencing extended unease or discomfort. Grote pejoratively compares the sitcom to the traditional literary comedy, suggesting that the narrative as lacks any impetus to change: "...the messages that accompany those weekly appearances are the messages of defense, of protection, of the impossibility of progress or any other positive change" (qtd. in Feuer 122). Similarly, in Himmelstein's investigation of the genre, he delineates different subcategories of sitcom: ironic, mimetic, leader-centered, romantic, and mythical. The most highly represented type is mimetic: that which places the main characters in a reflexive relationship with the audience member, possessing similar intelligence and values. The show "becomes an agent for reinforcing traditional dominant value orientations and thus becomes a primary mechanism for socialization" (116–17).

Also present in Newcomb's analysis of the situation comedy format is an analysis of the characters themselves. He identifies and explicates the role of the secondary characters. Described as the characters with which the actual viewer can identify more fully, they live somewhere between the illogical world of the main characters and the real world of the audience. They possess a greater amount of insight than the main characters, spotting their weaknesses and foreseeing solutions to their weekly problems. It is these secondary characters who "stand closer to the value structure of the audience" (38).

These scholars have highlighted two characteristics inherent in the situation comedy genre: one, a reflection of dominant societal values, and two, a lack of situation development. By specifically looking at the lesbian characters in the television shows *Mad About You* and *Friends*, I will locate the effects of these generic characteristics. How do these marginalized representations manage to avoid alienating those who embrace the dominant mores of society? How do these portrayals reflect the static nature of the characters and situations of the genre? By looking at issues such as aesthetics, romantic involvement, motherhood, community, and conflict avoidance, I plan to uncover the inevitable influence of generic conventions on the representations themselves.

Enter the Lesbians

Each of the two shows features a lesbian couple. *Friends*, created in 1994, chronicling the lives and (mostly unsuccessful) loves of a group of six New York City friends (Monica, Phoebe, Rachel, Joey, Chandler, and Ross), introduced two lesbian characters in the show's first episode. Within the first ten minutes, the story line alerts the audience to the fact that Ross's wife Carol (Jane Sibbett) has left him for another woman. Soon thereafter he discovers she is pregnant with his child and must decide whether or not he is going to be a part of this nontraditional family. Through his decision to be an involved father to his unborn child, the lesbian couple becomes permanently tied to the heterosexual sextet. In the following seasons, Carol and her partner, Susan (Jessica Hecht), float in and out of the show's narrative.

Through the middle of the eighth season, Carol and/or Susan play a significant role in at least fifteen episodes.[3] Before that point, only two episodes of the series had depicted the couple physically separated, one of which revolves around Carol's preparation for a romantic evening with Susan. Previously, episodes showed them having a sonogram, discussing breast-feeding, meeting at Lamaze class, getting married, etc. Their involvement is linked to motherhood in over half of the fourteen episodes. For the most part, they are utilized solely as a vehicle for Ross' fatherhood, paranoia, and wisecracks.

Mad About You chronicles the life and love of Paul and Jamie Buchman. Present in the early ensemble are Paul and Jamie's families: mothers, fathers, Cousin Ira, and sisters, Debbie and Lisa. The character of Debbie (Robin Bartlett), Paul's sister, appears first in an episode in which Paul and Jamie take her son trick-or-treating. Debbie's husband and child eventually (and inexplicably) disappear from the story lines and, in the sixth season, Debbie discovers that she is a lesbian. While on a weekend skiing trip, she falls in love with a gynecologist, Dr. Joan Herman (Suzie Plakson), during a game of naked Monopoly (she was the shoe) and a backrub. At that point, Deb embarks on a partnership with Joan and her kid is never seen or mentioned again.

These basic descriptions of the characters and their roles in the narratives hint at the hegemonic leanings of respective constructions. As suggested by Newcomb, Grote, and Himmelstein, the conservative, coupled, and monogamous character development of these sitcom personae illustrates the programs' investment in the maintenance of the dominant social order. This investment tailors the image and actions of the various lesbian characters, avoiding their association with a community that lies outside of the affluent heterosexual one.

Anything You Can Do I Can Do Better

The secondary character types described by Newcomb better represent the aspirations of the (middle-class, heterosexual) viewing audience.[4] By relational, emotional, and social superiority, Carol, Susan, Debbie, and Joan not only pose no threat, but they present an image to which society encourages us to aspire. In both shows, the characters behave and appear in a manner that minimizes their lesbianism and highlights their successful assimilation into the heterosexual world of the main characters.

In both of these cases, the characters display more emotional stability through their relatively conflict-free relationships than the characters they support. The *Friends* ensemble continuously struggles to find love, but instead usually finds disaster. Those in long-term relationships, Chandler and Monica, and Ross and Rachel, frequently find themselves in the midst of conflict and confusion. Similarly, Paul and Jamie struggle through the everyday problems of married life. Yet the lesbian couples exist in a relatively problem-free world. They embody the ideal heteronormative relationship: bliss, monogamy, and a shared home.

Both series introduce lesbianism in the form of a monogamous couple. In the case of *Friends*, Carol's discovery of her true sexual orientation directly coincides with her finding of a lesbian life-partner. To emphasize their relationship, they commonly occupy the same geographical space, together either in body or conversation throughout the show. To further naturalize the lesbian bond, *Friends* provided network television with its first lesbian wedding. On January 18, 1996, Carol and Susan exchanged vows in aesthetically similar dresses as their son Ben (good women have children) was wheeled down the aisle in a flower-bedecked baby carriage. This final act of heterosexual privilege solidifies Carol and Susan as ideological members of dominant society.

Similarly, *Mad About You* introduces Debbie and Joan, a couple who also mirror the values and traditions of heterosexual expectations. Debbie floats from one socially sanctioned relationship to one that resembles (and is narratively accepted as) a socially sanctioned relationship. Early episodes depict Debbie's struggles as a married mother. More than one revolves around her marriage and child. In the middle of the fourth season, however, after her husband and child have disappeared from the narrative, she announces her lesbianism and enters a long-term relationship with Joan (mirroring that of Paul and Jamie). *Mad About You* better integrates its lesbian couple into narrative than does *Friends*. Though Debbie and Joan act more independently than Carol and Susan, the story line links Debbie to the plot by blood and Joan by profession (she becomes Jamie's gynecologist). As Paul and Jamie struggle with their lives and loves, Joan and Debbie share (for the most part) a blissful union. They move in together and become accepted by family and friends as just another "married" couple.

One episode of each series does depict conflict in the lesbian relationship, only to resolve it with a strengthened love bond. In each show, the women come to a crossroad at which they must decide if their relationship is more important than any external challenges. In the *Friends* episode entitled, "The One with the Lesbian Wedding," the couple fights over Carol's refusal to carry out the ceremony without her parents' blessing. In the end, Ross encourages Carol to continue with her plans, and the episode ends with a glamorous lesbian wedding at which Ross, in a grand gesture of acceptance, stands in for Carol's father. Similarly, in the *Mad About You* episode "Fire at Riff's," Debbie is incensed when she discovers that Joan has accepted a nomination as one of "The 20 Most Eligible Bachelorettes in New York." The conflict over Joan's willingness to pretend to be a single (straight) woman when she has been in a monogamous relationship with Debbie for the equivalent of two and a half seasons drives both women into a huff. Like *Friends*, however, the conflict is resolved when their devotion is tested and proven by a fire that endangers their lives. While the imperfect Jamie completely forgets about Paul's whereabouts and flees the fire alone, Debbie and Joan engage in a panicked search for one another. After locating each other, Joan proposes marriage; they kiss, and all their problems disappear. For Susan and Carol, and Debbie and Joan, the ease with which they can solve their conflicts highlights the strength and stability of their relationships. In contrast, the relationships of the straight couples (Ross and Rachel, Monica and Chandler, or Paul and Jamie) are not always so stable. Admittedly, the heterosexual couples carry the majority of the plot lines — stories which continually destabilize their relationships, while the lesbian couples control only one conflict-based plot each, thus limiting the appearance of recurring instability.

Another way in which both shows elevate the status of the secondary characters is through their association with successful motherhood. As the representation of "normal" womanhood, Carol and Susan are consistently depicted in their maternal roles. Unlike Phoebe, Monica, and (at least at that point) Rachel, Carol has fulfilled her "biological destiny."

She serves as a point of contrast for Monica who laments her childless state, going as far as to procure information regarding artificial insemination (a procedure often associated with lesbian or otherwise "unnatural" mothers). Similarly, Debbie and Joan stand in as knowledgeable mothers; Debbie as an actual mother through her previous marriage (though after she meets Joan, her children are not referred to again until the final episode of the series) and Joan as an OB/GYN. The lesbians are the natural mothers, highlighting the main character's foibles, immaturity, and shortcomings.

The lesbian characters also enjoy a greater level of maturity and financial stability than the main cast. Carol and Susan are always financially secure and professionally focused, unlike the rest of the characters in the *Friends* ensemble who are constantly moving from job to job. The lesbian couple's livelihood is never in question. In contrast, Monica, Joey, and Phoebe lose at least one job each (for accepting kickbacks, extreme stupidity, and suspected prostitution respectively). Ross' boss deems him mentally unstable and forces him to go on sabbatical, and Rachel, after having never worked in her life, moves from job to job until she establishes herself (quite unbelievably) in the fashion industry. Meanwhile, Carol and Susan maintain gainful employment and stay home taking care of their child. The narrative clearly establishes Carol and Susan as the more emotionally stable members of the group. Like the standard secondary characters, they are present to contrast the zaniness and irresponsibility of the main cast. In *Mad About You*, Joan's title of Doctor similarly elevates her social status. Although Jamie's advertising job and Paul's directorial success are nothing to sneeze at, it is Joan's position that begs respect and gains acceptance from Paul's parents.

The naturalization and stabilization of the lesbians helps to define the roles of the secondary characters as a site of positive contrast to the central figures. Although these lesbians are an improvement upon earlier television representations that render the lesbian poor, powerless, and loveless, such constructions, based on socioeconomic status, motherhood, and monogamous relationships, tend to prioritize lesbian types and behaviors. Rather than presenting an image which promotes acceptance, the static "accepted" lesbian is she who follows the codes of the heterosexual society to which, in reality, she does not have full access. Not only do the shows prioritize one relationship and social status, but they do so by promoting a sense of false consciousness. These shows only imply acceptance. Yes, lesbian representations are permeating the prime-time schedule; however, the automatic association of lesbianism with the three M's (marriage, money, and motherhood) becomes problematic. Paula Ettelbrick argues:

> Marriage runs counter to two of the primary goals of the lesbian and gay movement: the affirmation of gay identity and culture; and the validation of many relationships.... The moment we argue, as some among us insist on doing, that we should be treated as equals because we are really just like married couples and hold the same values, we undermine the very purpose of our movement and begin the dangerous process of silencing our different voices [qtd. in Strayer 179].

Both lesbian couples accomplish just this. By prioritizing lesbian marriage, the single or nonmonogamous subject is marginalized. Remaining invisible, they are denied access to mainstream culture and society. Similarly, racial and class diversity are not represented. In order to fulfill the role of the secondary character, the legitimized character type must be she who possesses some (in these cases many) forms of social privilege.

We're Just Alike, You and I

An additional requirement of the secondary character is that he/she serves as a reflection of the values of the targeted (heterosexual) viewer.[5] This character must interact with the narrative in ways which do not threaten, but affirm social norms. Consequently, there must be some concessions made if a member of a marginalized group is going to represent the general viewer. Both *Friends* and *Mad About You* accomplish this task in four ways: coding the lesbian characters as heterosexual, detaching them from any sense of community, removing any sexual threat levied at the heterosexual community in the narrative, and avoiding any signs of social conflict.

Carol, Susan, Debbie, and Joan are associated with the dominant society through their physical representation. The butch/femme dichotomy historically associated with the lesbian community and movement is almost completely absent in these characters. Aesthetically, all four are constructed as femme with occasional verbal references identifying one member of each duo as butch (although the visual representations belie this appellation).[6] *Friends* attempts to build a false dichotomy around the characters of Susan and Carol. Ross interacts with Susan as though she has simply been inserted into the masculine position, greeting her with a firm handshake and mimicking a football pass using a baby doll and shouting, "Hey Susan, go long!" Despite Ross' attitude, Susan appears and behaves like a traditionally feminine woman. She wears dresses and has long hair. Even in the episode "The One That Could Have Been," when Ross imagines what his life might have been like if Carol had not realized her lesbianism, Susan is wearing a long flowing dress; more ethereal than butch. Ironically, the scene portrays Carol, not Susan, as a masculine, flannel shirt-wearing, beer-drinking belcher. With this image, the audience is no longer asked to identify with Carol, but to sympathize with Ross and gawk at her aberrant behavior. However, this one divergent representation does not constitute an alternative lesbian construction. Aside from this dream scene, the show portrays both women as long-haired, dress-wearing femmes who subscribe to heterosexual standards of beauty. Similarly, Joan and Debbie conform to traditional standards of beauty, the former named one of "The 20 Most Eligible (straight) Bachelorettes in New York." Though Debbie is the only one of the quartet to sport short hair, she and Joan both fall within the boundaries of what is considered proper femininity, avoiding association with lesbian stereotypes and conforming to the expectations of the majority.

Another way in which both series reconcile the lesbian characters with their assumed (hetero) viewing audience is by avoiding interaction between the characters and the lesbian community at large. Secondary characters exist to serve the main plot, thus any ties between Debbie and Joan and the lesbian community would detract from the main thrust of the narrative — the lives of Paul, Jamie, and the rest of the Buchmans. Carol and Susan have some association with other lesbians in the series, but these serve almost exclusively as a source of amusement, lessening their threat to the heterosexual hegemony. In one case, Ross visits Carol and Susan's apartment and comes across a picture he thinks is Huey

Lewis. The photo turns out to be their friend Tanya, who is assumed by the viewer to be sporting the stereotypical lesbian mullet hairdo. In this one gag, the failure of lesbians to conform to the heterosexual standard of beauty marginalizes and trivializes them.

The guests at Carol and Susan's wedding act as another example of lesbian "othering." This episode, by placing the couple at the center of the main plot, provides an insight into Carol's and Susan's lives sans the six main characters. In this episode, both Candace Gingrich (the high profile activist and lesbian sister of Newt Gingrich) and butch lesbian stand-up comic Lea Delaria make guest appearances. Gingrich plays the part of the priest who marries the couple, while Delaria makes a pass at an unwitting Phoebe. Both women conform more closely to the butch aesthetic than either Carol or Susan and are intertextually associated with more radical politics than the show advocates. It is only in this scene, where heteronormativity is so highly represented through the institution of marriage, that alternative lesbian representations exist. This sudden inclusion of alternative lesbianisms into a show that has previously been uniform in its representations of the group intensifies the otherness of the lesbian extras. They also serve as a source of threat and humor: Joey says, "All these women and nothin'" to which Chandler responds, "The world is my lesbian wedding." By avoiding varied positive representations and contrasting the recurring characters with the other lesbians, the programs further naturalizes Carol, Susan, Joan, and Debbie.

Let's Not Get It On

A third way in which lesbianism is naturalized and social norms are maintained is through the shows' exclusion of sex from the lesbian relationship. By coupling immediately, the women cannot recruit any of the heterosexual characters. The single lesbian raises the specter of dating and potential sex; but with married lesbians, the only threat to any of the characters is to Ross' deflated ego. However, Ross is depicted as excessively insecure and neurotic early in the series; thereby the psychological and sexual threat of the lesbian representation is transformed into a source of humor.

Rather than focusing on sex, the narrative chooses to concentrate on romance and domesticity. Allusions to actual sexual activity are minimized. In *Friends*, references to Carol and Susan's sexual activity is intended to highlight Ross's awkwardness or naiveté. Examples include Ross' discovery that Susan has tasted Carol's breast milk and his unknowing interruption of their anniversary celebration. Despite Ross' queasiness, Susan and Carol, who are usually foregrounded as caring mothers and not sexual lovers, are only shown being affectionate with each other at their wedding. Debbie and Joan behave similarly, engaging in nonerotic romance and domesticity (e.g. holding hands, sharing a bed, and once kissing). The only allusion to any eroticism occurs when Debbie describes for Jamie her first encounter with Joan (skiing trip, naked Monopoly, backrub). Though the shows break the taboo of the gay kiss, they do it in a manner that disassociates it from sex and attaches it to heteronormative domesticity and marriage.

A final way in which the marginalized group sustains the cultural hegemony is through avoidance of any representation of social inequity or struggle. If the narrative does not acknowledge that social inequity exists or that the character with whom the audience must identify may suffer unjust pain, then another obstacle is removed from the representational threat. Both *Mad About You* and *Friends* cling to this political neutrality. Neither lesbian couple suffers any great loss or injustice because of their sexuality. Carol never runs the risk of losing her child.[7] The ensemble, minus insecure Ross, interacts with them as if they are a normative couple, belittling Ross for thinking otherwise. Aside from Carol's parents' refusal to attend the wedding, the show exhibits no evidence of negative ramifications of lesbianism. Similarly, Debbie and Joan fully assimilate into heterosexual society. The threat of familial rejection turns farcical when Debbie's mother, Sylvia, threatens to jump out of the window upon hearing of her daughter's same-sex orientation. However, upon meeting Joan, Sylvia is immediately welcomes her into the family, even favoring her over her heterosexual daughter-in-law, Jamie. The only other sign of family discomfort comes in a humorous double interchange. In "Speed Baby," Joan, lying in bed, answers a telephone call from Sylvia. Joan calls Sylvia "ma," to which Sylvia replies, "I'm not ready for you to call me that." Soon thereafter, Joan relays the call to Debbie, again referring to Sylvia as "ma" to which Debbie responds, "I'm not ready for you to call her that." Though a similar discomfort may occur between heterosexual couples and their in-laws, the narrative makes it obvious that Sylvia's discomfort comes from Joan's lesbianism. This interchange is the only evidence of any residual discomfort regarding their relationship. Both shows lack any significant representation of the inequities faced by gays and lesbians daily, such as legal and employment discrimination, social disdain, physical abuse, etc.

All of these characteristics — the heterosexual standards of beauty, the invisibility of the lesbian community, the desexualization of the couples' relationship, and the erasure of political struggle — promote the targeted heterosexual audience's identification with the characters. By minimizing the social threat posed by the stereotypical appearance, behavior, and treatment of the lesbian characters, the shows set a standard for the types of lesbian characters that are acceptable. In order to satisfy the needs of the secondary character vis-à-vis the genre, these lesbian characters must sacrifice their individuality, authenticity, and agency for the good of the show as a whole. To introduce significant characters who buck societal norms (of beauty, of sexuality, etc.) would be to undermine the central function of the recurring character — to promote audience identification.

Conclusion: It's Funny But...

The lesbian representations in *Mad About You* and *Friends* illustrate the limits of social tolerance in the genre. Its very formula impedes growth and development of sexual minorities. The idyllic portraits of the four lesbians hide the social struggles that actual lesbians face every day. Clare Whatling argues that the narrative's failure to address lesbian sexuality encourages the audience to leave with its "assumptions unchallenged" (88). The same can be said for addressing the lesbian without acknowledging the associated politics. The hetero viewer is not challenged to question the current oppressive system when social privilege and unequivocal acceptance shield inequality.

In *Unmarked*, Peggy Phalen warns of the type of monitored visibility encouraged by the situation comedy:

> Visibility is a trap; it summons surveillance and the law; it provokes voyeurism, fetishism, and the colonialist/imperial appetite for possession. Yet it retains a certain political appeal. Visibility politics have practical consequences.... While there is a deeply ethical appeal in the desire for a more inclusive representational landscape and certainly under-represented communities can be empowered by an enhanced visibility, the terms of this visibility often enervate the putative power of these identities [7].

This colonialist fetishism is well represented in the aforementioned television representations. The generic conventions set the trap. Voyeuristic by nature, television programs are inherently about looking. As Phalen further suggests, when one is looking at the "other," one is truly trying to see one's self. As proposed by television genre theorists, audiences utilize the secondary characters as a point of such identification. Therefore, if one is looking for oneself in the image of another, one is simultaneously naturalizing the other into an image of self (16).

How does the lesbian community escape this type of identificatory bondage? Phalen recommends invisibility, saving the lesbian image from heterosexual possession. I disagree. I believe visibility promotes knowledge (though often limited) and acceptance; however, as was illustrated by *Ellen*, attempts to push the envelope often end in audience alienation (the show lasted just one season after Ellen revealed her lesbianism). If progress is going to be made, it will not be accomplished by these secondary characters or even *Will & Grace*'s "but I play one on TV" Eric McCormack.[8] Rather, additional sites of representation must be explored, those which can avoid the traps of the inherently nonconfrontational situation comedy. Rather, gay and lesbian representations must find their ways to sites that better accept change and controversy. Perhaps a further investigation of the ideological underpinnings of generic formula may lead to this discovery, or perhaps ensemble "dramadies" can provide a space to diversify television's lesbian representations. In the meantime, the gay community must stay aware of the limitations of certain representations and recognize that, at the end of the day, the tallies on GLAAD's prime-time scoreboard mean very little.[9]

Notes

1. *Entertainment Weekly* and *OUT* are two notable examples of magazines that have glamorized the current portrayals of gays and lesbians on television without stopping to problematize the types of representations being shown. The cover of a recent *Entertainment Weekly* read "Gay Hollywood 2000." One aspect of the issue dealt with the proliferation of gay and lesbian characters on prime-time television. Svetsky writes, "They're here, they're queer ... and they'll be back after this commercial message. From *Will & Grace* to Richard on *Survivor*, gay TV is staking its claim," but it fails to cast a critical eye on the types of representations provided. Similarly, Jeffrey Epstein's interview with Eric McCormack (Will of *Will & Grace*) in *OUT* waves the banner of TV's gay revolution, but focuses on the depoliticization of the show. The show's creator, Max Mutchnick, says, "We will never tackle political issues. We won't do it because it's not necessary

2. For examples of this type of criticism, see Marlon Riggs' documentary film, *Color Adjustment*, as well as the work of Herman Gray.

3. Nine of these fifteen episodes occur within the first two seasons of the show. Throughout the rest of the run, the characters have been progressively phased out.

4. In this discussion, as in the one by Newcomb, I am referring to an idea of the viewing audience which represents those looking for identification with the social ideals and values considered to be the norm at the time of reception. These characters represent that which is expected out of the normal, successful American (which always implies heterosexual).

5. This assumes a homogeneous audience, which has well been ruled out by reception scholars. However, since the shows I am discussing are prime time vehicles, I will work under the assumption that the audience being courted is a middle-of-the-road mainstream audience, that which will provide the most capital to the advertisers.

6. Various theorists argue that rendering the butch — an image historically ingrained in lesbian culture — invisible, aids in veiling the lesbian herself, as well as making implied statements regarding acceptable lesbian socioeconomic class; it was the working-class lesbian who often played the butch role. Sue Ellen Case, surveys the butch's disappearance or disavowal as the feminist movement dubbed the role "politically incorrect" or unsavvy. As the butch was deemed passé or oppressive, a major semiotic signpost which marked lesbianism was shelved. Similarly, Chris Holmlund as well addresses the proliferation of femme images in film. Both of these shows suffer from this type of butch invisibility. Implied in the representations of Carol, Susan, Joan, and Debbie are both a certain socioeconomic standing and the safety-assumed heterosexuality that goes along with a desexualized femme in lieu of her butch lover.

7. Laws regarding child custody by gay or lesbian parents vary from state to state, but high profile cases, such as Sharon Bottoms vs. Kay Bottoms (a case in which the mother loses her child to the grandmother after revealing her lesbianism), illustrate the existent threat homophobia places on gay and lesbian parents. See the ACLU Website.

8. Eric McCormack, who plays the title role in the *Will & Grace* (the first lasting

sitcom to place a homosexual character in a leading role) often evokes his real role as married heterosexual in many television interviews, thereby creating a disconnect between the gay character and his "legitimate" heterosexual portrayer.

9. The GLAAD (Gay and Lesbian Association Against Defamation) website (www.glaad.org) keeps a running tally of gay, lesbian, bisexual, and transgendered characters on television.

Works Cited

ACLU Website. http://www.aclu.org/issues/gay/mothers.html 10 Dec 2001.
Bruni, Frank. "Culture Stays Screen-Shy of Showing the Gay Kiss." *Columbia Reader on Lesbian and Gay Men in Media, Society, and Politics.* Larry Gross and James D. Woods, eds. New York: Columbia University Press, 1999. 327–28.
Capsuto, Steven. *Alternate Channels: The Uncensored Story of Gay and Lesbian Images on Radio and Television, 1930 to the Present.* New York: Ballantine Books, 2000.
Case, Sue Ellen. "Toward a Butch-Femme Aesthetic." *Lesbian and Gay Studies Reader.* Henry Abelove, Michele Aina Barale, and David M. Halperin, eds. New York and London: Routledge, 1993. 294–306.
Collis, Rose. "Screened Out: Lesbians in Television." *Daring to Dissent: Lesbian Culture from Margin to Mainstream.* Liz Gibbs, ed. London and New York: Cassell, 1994. 120–46.
Color Adjustment. Marlon Riggs, dir. California Newsreel, 1991.
Epstein, Jeffrey. "Where There's a Will." *OUT* Nov. 2000: 80–85+.
Feuer, Jane. "Genre Study and Television." *Channels of Discourse.* Robert Allen, ed. Chapel Hill: University of North Carolina Press, 1992. 138–60.
Friends. NBC. 1994–2004.
Gray, Herman. *Watching Race: Television and the Struggle for Blackness.* Minneapolis and London: University of Minnesota Press, 1995.
_____. "Television, Black Americans, and the American Dream." *Television: The Critical View*, Fifth Edition, Horace Newcomb, ed. New York and Oxford: Oxford University Press, 1994. 176–87.
Himmelstein, Hal. *Television Myth and the American Mind.* New York: Praeger, 1984.
Holmlund, Christine. "When Is a Lesbian Not a Lesbian? The Lesbian Continuum and the Mainstream Femme Film." *Camera Obscura* 24 (1990): 144–79.
GLAAD Website. http://208.178.40.42/org/projects/tv/index.html 8 Nov. 2000.
Mad About You. NBC 1992–1998.
Moritz, Marguerite J. "Old Strategies for New Texts: How American Television Is Creating and Treating Lesbian Characters." *Columbia Reader on Lesbian*

and Gay Men in Media, Society, and Politics. Larry Gross and James D. Woods, eds. New York: Columbia University Press, 1999. 316–26.

Newcomb, Horace. *TV: The Most Popular Art.* Garden City: Anchor Press, 1974.

Phalen, Peggy. *Unmarked: The Politics of Performance.* New York and London: Routledge, 1993.

Riggs, Marlon, dir. *Color Adjustment.* California Newsreel, 1991.

Straayer, Chris. *Deviant Eyes, Deviant Bodies.* New York: Columbia University Press, 1996.

Svetkey, Benjamin. "Is Your TV Set Gay?" *Entertainment Weekly*, no. 562. 6 Oct. 2000: 24–28.

Tropiano, Stephen. *Prime Time Closet: A History of Gays and Lesbians on TV.* New York: Applause Books, 2002.

Whatling, Clare. *Screen Dreams: Fantasizing Lesbians in Film.* Manchester: Manchester University Press, 1997.

Masculinity and Male Intimacy in Nineties Sitcoms: *Seinfeld* and the Ironic Dismissal

Margo Miller

Before prime-time television had mainstreamed gay and lesbian characters, queer pleasures were widely available in sitcoms with same-sex intimacy and unconventionally gendered characters. Queer characters and queer moments may not have been definite, but they were rarely denied over the course of an episode.[1] During the nineties flood of gay and lesbian visibility, these queer pleasures receded. Coming-out narratives supplemented the system of codes for gay characters, but nonetheless, effeminacy in male characters became explicitly linked to homosexuality, both as a gay cue and as frequent comic fodder for straight men. In *Friends*, Chandler tries to entice his wife to move west by naming songs from the musical *Oklahoma*, to which she responds, "Are you trying to tell me we're moving to Oklahoma, or that you're gay?" These kinds of jokes facetiously censured straight men's queer behavior with exclusive and contradictory categories of "gay" and "straight."

Similarly, a dichotomy between friendship and intimacy supplanted television's history of ambiguous homoeroticism. Prime-time television avoided intimacy between gay characters and grew suspicious of bonds between straight men. In fact, sitcoms began to include comic denials of perceived homosexuality whenever male bonds were confirmed or prioritized. Straight male characters became aware of intimacy and gendered behavior that could signify gay identity and were quick to dismiss that possibility with a joke. After a series of flashbacks showing physical affection between Joey and Chandler in earlier episodes of *Friends*, for example, they make what may be called an ironic dismissal. Joey intercepts imagined accusations of homosexuality, asking, "Do we do this too much?" Chandler quickly agrees, "I think so. Yeah, get off me." The ironic dismissal defines intimacy between straight men against homosexuality, telling the viewer that the men's relationship was the opposite of what it seemed to be during physical, intensely emotional, or overly familiar displays of affection.[2] As a result, straight male characters could reflect modern masculinities by deflecting the queer implications of their same-sex intimacy with a quick one-liner: they hug, but they are not gay.

The ironic dismissal quickly became the standard method for sitcom characters to maintain their heterosexuality when their masculinity or male friendships were questioned. Though many ironic dismissals seem innocuous, this trend reflected a new hostility toward queerness in straight male characters. *Seinfeld* is a notable exception to this trend. This show rarely conflates effeminacy and homosexuality and accesses a continuum of men's relationships that include queer pleasures. It consistently experiments with masculinity and foregrounds homosocial relationships. At times, the expectation of an ironic dismissal endangers the men's friendships, but *Seinfeld* refuses to retract or reject its characters' intimacy in order to confirm heterosexuality.

Masculinity

Co-creators Larry David and Jerry Seinfeld conceived of a sitcom about the musings and complaints of an immature but intelligent clique with too much time on their hands. Their dialogue often examined the category of masculinity. Can a man order just a salad? When washing one's clothes, is it effeminate to use the gentle cycle? What about fine fabrics? The characters' questions — by turns frantic or facetious — reveal that masculinity is as fluid and artificial as femininity. Jerry, George, and Kramer exhibit unprecedented interest and comfort in discussions about attire, etiquette, and interpersonal relationships — concerns that often mark female characters and gay or gay-coded male characters. In the nineties, it was unusual for these obsessions to be articulated by ostensibly straight lead male characters without an accompanying ironic dismissal.

Seinfeld explores alternative forms of masculinity without linking effeminacy and homosexuality in an ironic dismissal. Although *Seinfeld*'s characters reject traditional aspects of masculinity and embrace activities like cooking, cleaning, and singing, they never approach the "sensitive guy" characters of other sitcoms. *Seinfeld* does not find it contradictory for men to act feminine or straight men to act gay. Instead, its characters mock masculine conventions and highlight the humor intrinsic to performing heteronormally.

Sitcoms like *Friends* and *Frasier* need the ironic dismissal to draw a line between masculine and feminine and straight and gay in the new male characters of the nineties. They often attempt to set up comedic contradictions in men acting gay—displaying stereotypically feminine qualities or stereotypically gay interests—if they are, in fact, heterosexual. The ensuing ironic dismissals are fraught with negative connotations toward gay men. Chandler's jokes, for example, are often self-deprecating acknowledgements of his suspicious masculinity—"I'm so gay!"—realizations that rely on broad stereotypes and judge his taste in clothes or knowledge of fine dining against Joey's crude behavior.

In *Seinfeld*'s world, there is no "man" against whom to judge Jerry, George, and Kramer. Their models of masculinity are absurd caricatures like the ancient-but-ultracompetitive Mandelbaums, Elaine's robust-but-tiresome boyfriend Puddy, and her imperious boss Mr. Peterman. When these characters appear, it is precisely their exaggerated or archaic masculinity that is mocked. Chandler, Ross, Niles, and Frasier feel compelled to defend themselves when confronted about their unmasculine traits. *Seinfeld*'s characters, on the other hand, compete to be the least manly. A *Seinfeld* joke that does question a character's masculinity finds humor in his resistance to proving his masculinity or in his excessive attention, but ultimate indifference, to gendered expectations.

Even within traditionally masculine spaces like sports culture, *Seinfeld* was brazen about its character's alternative masculinities. Even while they are eating hot dogs and discussing the Super Bowl, Jerry and George are "just a couple of gals out on the town, shopping and gabbing." Feminized terms are counterintuitive, but accurately describe these men's engagement in traditionally masculine activities. The show's sports references are informed but irreverent. Instead of arguing about who has the better team, the characters debate whether or not Joe DiMaggio dunks his donuts. When George asks Yankee Danny Tartabull to compare the team's cotton and polyester uniforms, Tartabull resists. Jerry, of course, answers with ease. This type of conversation is a skill, the show argues, that conventional men lack. When Jerry and George meet Elaine's father, Alton Benes, at a bar, George tries to engage Mr. Benes in a discussion about ordering ice with a beverage. Alton, already embarrassed by their choice of dainty drinks, is uncomfortable and, like Tartabull, first acts confused and then dismisses the conversation as if it were somehow queer.

Seinfeld always finds conventional masculinity comical, but in "The Jacket," it is also absurdly dangerous. Elaine's father's rigid masculinity ruins Jerry's expensive new coat. Jerry turns it inside out so snowfall will not ruin the suede, but Alton, seeing the pink-striped lining, barks, "You're not going to walk down the street with me and my daughter dressed like that. That's for damn sure!" Clearly suspicious of their masculinity, Mr. Benes questions Jerry's and George's heterosexuality: he compares Jerry to a sissy he served with in Korea and tells Elaine he thinks George is gay. George and Jerry do not compensate for their queer behavior by asserting their heterosexuality. Alton thinks George is gay because he (George) persistently sings "Master of the House" from *Les Misérables;* at one point, Mr. Benes says to George, "Pipe down, chorus boy." But Elaine explains that her father "thinks everyone is gay." The fact that Alton does not base his conclusions upon their "gay" behavior is humorous because it is surprising; in most sitcoms, the assignment of sexual orientation would be grounded in observations of mannerisms. The episode suggests that Alton thinks "everyone is gay" because he compares modern masculinity to his archaic expectations. And despite his masculine posturing, Mr. Benes is not incapable of being queer. When driving home alone at the end of the episode, Alton inadvertently offers his own husky rendition of the infectious *Les Mis* tune. His harsh criticisms of George's and Jerry's behavior become still more laughable when he demonstrates that even the most masculine men cannot perform heteronormativity flawlessly.

Jerry is more comfortable in the company of gay masculinity. In "The Wigmaster," he dines happily with a male acquaintance until another man approaches their table and propositions Jerry's friend. Jerry subsequently upbraids the interloper for his rudeness, wondering how the latter knows that he (Jerry) and his friend are not a couple. Seinfeld is as insulted at being overlooked as the potential partner of a gay man as he is when Elaine is asked out in front of him. He comically confuses stereotypes by joking that his failure to perform homosexuality adequately was "very emasculating." Jerry does not qualify his egotistical tirade; he presents himself as the man's partner and chases off the rival suitor. The incident suggests that Jerry's possessiveness could come from an emotion other than spite. In an episode of *Friends* with a similar premise, Chandler is mocked for defending his romantic prospects as a gay man. Chandler's co-worker sets him up with an average-looking male colleague and says that their better-looking colleague Brian is "out of his league." Unnerved that she thought he was gay and insulted that she does not think he could attract a more handsome man, he offers an awkward and conflicted dismissal: "You don't think I could get a Brian? Because I could get a Brian. Believe you me.... I'm really not."

Jerry is less concerned about being perceived as gay. He understands the cultural markers of sexual identity — he states, "People think I'm gay ... because I'm thin, single, and neat" — and does not resist these stereotypes. Chandler is surprised and disturbed to learn that people sometimes assume he is gay, and the series blames his "vague" gay "quality" on his cross-dressing father and hypersexual mother. His image is presented as problematic, and he jokes about it to police his own behavior, saying "Don't we look nice all dressed up today!" and then realizing "It's stuff like that" that makes him seem gay.

Sitcoms' gay guest appearances usually hinge on their sexuality, but *Seinfeld* establishes its gay male characters through cultural codes, not cliché narratives, and their story lines are independent of their sexual identities. In three episodes over the course of four seasons, a pair of gay thugs makes a mockery of the classic Hollywood convention of vilifying the sexually deviant. They terrorize Kramer, organizing a mob to force him to wear a ribbon during an AIDS walk in "The Sponge" and stealing an armoire he is guarding for Elaine in "The Soup Nazi." They exact cultural revenge for their vaguely ethnic, street-queen subculture. Although gay characters create opportunities for ironic dismissals, those in *Seinfeld* do not provoke one because they are superficially unlike its main characters. Usually, sitcoms humorously establish straight men's identities in the presence of characters who look and act just like them, but turn out to be gay. The gay male characters in *Seinfeld* are outrageous compared to the safe and highly homogenized representations in other prime-time sitcoms. Nonetheless, Jerry, George, and Kramer remained the defiantly abnormal outsiders of society even compared to these very queer characters.

Male Intimacy

Most nineties sitcoms also use an ironic dismissal to yank the queer subtext out of straight men's relationships. These jokes dissolve the romantic, domestic, or physical elements of a straight friendship with a preemptive statement that the men are not gay. *Seinfeld*, on the other hand, uniquely pulls its queer subtext slowly to the surface and anchors entire episodes with homoerotic undercurrents. It unabashedly displays the intense bonds shared by its insincere main characters. Jerry, George, and Kramer indulge each other's idiosyncrasies and share every detail of their lives. Their familiar commiseration and mutual antagonisms are consistent markers of their unusual intimacy. Selfish and unsentimental, they are more likely to thwart each other's success than encourage it, yet their relationships with each other are their only source of pleasure.

Jerry constantly makes futile attempts to set boundaries in his relationships with other men. He is suckered into buying dinner for fellow comic Bania, suffocated by Ramon-the-pool-guy's constant companionship, obliged to accept gum and wear glasses for George's old neighbor, Lloyd Braun, and forced to "break up with" his annoying childhood friend Joel just as he would a girlfriend. His interactions with other men playfully highlight the procedural similarities of making friends and making dates, the continuities between friends and more-than-friends, and the romantic overtones of professional relationships.

Narrative irresolution akin to the soap opera's circumvents an ironic dismissal in many *Seinfeld* episodes.[3] In "The Mimbo," George, always the loser, is infatuated with "cool guy" Tony. Jerry quickly explains that George's attraction to Elaine's new boyfriend is a "non-sexual crush," and the episode goes on to explore what this term might mean. When George becomes jealous of Kramer's budding friendship with Tony, Kramer says that he thinks George is in love with Tony. George reacts by telling Kramer he had better "watch it" on their joint rock climbing trip. George's abrupt exits and avoidance of the subject make the audience more aware of his ambiguous emotions.

Friends and *Seinfeld* both access their homoerotic undercurrents by performing heterosexual couplehood. When Joey monopolizes Monica's phone conversation with her husband, Chandler, it seems that Joey—not Monica—is the one in the long-distance relationship. As is often the case in *Friends*, after the homoeroticism is exposed, the scene abruptly ends. This parody further ingrains the differences between Chandler's two relationships: although Joey is unknowingly acting like a lover, he is clearly "just a friend." George and Kramer, on the other hand, do not accidentally "act like" Jerry's lovers, they are compared to — "are like" — his lovers. When Jerry and Kramer find themselves in bed together reading the paper, for example, their pillow talk resembles a married couple's dialogue.

Jerry's failed attempts at ironic dismissals often extend the homoeroticism of a scene. He and Kramer are seen in bed together despite Jerry's earlier attempt to snub Kramer with an ironic dismissal. When Kramer wants to sleep in Jerry's bed instead of on his couch, Jerry balks. "Why not?" Kramer wonders, and Jerry, annoyed, asks, "Do I really have to explain why?" When Elaine interrupts their argument, Kramer asks her to leave, explaining "We need to get to bed." As is often the case in *Seinfeld*, the ironic dismissal is ineffective. Jerry shares his bed with Kramer after acknowledging the homoerotic implications of the act. In the scene that follows, he is more threatened by the banality of the somewhat queer situation than the physical intimacy.

Comic dismissals of implied homosexuality presume that intimacy between straight men is inherently ironic. According to *Friends*' executive producer David Crane, Chandler and Joey's relationship "is about two straight guys behaving like a married couple"—"if they were two gay characters, it would be considerably less funny."[4] In fact, it might not be funny at all. Joey and Chandler's respectable relationship constitutes a recurring joke: "we're acting gay, but we're straight." None of *Seinfeld*'s comedy can be reduced to this formula. Episodes that examine Jerry's professional or highly scripted relationships with other men, for example, revolve around an ambiguity that is not directly linked to sexual identity. *Seinfeld* is generally more nuanced and instead of underlining categories of "gay" and "straight," has its characters' peculiar relationships cross boundaries and complicate viewers' expectations.

The intimacy displayed by straight men in *Seinfeld*'s satires of dating and marriage may be part of the reason viewers laugh at the show, but a scene is never funny solely because the men are supposedly straight. In "The Susie," George's girlfriend Allison asks Kramer to break up with George for her, and it becomes increasingly difficult to distinguish George's feelings for Allison from George and Kramer's feelings for each other. They meet unexpectedly in the doorway to Jerry's apartment, for example, and effectively parody awkward ex-lovers. Handled differently, the humor might hinge on the characters' heterosexuality, but the comic value in George and Kramer, two ostensibly straight men, attending the "Yankee Prom" as a couple is less significant than their increasingly convoluted relationship and farcical performance of George's fantasy. George makes his first "great entrance," but with Kramer, not Allison, twirling through the doors in a backless outfit just as he hoped Allison would wear. Kramer's tuxedo rips as George struggles to prevent him from stepping into the banquet hall. When Kramer, who has agreed to take George back without Allison's approval, tells George's boss that the two of them are "together," George seems to accept it as a fact. A viewer may find it humorous that, in this final moment, they appear gay, and there is no defensive affirmation of their heterosexuality.

In most sitcoms, the ironic dismissal supports men's friendships by dispelling the threat of homosexuality, but in *Seinfeld*, men's obligations to distance themselves from homosexuality are an obstacle in their relationships. When Jerry and New York Met Keith Hernandez meet, exchange numbers, and go to a movie together, their enthusiasm and insecurities make their attraction ambiguous but overt and suggest the continuities between friendship, romance, and erotic relationships. After Jerry gets back from his "date" with Keith, George asks, "Who paid?" and "Did you shake his hand?" George's usual attention to detail eroticizes the relationship and renders the questions themselves queer. Kramer and Elaine continually question the nature of Jerry and Keith's relationship, and it is difficult for Jerry to respond. He never defines his desires or emphasizes that he and Keith are "just friends." In the end, Jerry withdraws his offer to help Keith move into a new apartment because he considers it too intimate an act for men who have just met, and he ends the relationship to avoid further emotional turmoil. Jerry is not willing to make the ironic dismissals necessary in order to maintain a relationship with Hernandez.

Jerry and George's obliviousness to the ironic dismissal endangers their friendship in "The Outing," when an NYU reporter visits Jerry's apartment to interview him for an article in her university's paper. She is already under the impression that Jerry and George are a couple when she arrives, and she interprets their responses to her questions and their interaction as evidence. Signs that indicate Jerry and George are partners continue throughout the episode, and the viewer sees their behavior through the eyes of the reporter. George's persistent obliviousness to the reporter's point of view—he does not find the question, "Do you two live together?" at all unusual—shows how comfortable and unguarded they are in their relationship. They finally realize they must assert their heterosexuality to contradict their behavior, but by then, even Kramer and their parents will not accept their denials; Jerry and George continue fulfilling gay stereotypes and displaying familiarities that makes them "more than friends." After reading portions of the published article aloud—including passages such as "Within the confines of his fastidious bachelor pad, Seinfeld and Costanza bicker over the cleanliness of a piece of fruit like an old married couple...."—Jerry resumes the same argument with George, yelling, "I told you that pear was washed!" They are desperate to correct the reporter's mistake, but incapable of proving that they are not a couple because they continue to act in their usual fashion; their everyday behavior and entrenched intimacy are undeniably queer.

In this episode, it becomes clear how different Jerry and George's relationship would be if *Seinfeld* regularly made ironic dismissals of its queerness. Because of the turmoil the article inspires, Jerry's birthday gifts are ruined. He will not accept gay icon Bette Midler's *Greatest Hits* from Elaine, and he will take George's tickets for the Broadway musical *Guys and Dolls*, but will not let George accompany him as planned. As George concedes, "everything is tainted now!" Instead of reuniting by denying homosexuality, Jerry and George are pushed apart when forced to downplay their intimate connection. Homosexual inferences cannot be cleanly dismissed and are incorporated into nearly every moment of the episode. Intimacy and effeminacy do not threaten their friendship, but the expectations that others have for unambiguous sexual identity do. Ultimately, Jerry and George's "outing" is as inconsequential as any of the other events in their lives, and the repercussions are confined to one episode.

In its critique of homophobia, *Seinfeld* suggested that straight men may sublimate their desires for other men. In "The Boyfriend," for example, Elaine notices that Jerry sounds more jealous of her for dating Keith Hernandez than of Hernandez for dating her and asks which of them he wishes he was. Jerry stalls and pretends to look through his kitchen cupboards for a bottle of scotch, suggesting that liquor is the only honest response to her directness. Jerry recognizes his attraction to Keith and acknowledges his unwillingness to accept or pursue his desires in order to maintain his heterosexuality. George's satiric homophobia often morphs his fear of physical intimacy with other men into a form of homoeroticism. "The Outing" mimics the scene from "The Contest" in which an attractive female nurse attends to an equally sexy patient while George is desperately trying to refrain from masturbation. Exhausted from his futile attempts to prove he is not gay, George sees a hunky male nurse giving a handsome patient a sponge bath and is paralyzed by the men's silhouettes. In this episode, like many others, *Seinfeld* does not expose its homoeroticism like other sitcoms, but keeps its queerness far from subtextual.

Sitcoms that use the ironic dismissal depart from the queer past of television comedy. Sissy-buddy duos Martin & Lewis and Hope & Crosby were good friends overflowing with gay innuendo; the homoerotic subtext of coupled personality comedians Laurel and Hardy was accepted, if not widely acknowledged; half-hour television programs like *The Odd Couple* allowed audiences to read whatever they wanted into intense homosociality. In many nineties sitcoms, the ironic dismissal cancelled, or at least short-circuited many queer pleasures, but *Seinfeld* expanded the queer cultural legacy that came before it.

Seinfeld converged textual and subtextual readings with its commentary on the intimacy between Jerry and George. In the "The Cartoon" from the final season, George dates a woman who resembles Jerry, and Kramer and Elaine suggest that George likes this woman because he is actually attracted to Jerry. Neither Kramer nor Elaine is surprised, and Elaine initially finds the new evidence of George's attraction too ordinary to merit discussion. Kramer speaks with astonishing directness, and his pronouncements are given a humorous veracity by the episode's other thread, in which he tells a struggling comedian Jerry's true opinion of her talents. It is as if George's desire for Jerry has always been well understood.

Kramer tries to assuage George's fears by telling him, "just because they look alike, it doesn't mean you're secretly in love with Jerry." For George, hearing the formerly subtextual conclusion spoken aloud is even more shocking than his private ruminations about the similarity. Later, Elaine initiates a charged and self-conscious conversation between George and Jerry simply by mentioning that the girlfriend is "quite a handsome woman." George becomes visibly shaken when he hears Jerry's defensiveness. Together, they address their friends' insinuations, casually denying resemblance between Jerry and the girlfriend. When there seems to be nothing more they can say, but the tension between them remains, Jerry utters the final safeguard: "I'm not gay." However, his attempt at a dismissal fails. Even this statement is insufficient to deny the "evidence" that they are, on some level, attracted to each other. George replies, "Neither am I," uncertainly, as if he hopes that his concurrence will end their embarrassment, but knows that affirming their heterosexuality is beside the point; their predicament is not as simple as a miscommunication or mistaken identity. Theirs is not the typical dismissal; the scene argues that their relationship is as queer as it seems.

They turn to Kramer after this unfamiliar territory leaves them uncertain about how to interpret and explain their feelings for each other.

Kramer's insouciance about George "dating a lady Jerry" emphasizes their discomfort. He reiterates the implications by peppering a self-indulgent tirade with references to the situation: "George has a new femme–Jerry friend"; "George is all mixed up in a perverse sexual amalgam of some girl and his best friend"; and "George's parents' reaction upon hearing their son's man-love toward she–Jerry." In Kramer's mind, it is more perverse for George to date a woman who looks like Jerry than it would be for George to date Jerry.

The audience enjoys seeing Kramer textualize — and sexualize — the homoerotic undercurrents of Jerry and George's relationship, hearing that which is not customarily said but is known to have some elements of truth. Watching his girlfriend, George's paranoid thoughts are heard in voiceover: "So what if she does look like Jerry.... What does that mean? That I could have everything that I have with Jerry but that because it's a woman I could also have sex with her? And that somehow that would be exactly what I've always wanted...."

Conclusion

Jerry, George, and Kramer evaded ironic dismissals at a crucial moment in television history. As gay visibility increased, queer pleasures in straight characters were quietly jeopardized. Throughout the nineties, *Seinfeld* presented a queer challenge to this new incarnation of primetime heteronormativity, as the critical exception to sitcoms' standardized rejection of gay codes in straight male characters and of intimacy between straight men. The show found a way to highlight queer pleasures without limiting them with an ironic dismissal and persistently incorporating homoeroticism into its episodes. The precedent of an ironic dismissal abruptly queered every "unmasculine" moment and then pretended it had never happened. *Seinfeld*, though, would not let this queerness be forgotten.

Notes

I would like to thank Laura Ring, Ron Gregg, and Anthony Ruth for their help with this essay.

1. See Alexander Doty, *Making Things Perfectly Queer: Interpreting Mass Culture* Minneapolis: University of Minnesota Press, 1993.
2. My theory of the ironic dismissal owes a great deal to Mark Simpson's essay "The Straight Men of Comedy" in *Because I Tell a Joke or Two: Comedy, Politics and Social Difference*, Stephen Wagg, ed. (New York: Routledge, 1998).
3. John Fiske, *Television Culture: Popular Pleasures and Politics* (New York: Routledge, 1988).
4. David Kirby, "Open Secret: The Subtle Shift in the American Sitcom," *The New York Times* (18 June 2001).

Seinfeld episodes discussed: Male Unbonding (14 June 1990), The Revenge (18 April 1991), The Jacket (6 February 1991), The Note (18 September 1991), The Red Dot (11 December 1991), The Boyfriend (2, 12 February 1992), The Outing (11 February 1993), The Stall (6 January 1994), The Pledge Drive (6 October 1994), The Soup (10 November 1994), The Label Maker (19 January 1995), The Jimmy (16 March 1995), The Wink (12 October 1995), The Soup Nazi (2 November 1995), The Pool Guy (16 November 1995), The Sponge (7 December 1995), The Gum (14 December 1995) The Wig Master (4 April 1996) The Invitations (16 May 1996), The Susie (13 February 1997), The Betrayal (20 November 1997), The Apology (11 December 1997), The Cartoon (29 January 1998), The Puerto Rican Day (7 May 1998).

Friends episodes mentioned: The One Where Nana Dies Twice (10 November 1994), The One with Mac and C.H.E.E.S.E. (13 April 2000), The One Where Emma Cries (3 October 2002), The One with the Pediatrician (10 October 2002).

Gay Performativity and Reality Television: Alliances, Competition, and Discourse

Christopher Pullen

James Getzlaff, leading man of television's first gay male dating show, *Boy Meets Boy*, tells his fellow (straight) cast member (and best friend) Andra that his objective for participating in the series is to demonstrate to a skeptical and even hostile world that gay men are no different than heterosexuals save in the choice of sexual partners and that their sincere love for each other should warrant inclusion in exclusive heterosexual institutions such as marriage. James, like many other gay individuals, involved himself in reality television for the purpose of reforming dominant ideas concerning sexual identity. A format twist in *Boy Meets Boy* required that James strengthen his alliance with Andra to resolve his search for romance and to achieve his political objectives. This developing relationship between James and Andra may be indicative of a recurring feature in contemporary reality television — the alliance between gay and straight cast members. This essay consequently discusses such strategies of alliance, relating this both to internal alliances within the cast and alliances between producers and performers.

The formation of alliances is not new to gay identity politics and reality television. The appearance of Lance Loud as a contented, if somewhat precocious, young gay man in the groundbreaking observational documentary *An American Family* may be considered a defining moment in TV history and gay representation (Pullen; Rouff). In what may be considered by some the first televisual coming-out sequence, Lance socially performed codes, gestures, and behaviors that signified a homosexual identity.[1] This marked not only the emergence of the openly gay man appearing on serial television, but also the importance of forming alliances with those responsible for broadcasting one's image. Although Lance (at the time) became disheartened when he saw the represented version of himself (qtd. in *Lance Loud! Death in an American Family*), it has been the willingness of gay citizens, such as Loud, to commit aspects of their personal lives to the camera and to public scrutiny that has produced the powerful presence of gay performativity in contemporary reality television and has resulted in a greater visibility for the gay community.

When discussing the presence of gays and lesbians in contemporary reality television, one must consider the potential for exploitation both by producers who see in gay narratives a lucrative and appealing subject matter and by gays and lesbians themselves who participate for financial purposes rather than the edification of the public. While the motivation for inclusion of gays and lesbians in reality television may be commodification, this programming, nevertheless, provides both a platform for the public performance of gay identities and an arena for social debate.

This essay discusses the voluntary appearance of gay performers in reality television, focusing on the potential of such imagery to generate alternative discourses. The essay examines performances in *Boy Meets Boy* within the broader context of the highly successful reality programs *The Real World* and *Survivor*. Producer Jon Murray of *The Real World* created one of the first powerful alliances between producers and performers, creating positive representations of gays and lesbians and thus stimulating a welcome environment for gay subjectivities on television —*Survivor* and *Boy Meets Boy* have continued this process, both overturning negative stereotypes about alternative sexual identities. The performances of Richard Hatch (of *Survivor*), a 39-year-old corporate trainer, and James Getzlaff (of *Boy Meets Boy*), a 32-year-old benefits administrator, inverted public expectations regarding gay identity; the former becoming a leader in a survival game and the latter an object of desire in a gay dating show. The discursive power of these performances creates the potential for the transgression of identity constructs.

Performative Potential

Richard Schechner tells us that performativity "points to a variety of topics, among them the construction of social reality, including gender and race" (110). Marvin Carlson further suggests that "[p]erformance can work within society precisely to undermine tradition to provide a site for the exploration of fresh and alternative structures and patterns of behavior" (15). Consequently, the performances are discussed here for their potential to reinvent and reformulate identity constructs. In order to evaluate this performative/transgressive potential, Mikhail Bakhtin's idea of the carnival and Michel Foucault's ideas on discursive power must be foregrounded.

The Bakhtinian carnival often involves identifying binary oppositions and inverting their hierarchical relationship. This may be evident in the representation of homosexuals as dominant providers (as occurs with Richard Hatch) or as romantic partners (as is evident with James Getzlaff): this practice inverts the alleged natural sexual order. In this context, the gay male is no longer a lone subject (of derision or entertainment); he plays a central role in the development and resolution of the narrative. In their analysis of the Bakhtinian carnival, Peter Stallybrass and Allon White have acknowledged the potential to shift "the very terms of the system itself by erasing and interrogating the relationships which constitute it" (58). The removal of traditional power bases which form cultural hegemony (such as the dominant role of the heterosexual male) may result in "a potent, populist, critical inversion of ... official worlds and hierarchies" (7). Reality television retains a great deal of "carnivalesque potential" in the replacement of the heterosexual with the homosexual as the central impetus behind the narrative action.

The narrative and the discursive performativity of gay cast members challenge established sites of power. This may be possible if we consider Michel Foucault's postulate that power is "everywhere; not because it embraces everything, but because it comes from everywhere" (93). Foucault proposes that power can be fluid, a dynamic interaction between individuals, organizations, and hierarchies, as well as a source of resistance. Although the texts discussed here may be termed mainstream, the inclusion of gay performers generates the potential for resistance. Such opportunities may be created through the alliances between gay performers and producers or other cast members; relationships that challenge and overturn the idea of "heterocentric closure" as a textual norm. In order to discuss this further, it is important to establish the textual and discursive circumstances that have contributed to the heightened visibility of gay identity within reality television. Competition oriented reality television and its romance with gay subjectivity (as illustrated in *Survivor* and *Boy Meets Boy*) is not a new development; it is further evidence of a progression initiated by *The Real World*.

Starting Alliances with The Real World

Since its inception in 1992, *The Real World* has consistently included gay participants as a recurring feature in the social profiles offered by the series,[2] thus creating a format that has provided multiple opportunities for the articulation of gay political and social issues for the edification of a mass audience. Jon Murray, co-creator of *The Real World* and an openly gay man, regards himself as a political agent with a personal agenda to promote gay visibility through his series.[3] Jon Murray also discloses personal details concerning his sexuality in order to reinforce the personal political necessity of openness and visibility:

> I knew I was a gay teenager. But concealing that kind of knowledge was the norm at the time.... I was much happier when I was ultimately able to embrace and reveal my sexuality [qtd. in Solomon 4].

Jon Murray's casting priorities in *The Real World* helped to break down barriers against the depiction of gay romantic love on television, initiating a process that would result in more overt representations such as *Boy Meets Boy*.

Most notably, the San Francisco series of 1994 and the New Orleans series of 2000 included representations of intimate relationships between male lovers: Pedro and Sean (in the former) and Danny and Paul (in the latter). The representation of Pedro and Sean's wedding ceremony remains a landmark in television representations of same-sex couples, one yet to be equaled. Danny Roberts' romance with Paul is an equally progressive statement. This may be seen not as much in its sensitive display of affection between the couple as in its political commentary and aesthetic choices: because Paul was enlisted in the army during the series, his face could not be revealed. This type of textual seduction made the romance between Danny and Paul intriguing (everyone wanted to know what Paul looked like). It also generated a torrent of highly contentious political discourse, criticizing the American government for not promoting legislation that would allow gay men and women to state openly that they are in the employ of the armed forces. The inclusion of Pedro Zamora (a man who was dying from AIDS) and Paul (a man who risked his career by participating in the series) embodies the political/polemical posture adopted by both performers and producers. While not every example of gay performance in *The Real World* is as progressive as those above, the alliance between producers and performers remained a constant site of resistance to the conservative proprieties.

Not only have the producers of *The Real World* provided a vehicle for broadcast of gay friendly discourse, but they have also revealed a conspicuous bias towards the inclusion of gay people. Evidence of this may be seen in casting statistics provided by Murray: "while roughly 35,000 people audition for *The Real World* and *Road Rules* [(another Bunim-Murray show)] each year, only about 200 are openly gay" (qtd. in Epstein 50). The predisposition recounted by Jon Murray is substantial: openly gay people represent 0.5 percent of the potential cast availability, yet constitute to 12 percent of the cast,[4] a 2,400 percent bias in favor of casting gays Such motivation for inclusion no doubt outstrips the possible narrative appeal of gay people. Jon Murray's determination to broadcast a persistent progay message on *The Real World,* combined with the cultural power of MTV, seems to have had a permanent impact on the genre: gay people are consistently included as part of the social lineup in the reality television household.

Competition and Narrative Tension in Survivor *and* Boy Meets Boy

Survivor and *Boy Meets Boy* may be seen as a variation on the "reality" format of *The Real World.* While *The Real World* established the impetus to record social actors for the purpose of television drama, *Survivor* and *Boy Meets Boy* modify *The Real World* format, moving from a mostly anthropological (observing behavior, even if it is within a fabricated environment with certain rules)[5] approach to reality drama to a competition oriented narrative. These newer programs expand upon Murray's inclusive paradigm by actually placing the gay cast members in competitive contexts with heterosexuals and observing their relative successes (allowing for a potential public relations boon should the gay performer win or succeed). While this does not equate to an assurance that narratives will be beneficial to the winners (the gay performer may still not appear in an advantageous light), the competitive opportunities do allow the gay participants to test the equity of their skills in a mass media context, a circumstance which has the potential to transform public opinion and undermine negative stereotypes.

Therefore, while Jon Murray and *The Real World* make alliances with preferred gay performers to promote gay visibility through a joint narrative venture (selecting Pedro in San Francisco and Danny in New Orleans), Richard Hatch of *Survivor* and James Getzlaff of *Boy Meets Boy* become more prominent through their competitive engagements in their respective contexts. Although there was much potential for failure, each managed to pluck victory from their respective engagements and subsequently improve public perceptions of gay men as competitors, thus undermining the stereotype that gay men are helpless, feckless, or ineffectual, particularly in confrontation with heterosexual males. Through internal (cast orientated rather than production orientated) alliances, the gay performers in *Survivor* and *Boy Meets Boy* succeeded in an environment where most would have predicted their failure.

Boy Meets Boy necessarily focuses on the representation of homosexual desire (a gay dating show), and *Survivor* focuses on various social groups and identities (a survival game that presents an imagined microcosm of society). In each, an opposition between homosexuality and heterosexuality is set up from the outset. Evidence of this is seen in the opening episode of *Boy Meets Boy* where we are told that Getzlaff (the central object of desire and date selector) does not know that some of his potential dates are straight. On day one in *Survivor,* elder cast member Rudy comments that he does like homosexuals. Consequently, both textual sites foreshadow conflict between sexual identities, as Getzlaff may inadvertently select a straight man for his romantic date, and Hatch may be rejected immediately by the other castaways (or at least by Rudy) if he reveals his orientation. Therefore, although it may be imagined that *Boy Meets Boy* would be a simple matchmaking game resulting in romance, we find out that an undisclosed format twist (not revealed to Getzlaff until episode four) reinvents the series as a precarious journey to discover the authentic gay man. Similarly, although the focus on homosexuality so early in *Survivor* suggests that Richard Hatch may be a strong contender in the series, at the same time, it suggests that there will be conflict.

Survivor: The Gay/Straight Alliance and Bodily Performance

While Richard Hatch's motives for competing in *Survivor* may be solely related to money (the prize was a million dollars and a car), it is evident that Hatch nevertheless wanted to make a stand regarding his gay sexual identity. After certain cast members complain that he should remain dressed (he appears naked to celebrate his birthday), he responds, "If I lived my life based on what made other people uncomfortable, I wouldn't be living my life." His unashamed and confrontational style made Hatch a central narrative provider in the first *Survivor* series. Since Hatch was the overall winner in the survival game (endorsed by the other cast members), his success may have led to the inclusion of gay people in later programs.[6] He is remembered as much for his cunning, guile, and productivity, as for his sexual orientation. His success was mostly attributable to his ability to win the trust of other cast members (the voting alliance).

From an early stage in the game, Richard Hatch formed and led an alliance that resulted in opposing cast members being voted off almost to his order. This alliance most notably included Rudy (who, as discussed above, expressed his distaste for homosexuals), Sue (a heterosexual redneck), and Kelly (a younger female). His organizational skills included gaining support from people who might have appeared to be unlikely heterosexual allies. Similarly, Richard Hatch established himself as major food provider: he caught more fish/provisions from the sea than anyone else. Consequently, his role was functional: he organized a voting strategy that would support a small dominant group that he led, and he provided nutrition to the cast in an environment where it was difficult to obtain food. This strategy ensured that he would remain an obligatory participant until the end of the game.

During episodes eight and nine, Hatch's central role came under attack, first from Greg and later from Jenna, who formed an opposing alliance aimed at dispatching Hatch. In both of these episodes, Hatch cunningly engaged with opposing cast members to determine their weaknesses and vulnerabilities. During episode eight (in which Greg was to be voted off), Hatch admitted he was attracted to Greg and instigated a conversation, revealing that Greg may be interested in sexual experimentation. This exchange established Hatch's control, revealing that he is sexually aware and fulfilled while Greg may be uncertain, vulnerable to sexual deviation. Similarly in episode nine (in which Jenna was to be voted off), Hatch appeared naked (allegedly in celebration of his birthday). This upset a number of cast members, but particularly Jenna who used the occasion to comment on Hatch's sexuality: "It felt awkward sitting next to a naked gay man." In a manner reminiscent of Bakhtin's carnival, Hatch used his body as a site of performative resistance where "status degradation through exposure of the grotesque aspects of the body ... [is presented] over the rational and spiritual control of the head" (Stallybrass and White 183). Hatch's naked overweight and hirsute body was a carnivalesque/grotesque spectacle calculated to be an affront to Jenna. Her response revealed her vulnerability and disempowerment. Hatch mobilized his alliance to vote against Greg and Jenna respectively. However, in order to justify this, he first disempowered them. These eliminations were not only helpful in maintaining his alliance, but useful in ensuring his pathway to the finale.

The representation of Richard Hatch helped break down traditional stereotypes of gay males on mainstream television; an overweight, overbearing, masculine gay man dismantled commonplace images of gay identity — "effeminacy, sensitivity ... [and] isolation" (Clum 77). Hatch demonstrated that gay people can be productive in the formation of successful social alliances. Moreover, Hatch's performance can be seen as a building block in reality television texts, one which prepared the way for *Boy Meets Boy*, where the gay performance involves a potential romantic attachment.

Boy Meets Boy *and the Heterosexual as the Hidden Other*

The initial episode of *Boy Meets Boy* introduces its central performer and unashamedly tantalizes the audience with a format twist, revealing that there are hidden heterosexual participants in the contest. This format ruse also allows for a reversal of roles. Alluding to the idea that gay people have been forced to live covert lives in order to protect themselves (from abuse, segregation, devaluation, and confinement), the series places the heterosexual male in the role of the "hidden other," whose success in the artificial environment is determined by his ability to conceal his sexual orientation. As openly gay series producer Douglas Ross tells us, "it's impossible to tell who's gay and who's straight" (qtd. in Sigesmund 52); thus the show becomes an exercise in evaluating the propriety of the stereotypes often applied to gay and straight men.

Although we are aware that the gay contestants may have agreed to be participants in the show for the purpose of breaking stereotypes (and possibly finding romance or achieving personal fame), it is debatable whether the straight contestants have the same lofty goals (as they are able to win a cash prize should they be selected by James). This element makes the text hard to evaluate in its effort to reverse "the outsider role," as dialogue provided by straight contestants may be intended to excuse them for deceiving the openly gay men honestly participating in the show.

Statements provided by straight contestants following their elimination reveal the effort of producers to advance a political agenda through the show. Episode two concludes with the elimination of straight contestant Jim who succinctly relates a connection between his experience and normal experiences of closeted homosexuals, telling us: "My [covert] experience here has been a mirrored image of how people in the closet are still experiencing daily life." Although the audience may have been uncertain about Jim's sexual identification, the same cannot be said of contestants Dan and Michael. These straight participants were much more successful in masquerading as gay. Consequently, when both are eliminated in episode three, their coming out as straight men is surprising, but they offer a commentary on the difficulty of concealing their true sexual orientation.

Although both performers expressed an appreciation for the struggle of gay men to conceal their sexual identities in order to function in a prejudicial society, it is doubtful that producers would have used any disconsolate discourse critical of gay men. In other words, there is no detailed or unedited commentary provided that would reveal the reason these men agreed to participate in the program or their feelings about their failure to win the prize — information provided by the rejected gay participants.[7] In place of this, the producers include only the dialogue that supports a progay stance by suggesting that rejected straight contestants only became involved because they had an interest in breaking stereotypes. This type of "production determinism" is most centrally foregrounded in the final episode when the last straight guy (Franklin) is eliminated. In the lead-up to this finale, alliances and coalitions are foregrounded in an effort to close the emerging homocentric narrative.

Although the series commences with a heterocentric narrative, suggesting that James is an object for the entertainment of heterosexual audiences since he is not aware of the complication in the plot line, the balance of power shifts in his favor after episode four (when James is informed of the format development). At this point in the series, the confrontation becomes more equitable; James, no longer ignorant of the conditions of the game and likely to be tricked into dating a straight man, is instead challenged to identify the remaining straight man. While this development takes the focus off romance and fulfillment, it also generates the potential for resistance to the heterosexist hegemony. Should the infiltrator be discovered, he can be punished with rejection. In terms of Foucaultian power, this provides the opportunity for a performance of power resistance. Had James simply chosen a gay guy (by luck) or had there been no straight guys within the lineup, this opportunity would not have been created. Consequently, after episode four, the tone of the series, not surprisingly, changes. James no longer tries to find the ideal lover, but must instead identify the outsider. His alliance with his friend Andra (a straight girl who helps him select the guys) becomes more central to the narrative. Also, the remaining gay men become closely allied, generating another symbolic social reversal by casting the straight guys in the role of outsiders.

The remaining three contestants for the finale were Wes (gay), Brian H. (gay), and Franklin (straight). Although the audience is not privy to each participant's sexual identification until the end of the series, it is easy to perceive that Franklin is the straight outsider. The selection/rejection process involved cast members being brought together in small groups from which James was required to reject only one.[8] Consequently, the pairing of Franklin and Sean in episode four (from whom James chooses the former and rejects the latter) implies that both men are straight and must be eliminated separately.

James and Andra go on the offensive. Earlier, James had suggested that Franklin might be the straight guy. In order to test his theory, he arranges a date with Franklin at a sauna so that he can evaluate the level of discomfort generated by the close physical proximity. James does not reveal (before the finale) whether this experiment exposed Franklin as the outsider. Andra also confronts Franklin, telling him that she would be unhappy if anyone were lying to her best friend (James). The finalists also discuss sexual stereotypes that surround gay sexuality. Franklin recalls his history of identification as a sexual rather than a social object, complaining "there is nothing more I wanted to hear [from gay men] than about a person's day, not about how pretty I am." Andra responds "You're pretty?" Andra's aggressive riposte reveals her close, protective alliance with James and her possible identification of Franklin as the outsider.

While James and Andra move in on Franklin, the former testing his physical comfort with gay men and the latter challenging him verbally, the remaining gay contestants are represented as a separate group who focus on Franklin as an object of desire/difference. This may be seen on the final night before the selection ceremony when Wes, Brian H., and Franklin involve themselves in "carnivalesque" play. Wes prompts the group to bring a production camera and film with them so they can film their interaction. While all three are involved in this sequence, the focus of attention is drawn towards Franklin, whom they encourage to have sex with them.

Wes and Brian H. identify Franklin as an object of sexual desire and at the same time, in the manner of carnival play, engage in an inversion that parodies the dominant paradigm of the heterosexual male who seeks the female object of desire while the homosexual remains the peripheral, disempowered outsider. Through this inversion, the homosexual is placed in a position of power. In a manner reminiscent of the observations of Stallybrass and White concerning carnival culture and iconography, *Boy Meets Boy* is a "'world upside down' which inverts the everyday hierarchies, structures, rules and customs of its social formation" (183). The traditional idea of male/female romance is replaced by a playful performance of male/male sexual engagement. This is particularly relevant in terms of parody, as the pursued individual (Franklin) is heterosexual. One must assume that he would not welcome such advances, and, therefore he is identified as the "other" (Hall 225).

Boy Meets Boy is an oppositional text. Not only do James and Andra work together in order to discover/eliminate the infiltrator, but also the remaining gay participants (now the dominant group) bond together to identify and harass the straight outsider. Thus, the program, from the end of episode four until the finale, becomes a site of resistance with all remaining cast members posed in opposition to the straight outsider. The effort to root out the remaining heterosexual, rather than the selection of Wes as the romantic partner, provides the narrative crisis and culmination of that program.

In the concluding remarks between James and Franklin, the latter protests that he had agreed to participate because he wanted to combat gay stereotypes. However, James is not convinced of Franklin's philanthropic motivations; using the opportunity to protest the inclusion of heterosexual suitors and the subsequent undermining of the romantic narrative; complaining that gay men face enough obstacles without having to combat the deceit of those who would, for entirely mercenary reasons, undermine the effort to achieve sincere romance. Thus, James repudiates the straight outsider. Although one may read *Boy Meets Boy* as heterocentric text since it supplies a format twist intended to gain a mainstream audience, the program, nevertheless, concludes with a socially defiant statement rather than a capitulation to mainstream dominant sexual ideology — a conclusion enabled not only by producers, but also by cast members who came together in a collective effort to resist the appropriation of gay narratives to a heterosexist agenda.

Conclusion

While there has no doubt been a commodification of gay identity on reality television, examples of resistance are increasingly in evidence. These instances of progressive performativity have become possible through heterosexual/homosexual alliances formed within the structure of the programming. While Jon Murray's standing as an openly gay man influenced the inclusion of gay participants in *The Real World*, this type of early alliance (a gay producer aligning himself with gay performers) has been displaced by alliances within the text. Consequently, Richard Hatch's success may be deemed to have been possible though his alliance with nongay performers, and James Getzlaff's success may have been possible through his close friendship with heterosexual female Andra and their impromptu alliance to ostracize the presumptuous intruder.

No doubt *Boy Meets Boy* is a landmark work. It co-opted successful representational paradigms of gay male identity and homosexual romance from the groundbreaking reality shows *The Real World* and *Survivor*. *Boy Meets Boy* attempted to undermine behavioral stereotypes by placing a gay man in competition with heterosexual males. Although James Getzlaff may have little in common with Richard Hatch, both represent emerging gay power bases within reality texts — representations that counter subjugation.

The future of gay performance in reality television is currently under review. The outstanding success of *Queer Eye for the Straight Guy* suggests that alliances between gay and straight performers will become more central. *Queer Eye* includes a cast of gay men who involve themselves with a heterosexual male in order to improve his social/romantic prospects. While the show is (currently) growing in success (with the format sold to 20 counties worldwide [TV Barn]), this type of alliance is inherently unbalanced and is a regressive depiction of gay identity. The irony of *Queer Eye for the Straight Guy* is that while it foregrounds the talent, sophistication, and charisma of gay males, revealing their social skills and their impeccable judgment in affairs of the heart, the fruition of these aptitudes is denied them within the programming format. Homosexual fulfillment is rejected, creating a division that involves not only subjugation, but also disavowal: "a strategy by means of which a powerful fascination or desire is both indulged and at the same time denied" (Hall 267). Consequently, *Queer Eye* swiftly returns gay identity to a wholly commodified heterocentric entity.

In order to build upon the anthropological bedrock provided by Jon Murray and *The Real World*, the gay performative presence of shows like *Boy Meets Boy* needs to be contextualised within a more welcoming environment. In this way the inheritors of gay performance and transgressive reality television may be shows like *Experiment: Gay and Straight*,[9] which foregrounded gay performative desire within a *Real World*–like household. Five gay and five straight cast members were brought together to discuss sexual identity differences in open debate. Seen more as a documentary (there is a distinct purpose and no format twists), the text attempts to resolve issues between gays and straights by bringing together oppositional identities. However rather than being tension- or formula-based, designed to appeal to a heterosexual audience (as in *Boy Meets Boy*), *Experiment: Gay and Straight* emphasizes education and understanding as the operative element in producing harmony.

The ideal performative context for gay identity in reality television should include the provision of discursive arenas less concerned with format obstacles and twists (designed to entertain the heterosexual majority) and more concerned with issues that directly impact the gay community, such as marriage and adoption rights, as well as legal protections. Building on the anthropological base provided by *The Real World* and creating scenarios in which the discursive balance is equitable, the producers of future reality television may allow gay performance and positive identification to progress from the periphery to the center of popular culture and consciousness.

Anthony Giddens tells us that, "In conditions of modernity, in sum, the media does not mirror realities but in some part forms them" (27). Therefore, while high profile, mainstream, audience-pleasing, gay performances undoubtedly raise the profile of gay identity, the character and context of such performances is not always positive or accurate. If, as Giddens suggests, media texts inform and mold the attitudes of audience members, then the gay collective must demand a truthful, equitable, and diverse representation of gay subjectivity. Consequently, should the progression continue in reality television in the manner that *Boy Meets Boy* suggests (placing emphasis on entertainment, conflict, and plot), potential resistance may be undermined, and reality representations like those currently proffered in *Queer Eye* (with emphasis on theater and commodity) may inadvertently return gay representation and identity to the days of the sissy and the dyke so aptly defined in Vito Russo's seminal text (4).

Notes

1. "Whilst Lance Loud did not openly discuss his homosexuality on the series as it aired, discourse was generated within the text which signaled him as homosexual" (Pullen 214). Furthermore after the series commenced, Lance openly discussed his identity as a gay man.

2. Openly gay cast members in *The Real World* to date have been: Norman Korpi (New York—1992) (identified as bisexual in the series), Beth Anthony (Los Angeles—1993), Pedro Zamora (San Francisco—1994), Dan Renzi (Miami—1996), Genesis Moss (Boston—1997), Ruthie Alcaide and Justin Deabler (Hawaii—1999), Jason Daniel "Danny" Roberts (New Orleans—2000), Chris Beckman and Aneesa Ferreira (Chicago—2002), Simon (Paris—2003). Also, the fictional *The Real World* Lost Season, set in Vancouver in 2002, includes a gay fictional character.

3. Each text discussed here may have the political support of a gay producer. Like Jon Murray, Charlie Parsons (*Survivor*) and Douglas Ross (*Boy Meets Boy*) are influential openly gay media producers.

4. This relates to the percentage of the mix of gay characters in the cast breakdown of all 13 series up to 2003.

5. *The Real World Paris: Culture Shock* (Squires, 2003) lists producers rules and expectations under a recurring heading called "The Real Deal" (pages: vi, 32, 80, 92, 100, 106, 110).

6. Other openly gay male participants in *Survivor* (CBS) have been Brandon Quinton, *Survivor Africa* (2001) and John Carroll, *Survivor Marquesas* (2002).

7. Darren (gay) expressed disappointment at rejection by James. While Mark and Matt (both gay) suggested that although they participated in the show hoping to find romance respectively, rejection by James was inconsequential as they were not attracted to him.

8. James is not aware of anyone's sexual identity: he believes they are all gay

until the last three remain in episode four when he is told one of the remaining three is straight. Although in episode one James can freely choose whom he wishes to reject (from the initial fifteen suitors, which includes seven straight guys), from episode two he is presented with limited choices of rejection. Cast members are brought together in groups of four, three, and then two from which he can reject only one in each group (making him keep a mixture of gay and straight contestants)

9. *The Experiment: Gay and Straight* was originally transmitted in eight-minute segments over the course of a week in November, 2002, as part of WFLD-TV FOX Chicago's evening news reports. The text discussed here, however, is a showcase documentary version which is 90 minutes in length (including 45 minutes of previously unseen and unaired material). Most notably, it has won numerous media and documentary/film festival awards (Experiment).

Works Cited

Bakhtin, Mikhail. *Rabelais and His World*. Translation by H. Iswolsky. Cambridge: Mass MIT Press, 1965.
Carlson, Marvin. *Performance: A Critical Introduction*. London: Routledge, 1996
Clum, John M. *Still Acting Gay*. New York: St Martin's Griffin, 2000.
Epstein, Jeffrey. "Gaytime" in *OUT*, July 2001. 48–55.
Foucault, Michel. *The History of Sexuality Vol. 1*. London: Penguin, 1998.
Giddens, Anthony. *Modernity and Self Identity*. Cambridge: Polity Press, 1992.
Hall, Stuart. "The Spectacle of the 'Other,'" in Stuart Hall (ed.) *Representation: Cultural Representations and Signifying Practices*. London: Open University (1997): 223–279.
Pullen, Christopher. "The Household, the Basement and *The Real World*," in Susan Holmes and Deborah Jermyn (eds.). *Understanding Reality Television*. London: Routledge, 2004: 211–232.
Ruoff, Jeffrey. *An American Family: A Televised Life*. Minneapolis: University of Minnesota Press, 2002.
Russo, Vito. *The Celluloid Closet* (rev. ed.). New York: Harper & Row, 1987.
Schechner, Richard. *Performance Studies: An Introduction*. London: Routledge, 2002.
Sigesmund, B. J. "Boys R Us" in *Newsweek*, July 21, 2003: 52–23.
Solomon, James. *In the House, the Real World Seattle: Behind the Scenes with the Seattle Cast*. New York: MTV Books/Pocket Books, 1998.
Squires, K. M. *The Real World Paris: Culture Shock*. New York: MTV Books/Pocket Books. 2003.
Stallybrass, Peter, and Allon White. *The Politics and Poetics of Transgression*. New York: Cornell University Press, 1995.

TELEVISION PROGRAMS

An American Family. Craig Gilbert, and Alan and Susan Raymond. PBS — WNET-13. 1973.
Boy Meets Boy. Produced by Evolution Film and Tape. NBC/Bravo. July–September 2003.
Experiment: Gay and Straight. Written and directed by Mark Saxenmeyer. WFLD-TV Chicago (November 2002). CAN TV Chicago (June 2003).
Lance Loud! A Death in an American Family. Alan and Susan Raymond. PBS — 12WHYY. 6 Jan. 2003.
Queer Eye for the Straight Guy. Produced by Scout Productions. NBC/Bravo. 2003–present.
The Real World. Produced by Bunim Murray. MTV. 1992–present.
Survivor. Produced by Survivor Productions. CBS. 2000–present.

INTERNET SOURCES

Durdale, Alonso. 15 May 2004. "Meet the Boys" posted September 5th 2003. http://www.advocate.com/html/stories/898/898_boymeetsboy.asp
Experiment. 15 May 2004. "Experiment: Gay and Straight." http://www.whatsup.com/experiment/
MTV. 23 February 2004. "*MTV Media* International Distribution." http://www.mtv-media.com/build2003/sql/grb_2_1.asp
TV Barn. 14 May 2004. "NBC PR: 'Queer Eye' sold in 20 countries." http://www.tvbarn.com/ticker/archives/017809.html

Altar Ego: GLAAD Sacrifices Male Intimacy and Commitment Ceremonies to the Media Gods

James Black

In 2002, World Wrestling Entertainment, Inc., a.k.a. WWE, included a gay story line on its program *Smackdown*. The wrestlers, "Billy" and "Chuck," were relatively typical in appearance to other wrestlers and somewhat renowned for their abilities; however, as a newly formed duo, their behavior hinted that they were more than tag-team partners outside the ring. The story line became detectable in December 2001. The WWE web site promoted the tag team, telling fans that Chuck "really likes his tag-team partner — a lot." Billy was described as having "a spring in his step — and a glimmer in his eye." The first overt suggestion of romance happened on Valentine's Day when Billy and Chuck exchanged chocolates and hugs in the ring (Miller 12). The story line continued for months, as the wrestlers provided stereotypical indications that they were gay: they hugged a little too long when offering congratulations, gave each other lingering glances, and performed suggestive stretching exercises allowing for easy rear entry. Their manager, Rico, doubled as their personal stylist.

Scott Seomin, Entertainment Media Director for the Gay and Lesbian Alliance Against Defamation (GLAAD), supported the story line and its representation of gay men because WWE officials promised that they wanted to build on the success of gay-themed television programs. Seomin hoped to show WWE's decidedly gay-unfriendly audience that gay men could play tough too. In early September, Chuck knelt down in the ring and proposed that Billy and he become partners for life. In an interview for the *Washington Post*, Seomin called the stunt a "hoot." He suggested that the audience actually rooted for the couple, adding, "While it's entertaining for viewers, it's also enlightening. Because of its teenage audience, *Smackdown* reaches a lot of potential bullies and gay bashers out there, and what Billy and Chuck are saying is not only 'We're here,' but they also say, 'Don't mess with us'" (Stuever C1). Seomin went so far as to have *Today* show host Matt Lauer present the couple with a gravy boat from Pottery Barn on GLAAD's behalf.

However, Seomin's plan backfired. In interviews, the men who played Billy and Chuck carefully confirmed their heterosexual orientation. According to Wade Keller, editor of the *Pro Wrestling Torch* newsletter, on the night of the so-called commitment ceremony, the crowd chanted "just say no" as the wrestlers were about to agree to the vows (Stuever C1). Billy and Chuck revealed to the crowd that they had pretended to be gay for the sake of publicity; then their rival sent his cronies into the ring to beat up Billy and Chuck, a scene that John McClelland, a freelance sportswriter and 20-year fan of pro-wrestling, compared to a gay bashing.

Based on a history of hateful portrayals of gay men in professional wrestling, some argue that the Billy and Chuck story line suggests that attitudes are changing. Jonathan Miller wrote in the *New York Times*, "While characters like Exotic Adrian Street and Adorable Adrian Adonis romped around the ring in dresses, bows, and makeup in the '70's and '80's, Billy and Chuck appear in basic red hot pants and white robes" (sec. 9: 12). To be sure, Billy and Chuck were more subtle than previous caricatures, especially by pro-wrestling standards, earning them the nickname "The Ambiguously Gay Duo." Dr. Sut Jhally, a professor of communications at the University of Massachusetts at Amherst, believes that something more complex is going on. "Talking about gayness is not so weird these days[...]. I don't think the homophobia is as explicit. It's much more nudge, nudge, wink, wink. There's a level of parody" (Miller sec. 9: 12).

But it's not likely that the WWE had such complex motivations. WWE net income in the first quarter of 2002 was down 79 percent over the same quarter in the previous year, and its TV ratings were down 20 percent (Miller sec 9: 12). The gay wedding earned *Smackdown* its highest ratings in five months. Furthermore, the story line certainly did more to reinforce stereotypes than to change attitudes. According to an anonymous gay wrestling promoter interviewed by McClelland, the crowd booed during the commitment ceremony until Billy and Chuck announced that they were straight, at which time the crowd cheered louder than it had all night. Michele Orecklin wrote in *Time*, "The approving cheers of the crowd [at the commitment ceremony] suggested that wrestling fans don't mind watching preening, scantily clad men roll around on the floor together, as long as they go home with women" (89) or, in this case, as long as they do not go home together.

Curiously, GLAAD's handling of this situation was not consistent with its stance a few years before when World Championship Wrestling (WCW) had a gay tag team called Lenny and Lodi. GLAAD denounced the way the characters, who hinted that they were gay, were beaten up, charging, as McClelland did about the events at Billy and Chuck's faux ceremony, that such situations symbolize gay bashings. However, Seomin apparently did not anticipate such an end for Billy and Chuck and seemed surprised by how the story line played out. Afterward, Seomin spoke out against WWE for betraying GLAAD by lying about the ceremony. He also lamented the wrestlers' return to the closet ("GLAAD"), apparently unaware of (or in denial about) pro-wrestling's decidedly melodramatic conventions. While the wrestlers' ability to queer it up may support the notion that no one is absolutely straight, Seomin assumed that they had a greater investment in the story line than they did. Furthermore, he did not seem to understand that WWE's offense began when they created the story line, continued in the way they stereotyped gay male behavior, and culminated in their decision to mock the ceremonies that real nonheterosexual people design because their unions are not legitimized by the laws of the dominant culture.

Ordinary LGBT people courageously fight small but extraordinary battles to secure the right to live and love openly by publicly announcing their commitment to their partners. For professional wrestling to mock us is not surprising; for GLAAD, our watchdog organization, to join the offensive is not only wrong, but counterintuitive and not in line with the organization's mission to promote and ensure "fair, accurate, and inclusive representation" ("Our Mission"). The gay story line was obviously a sham long before the ceremony turned into a brawl. Perhaps Seomin truly intended to show that gay men can be as masculine as straight men and thus win a minor cultural victory. Unfortunately, Seomin's presumed spokesmodels of straight-acting gay maleness did more to polarize than mitigate the extremes of gender and sexuality in American culture. They served as composites of the worst gay and straight male characteristics, valorizing violence while emphasizing stereotypically gay behaviors.

Seomin's choices — on behalf of GLAAD and LGBT people — suggest confusion about how sexuality and gender relate, and the situation provides an opportunity to examine how these aspects of identity bleed together. Seomin was clearly motivated by Billy and Chuck's hypermasculine portrayal of gay men. His focus on their toughness illustrates the tendency for gay males to surrender to internalized homophobia and assume a "straight-acting" persona in an attempt to revise how the gay male role fits into the American cultural narrative. Most gay men are trained to believe that being gay prevents them from becoming real men. Straight-acting gay men, who are almost always self-proclaimed, buy into the common misconception that gendered behavior inexorably indicates (i.e., predicts) sexual orientation. Given so little room for error in the vital cultural work of confirming his masculinity and having already erred by desiring other men, the straight-acting gay man has limited opportunities for intimacy with other men because, presumably, intimacy is woman's work.

To better understand the straight-acting persona, we must challenge the validity of the science of gender and sexuality. Experts question whether masculinity is a natural extension of maleness or, for that matter, whether gender is solely determined by biological factors, because such beliefs are based on inherently subjective scientific studies. For example, cadavers used to study the biology of gender are themselves attributed gender based on visual assessment, not by biological facts (Kessler and McKenna 75). Such interpretation encourages experts to erroneously naturalize that which is socially and culturally determined. Anne Fausto-Sterling observes that scientific writing is a form of cultural interpretation in which "the enculturated scientist [...] uses that interpretation to reinforce old or build new sets of social beliefs" (133). Because of its presumed credibility, this scientific narrative goes unscrutinized and feeds into the larger cultural narrative.

By confirming masculinity, the male writes himself into the American cultural narrative; the necessity of such confirmation supports the idea that masculinity is culturally constructed. Success is achieved through convincing displays and behaviors that will cause the individual in question to be interpreted as heterosexual. Hegemonic masculinity is not so much flexible as it is adjustable, its guidelines firmly set at the given historical moment but subject to change (Ross 172). Models and symbols of normative masculinity are readily available, but are surprisingly fluid, having changed considerably in the last hundred years. For example, the symbolic value of the colors blue and pink have changed. Before World War I, blue signified delicateness, while pink indicated strength. Today, of course, pink clothing for men and boys is rare because, as Phyllis Burke notes, "it would be considered 'unnatural'" (141). Susan Faludi identifies the end of World War II as a significant point of change in masculinity: "The United States came out of World War II with a sense of itself as a masculine nation, our 'boys' ready to assume the mantle of national authority and international leadership. The nation claimed an ascendancy over the world, men an ascendancy over the nation, and a male persona of a certain type ascendancy over men" (16).

In this spirit, violence is the ultimate, although all-too-common, way for a man to publicly confirm his masculinity. Michael S. Kimmel asserts, "The spectre of the 'sissy'—encompassing the fears of emasculation, humiliation, and effeminacy that American men carry with them—is responsible for a significant amount of masculine violence. [O]ne is a 'real' man because one is not afraid to be violent" (253). Hegemonic masculinity is about dominance, whether over women or men, which allows dominant males, as Nancy Chodorow states, "to dominate subordinate males culturally, psychologically, and even sexually" (80). So-called straight and straight-acting men are granted permission to punish non-heterosexual males — or those they perceive to be feminine — as they wish.

Thus, Billy and Chuck's early victories in the ring against presumably heterosexual and (also presumably) more masculine opponents may have convinced some viewers that gay men could play by the rules of masculinity.

Furthermore, because masculine norms become firmly established through traditions and media displays, we might assume that the image of two gay professional wrestlers would have challenged gay stereotypes to the point of forcing a revision of the American cultural narrative. As life in western culture has become less physically strenuous for many men, maintaining an image of masculine strength has become important. Faludi compares women at the middle of the twentieth century to today's men, who have been "stripped" of their "connections to a wider world and invited to fill the void with consumption and a gym-bred display of his ultramasculinity" (40). This phenomenon is illustrated in the Charles Atlas advertisements from the 1940s, which provided a brief narrative (in comic strip form) about a "ninety-seven-pound weakling" who, by increasing his muscle mass, transformed himself into a real man. Chris Weinke explains that "being a 'man' means having a formidable presence in the world, one that conveys in an instant notions of power, control, and invulnerability, not to mention the capacity to exercise violence, when required." Weinke confirms his point by describing a study in which men were found to equate building up their bodies with taking control of their lives. Several men in the study perceived that building a muscular body was an investment of time, energy, and money that would pay off in the form of self- and social acceptance (Weinke).

The muscular body indicates power and shows potential for violence. Males who are perceived as soft are pressured to prove they are not. Susan Bordo writes, "If a man is seen as soft at the core [...] he is permitted much less latitude and constantly has to prove that he can 'play hardball,' 'take a firm stand,' and so on." However, if a man proves himself, he is allowed some softness. "Tears are permissible, even admirable, when they fill the eyes of an old warrior reminiscing about battle or a jock talking about his teammates. In such contexts, tears are like the soft penis after satisfying sex: they don't demean the man but make him lovable and human — because he has proved his strong, manly core" (55). Considering the importance of muscularity and violence in confirming masculinity, it would seem that Billy and Chuck did a fine job of overcompensation. Shouldn't they have been entitled to a little cuddling after fending off their enemies in the ring? The dominant cultural consensus, of course, is no.

Even the most masculine heterosexual males must work hard to confirm masculinity by avoiding behaviors and characteristics that suggest softness. Thus, gay men cannot be given a break because they are perceived as inherently soft. In explaining its influences on heterosexual men, Kimmel defines homophobia as "the fear of being perceived as unmanly, effeminate, or, worst of all, gay...." Based on the presumption that homosexuality is about gender inversion, homophobia inspires men to perform exaggerated, stereotypically masculine behaviors, reinforcing "the gender of [normative] sex, keeping men acting hypermasculine..." (Kimmel 238–39). Gay men are certainly not immune to homophobia; to prove they are not soft, they may take on activities, behaviors, clothing, etc. that are characterized as masculine, avoiding anything stereotypically feminine. Leo Bersani argues that gay men risk "identifying with culturally dominant images of misogynous maleness. [...] A more or less secret sympathy with heterosexual male misogyny carries with it the narcissistically gratifying reward of confirming [gay men's] membership in (and not simply our erotic appetite for) the privileged male society" (116–17). While he may challenge some of the most obvious gay stereotypes, the straight-acting gay male buys into the American cultural narrative more than he revises it.

It is important to address how misogyny and homophobia are related for gay males. While there are undoubtedly gay males who hold some kind of irrational hatred for women, the term is likely not quite accurate in this context, where misogyny connotes hatred of what is feminine, particularly in other gay males, but not necessarily in women. Such misogyny is based not only on fear and ignorance, but also on due to the ramifications of that automatic, inherent association of the gay male with femininity. Even if gay masculinity is arguably a legitimate variation of the hegemonic standard, hegemonic masculinity is, as Cliff Cheng argues, a relational construct and thus, "needs gayness as a contrast, as something to be more than, something to be against." Through the lens of queer theory, we can see this relationship differently. Butler asserts, "The replication of heterosexual constructs in nonheterosexual frames brings into relief the utterly constructed status of the so-called heterosexual original. Thus, gay is to straight not as copy is to original, but, rather, as copy is to copy" (Butler Gender 31). The straight-acting gay male strives to be normal, but his model of normality is as variable as his own identity.

The defeat of Billy and Chuck (*after* they announced that they had only played gay) indicates the fragility of masculinity and the need for confirmation. If they had simply hid their respective, authentically masculine selves in order to play gay characters, there probably would have been no problem. Instead, they embodied otherness. Their ability to perform gayness and thus not confirm their masculinity for months, made them suspect to the crowd. For such insubordination, they had to receive their punishment. Through the ritual of violence, residual feminine and gay traits were purged, and the men began the process of reestablishing their masculine personae (as individuals, of course — not as a couple).

Suppressing culturally feminine inclinations causes men to avoid and ignore certain desires (Bem 150). Understandably, men who avoid what they perceive to be feminine limit the range of relationships they can have with other men. It is not uncommon for two males who see a movie together to leave an empty seat between them (Kimmel 212). While we might assume that straight men are more likely to do this, many gay couples do the same. The dangerous relationship of misogyny and homophobia is commonly revealed in personal ads in which gay men label themselves straight-acting and bluntly state that feminine guys need not respond. Of course, the strength of their protestations does not guarantee the accuracy of these men's self-perceptions. Nor do such avoidance tactics, regardless of how well the straight-acting gay male performs masculinity, change the fact that it is his own desire for other males that prevents him from becoming a full member of the dominant culture.

Butler suggests that male/male attraction — or the denial of it and emotions related to such attraction — may serve as a foundation for masculinity, a phenomenon she calls heterosexual melancholy:

> [W]hat constitutes the *sexually* unperformable is performed instead as *gender identification*. To the extent that homosexual attachments remain unacknowledged within normative heterosexuality, they are

not merely constituted as desires that emerge and subsequently become prohibited; rather, these are desires proscribed from the start. And when they do emerge on the far side of the censor, they may well carry that mark of impossibility with them, performing, as it were, as the impossible within the possible. As such, they will not be attachments that can be openly grieved. This is, then, less the *refusal* to grieve [...] than a preemption of grief performed by the absence of cultural conventions for avowing the loss of homosexual love" [Butler *Melancholy* 34].

We can see evidence of this phenomenon in popular entertainment, which depends on gay jokes and images of obviously masculine men in drag. While such comedic devices do not provide positive representations of queerness, their visibility indicates acknowledgment of queer maleness by the dominant culture. However, there are few cultural instructions for dealing with queerness of any kind, so these representations rarely do more than dismiss gay men as comedic fodder, whether or not the text is comedic and regardless of the artistic value the producers strive to attain. The laughter preempts the possibility of attraction and thus, grief. Professional wrestling exemplifies this phenomenon, with characters that are painted in broad strokes, inspiring emotional responses that are, subsequently, as broad: anger, revulsion, hate, triumph — but nothing as complex as grief.

Male/male intimacy can flourish in private settings. Susan Faludi found that the environment at the Citadel allows for nurturing relationships between men: "The intimacy these men seek is physical and sensual, though not necessarily sexual; it is a dram of blissful oneness, a sensuality more closely associated with mother and child" (131). But these men must provide public disclaimers for their private associations, which could be enjoyed only by those who publicly promoted their contempt for homosexual love and who were shielded from the assumedly disapproving gaze of women. As (Col. James) Rembert [a teacher at the Citadel] put it to the class, "With no women, we can hug each other. There's nothing so nurturing as an infantry platoon" (Faludi 127). Ironically, veterans of World War II were more inclined to "embrace a masculine ideal that revolved around providing rather than dominating. Their most important experiences centered on the support and comfort they had given one another in the war, and it was this that they wished to preserve" (Faludi 23).

The Citadel serves as a microcosmic example of queer relationships in general. Nonheterosexual couples may vow eternal love and monogamy, but such vows are rarely acknowledged in public forums and never honored by the dominant culture. While same-sex couples can share intimacy in ways similar to heterosexual couples, society does not promote intimacy between individuals in these relationships. Although we are shown same-sex relationships in popular texts, they are typically exploited rather than promoted. Regardless of the producers' intentions, Billy and Chuck never had a chance. Even if their narrative had kept them together until they both died in their San Francisco retirement condo, it would have been played for laughs because a gay relationship is still, as yet, unacceptable in a text as public as professional wrestling. The entertainment value of Billy and Chuck for the mainstream audience was not in the telling of their love story, but rather in presenting them as a sideshow attraction: The Ambiguously Gay Duo.

Conversely, great importance is placed on intimate behavior in heterosexual marriages. Stephen Nock observes three major guidelines: sexual intercourse is the right of both spouses; other parties have no right to sexual intercourse with married spouses; and society enforces the sexual rights of married spouses (30). At present, a marriage of two men would defy all three guidelines. Despite limited acknowledgment that gay sex occurs, cultural prescriptions obviously do not grant two men the right to have sex. However, it is the second guideline that is most problematic. Entitling two men to have committed sex exclusively with each other would require changing more than laws: it would indicate a complete change in hegemonic masculine ideology. Committed relationships between two men have little credibility in mainstream society whether or not they are announced in the *New York Times*. The image of the "(white) middle-class gay man, unfettered by dependents but earning an income that is geared to supporting a family, is a central axiom in the homophobic construction of queers as a privileged minority undeserving of human rights protection" (Fung 293). Male/male sex does not necessarily bother the mainstream, but when faced with the possibility that sexual relations between men can function as expressions of deeper, lasting commitments, the dominant culture fortifies its defenses. Even the fictional relationship of Billy and Chuck proved threatening to mainstream values and although the audience's increasingly negative responses were no doubt heightened by the environment of the wrestling arena, their disapproval was quite genuine and representative of societal opinions.

As GLAAD tells us on its Web site, "Words [and] Images Matter," and this observation is especially true when we consider how dominant cultural messages, like those conveyed by and about Billy and Chuck, affect young people — especially adolescent males, the group Seomin hoped to educate. How boys and young men learn cultural expectations is important. In environments that are supportive of less traditional roles, boys and girls prove capable of more varied gendered behaviors (Golombok and Fivush 50). But gender training is based on the perceptions of whoever raises a child; if the child was labeled male as a newborn, the child's behavior is usually interpreted differently than if the child was deemed a female. Boys are perceived as stronger and tougher than girls (Golombok and Fivush 225), thus, they tend to "overconform to [meet] the expectations of their peers" (Kimmel 161).

Children quickly learn the rules of gender and "the penalties for challenging those norms..." (Burke 4). As children's correct behavior is reinforced, the rules of gender become programmed or naturalized. William Pollack observes that by the second grade most boys are on guard to avoid behaviors deemed inappropriate; they "seem far less attuned to feelings of hurt and pain in others and begin to lose their capacity to express their own emotions and concerns in words" (Pollack 347). Ironically, the masculine world of sports can be a safe haven, allowing boys to express emotions and experience levels of intimacy not allowed in other parts of their lives. Pollack states that the "team concept" and focus on specific athletic goals allows boys to care for and nurture one another in athletic contexts (276).

Besides sports, there are few forums in which male intimacy is acceptable, leading some males to label themselves as gay based on only a few instances of nonconformity. Despite concerns about how early children should learn about sexuality, children's behavior is regularly and rigorously sexualized. "In contemporary American society, boys identify themselves or are identified as homosexuals earlier and on the basis of fewer same-gender sexual experiences than girls because one of the main components of hegemonic masculinity is constant sexual interest in women. Femininity, in contrast, is not contradicted by a romantic attraction to other girls or women" (Lorber 60). Boys are discouraged from building intimate friendships with one another; they prohibit themselves, fearing accusations that they are gay, and others (adults and children) may discourage such friendships for the same reason. Then boys are unfairly accused of being incapable of maintaining intimate friendships (Pollack 185–87).

Nock asserts that, despite the expectation for males to "be men" the guidelines on how to achieve that goal — and the goal itself— extraordinarily vague (44). Ray Raphael argues that when such rituals occur, their purpose is summative, not formative (Raphael 189). Lack of ritual causes many to look to popular media for guidance, where boys are not provided with many positive models of intimacy and masculinity. While in the last few decades female characters in story books are less likely to model traditional gender roles, "[t]here has been no comparable change in the depiction of men or boys ... no movement of men toward more nurturing and caring behaviors. As in real life, women in ou[r] story books have left home and gone off to work, but men still have enormous trouble coming back home" (Kimmel 156). Similarly, in TV depictions, "men cannot find a way back into domestic life without being emasculated" (Kimmel 157). Even in depictions of heterosexual relationships and traditional families, men capable of intimacy are often portrayed as unusual, even out of place.

To be sure, gay male intimacy is virtually nonexistent in popular media. Gay men are allowed to live and love — or fail to do so in all our wonderful complexity — only in contained narratives. We thrive on premium cable channels, in independent films, community newspapers, graphic novels, and literature: narrative spaces in which makers and readers of texts — rather than corporations and politicians — have some say about how our stories are told. Perhaps, then, Billy and Chuck's relationship was somewhat daring because it implied some level of intimacy between the two men. Meditating on the meaning of WWE's "Ambiguously Gay Duo," Hank Stuever writes, "If wrestling fans can let a gay wedding — even a sham one — onto their big-screen TVs, is it possible that things could also change in churches, legislatures and city hall? The wedding is a ratings stunt for an increasingly desperate WWE, but what else does it portend?" (Stuever C1). Stuever's question rhetorically suggests that visibility is a step in the right direction and better than nothing. Seomin apparently agreed; his support of the gay story line seems to have been an attempt to teach wrestling fans — and anyone else paying attention — about the diversity of gay men, albeit, a very limited diversity of butches and femmes.

However, the profound emphasis on one representation of gay male life simply created a minor stir: while it may have challenged some of the obvious stereotypes of gay men, it did not represent truth; it was not what educators would call a learning moment. The visibility of gay men provided in the form of Billy and Chuck failed to acknowledge the diversity of the group in question. Their stereotypically gay behavior belied their athletic physicality — nothing new there. Furthermore, they did not amend the image of whiteness that dominates representations of gay male culture.

The wrestling ring is certainly not the ideal forum for depicting the complexities of any relationship, particularly a supposedly romantic relationship between two men. And even if the wrestlers had said, "I do," the superficial depiction only reinforced the idea that gay men lead superficial lives. As narrative, the Billy/Chuck storyline simply reinforced normative values of gender and sexuality. As Judith Roof observes, citing Propp, narrative does not necessarily reflect the social order as it stands; rather, it suggests how the group wishes to see itself, especially in times of conflict (8). Thus, WWE fulfilled its promise of capitalizing on the popularity of gay media texts, but it did so without approving of the trend. On the contrary, WWE used the popularity of gay male culture to wage a minor war against it. The tag-team duo of masculinity and heterosexuality defeated its perverse enemy, and those fans that worried that wrestling had gone gay were treated to a decisive victory that served to reinforce their patriarchal beliefs.

Seomin tried to play along, but his comments and actions suggest an unreasonable investment of faith in the story line and more than a little hubris in his hope that Billy and Chuck's hypermasculine displays of violence would temper homophobic attitudes. The effects have been minimal. Keller recounts, "It wasn't long ago that you would go to a wrestling event and be sitting next to kids who were encouraged to chant 'faggot, faggot, faggot' This time the audience responds to the gay, or effeminate, characters in a fun way, instead of as a way to express hate'" (Stuever C1). He does not describe the crowd's "fun" response, but we can assume that the laughs did not signify acceptance.

I do not agree with Seomin's assertion that "bringing camp to the masses is always a good thing" (Stuever C1), especially considering that we do not yet have the masses in our camp. As Richard Goldstein argues, "It's still necessary to maintain the illusion that only straight men can kick ass. To demonstrate otherwise is to raise the ever present dread of rape that animates so many nightmares about homosexuals. Any pushy queer is regarded as a threat to the sphincter of man and God. To worship a gay champion merely places this ravishment fantasy on a more sublimated plane" (Goldstein). For fear of domination by gay men, hegemonic masculinity stays on red alert and perpetuates its preemptive strikes. By fighting back according to the dominant culture's rules, we gay men get the public's attention, but they learn little about us.

We must select our battles more carefully than GLAAD did in supporting portrayals of LGBT life. Such support suggests a stamp of approval, and few portrayals are worthy. Likewise, we should not devote much time or energy to fighting negative portrayals from predictable outlets. Those battles cannot be won because they challenge such deeply entrenched cultural assumptions about gender and sexuality. Considering our culture is already on a "war footing," our resources can be put to better use in a long-term, more subversive strategy; our best bet is to take an ambivalent stance and encourage discussion about selected problematic portrayals. While this approach will not be particularly dramatic, it allows us to avoid the mistake of choosing a side. If we do not believe that gender and sexuality can be summed up in binary sets, why should we take such a reductive approach to challenging cultural assumptions? Activism can and must be more subversive — and more complex — successfully replacing cultural war plans with educational strategies.

Works Cited

Bem, Sandra Lipsitz. *The Lenses of Gender: Transforming the Debate of Sexual Inequality*. New Haven: Yale University Press, 1993.
Berger, Maurice, Brian Wallis, and Simon Watson, eds. *Constructing Masculinity*. New York: Routledge, 1995.
Bersani, Leo. "Loving Men." Berger, Wallis, and Watson, 115–123.
Bordo, Susan. *The Male Body: A New Look at Men in Public and in Private*. New York: Farrar, Straus, and Giroux, 1999.
Burke, Phyllis. *Gender Shock: Exploding the Myths of Male and Female*. New York: Anchor Books, 1996.
Butler, Judith. *Gender Trouble*. New York: Routledge, 1990.
Butler, Judith. "Melancholy Gender/Refused Identification." Berger, Wallis, and Watson 21–36.
Carrigan, Tim, Bob Connell, and John Lee. "Toward a New Sociology of Masculinity." *The Making of Masculinities*. ed. Harry Brod. Boston: Allen & Unwin, 1987. 63–100.
Cheng, Cliff. "Marginalized Masculinities and Hegemonic Masculinity: An Introduction." *Journal of Men's Studies*. 7.3 (1999): 295. Infotrac. Blough-Weis Library, Susquehanna Univ. 24 Mar 2003 http://web5.infotrac.galegroup.com/.
Chodorow, Nancy. *Femininities, Masculinities, Sexualities: Freud and Beyond*. Lexington: University Press of Kentucky, 1994.
Faludi, Susan. *Stiffed: The Betrayal of the American Man*. New York: William Morrow, 1999.
Fausto-Sterling, Anne. "How to Build a Man." Berger, Wallis, and Watson, 127–134.
Fung, Richard. "Burdens of Representation, Burdens of Responsibility." Berger, Wallis, and Watson, 291–298.
"GLAAD: We Were Lied To." *Outsports.com*. 13 Sept 2002. 24 Mar 2003 http://www.outsports.com/columns/20020913glaadwwe.htm.
Goldstein, Richard. "Pushy Queers: Two Plays and a Smackdown Augur a New Gay Image." *The Village Voice*, 18–24 Sept 2002. 24 Mar 2003 http://www.villagevoice.com/ issues/0238/goldstein.php.
Golombok, Susan, and Robyn Fivush. *Gender Development*. New York: Cambridge University Press, 1994.
Kessler, Suzanne J., and Wendy McKenna. *Gender: An Ethnomethodological Approach*. New York: John Wiley, 1978.
Kimmel, Michael S. *The Gendered Society*. New York: Oxford University Press, 2000.
Lorber, Judith. *Paradoxes of Gender*. New Haven, CT: Yale University Press, 1994.
McClelland, John. "Billy and Chuck's Big Fat Wrestling Non-Wedding."

Outsports.com. 13 Sept 2002. 24 Mar 2003 http://www.outsports.com/columns/20020913mcclellandwedding.htm.

Miller, Jonathan. "Billy and Chuck, Accidental Crusaders," *New York Times*, 25 Aug 2002, Late ed., Sec 9, p. 12, column 3. Lexis-Nexis. Blough-Weis Library, Susquehanna Univ. 24 Mar 2003 http://web.lexis-nexis.com/universe.

Nock, Steven L. *Marriage in Men's Lives.* New York: Oxford University Press, 1998.

Orecklin, Michele. "Back to the Headlocks," *Time*, 23 Sept 2002, vol. 160, issue 13, p. 89.

"Our Mission," *GLAAD: Fair, Accurate and Inclusive Representation.* 30 Mar 2003 http://glaad.org/about/ index.php.

Pollack, William. *Real Boys: Rescuing Our Sons from the Myths of Boyhood.* New York: Owl, 1999.

Raphael, Ray. *The Men from the Boys: Rites of Passage in Male America.* Lincoln: University of Nebraska Press, 1988.

Roof, Judith. *Come as You Are.* New York: Columbia University Press, 1996.

Ross, Andrew. "The Great White Dude." Berger, Wallis, and Watson, 167–175.

Stuever, Hank. "Wrestlers Going to the Mat for Gay Rights? Not Exactly," *Washington Post*, 12 Sept 2002, final ed., p. C1.

Wienke, Chris. "Negotiating the male body: men, masculinity, and cultural ideals." *The Journal of Men's Studies*, Spring 1998 v6 n3 p255(28). Infotrac. Blough-Weis Library, Susquehanna University. 24 Mar 2003 http://web5.infotrac.galegroup.com/.

Lesbians and Serial TV: *Ellen* Finds Her Inner Adult

Becca Cragin

The significance of *Ellen*'s coming out in 1997 is best understood when placed in the larger historical context of lesbian representation on U.S. television. This paper argues that the episodic coming-out and the variety of coming-out events associated with it were shaped by several factors: the personal history and politics of Ellen DeGeneres; the ideological and generic expectations and constraints of the sitcom form, of *Ellen*'s producers, and its audience; and the contentious understandings of the role sexuality plays in defining and marketing lesbianism. The history of *Ellen* and its reception provides an instructive example of the difficulties of integrating politics into sitcoms; and also of the importance of retaining gender specificity when analyzing queer media representations. One could easily analyze *Ellen* and the reaction to it in the generalized terms of homophobia. I will argue, however, that the divergent reactions to the series' turn of events reflect an ambivalence toward lesbianism that at times overlaps with the homophobia directed at gay men; and at times is distinct from it. One key difference is the historical and cultural linkage between lesbianism and feminist politics, which frames lesbianism (and its relationship to sexuality) differently than male homosexuality.

Lesbian Chic: Sexuality and (Post)Feminism

As gays and lesbians began to be represented more frequently on U.S. television in the mid–1980s and early 1990s, lesbian images in particular seem to have been impacted by the concurrent rise of postfeminism, a deeply anxious response throughout the culture to both feminism and the social and economic changes brought about by large numbers of women entering the workforce. Sasha Torres alludes to these trends as she connects the rash of lesbian characters that popped up on television series in the 1980s to the networks' attempts to capture the lucrative demographic of professional women. She argues that as television focused on groups of women, secondary lesbian characters were included — both to represent feminism and to locate lesbianism within a single character, assuring the audience that the female relationships they were enjoying were not lesbian (179). This seems to explain the odd phenomenon of so many dramatic and comedic series in the '80s all suddenly and simultaneously airing single episodes or briefly extended story lines involving lesbians (*Golden Girls, Kate and Allie, Cagney and Lacey,* etc.) The strategy connected lesbianism to feminism, yet limited both to temporary plot points.

This history of 1- or 2-episode arcs that Torres identifies suggests that the notion of scarcity needs to be complicated. While gays and lesbians have been underrepresented for many years, in the current, rapidly evolving context, the significant issue is not how little we are represented, but how we are represented. That is, despite several notable exceptions, such as *The L Word, Queer as Folk,* and *Queer Eye for the Straight Guy,* in both fiction and nonfiction television, we are still far less likely to be portrayed as main characters than as sidekicks. Fleeting and subordinate representations may increase marginality however much they may aim (or claim) to reduce it. Routinely framing lesbianism as an issue, situation, or event increases the likelihood that it will not be included more extensively as an ongoing part of the narrative. Apart from the occasional lesbian guest, heterosexuality is presented everywhere else on TV as the norm — as the natural background for all action. The occasional lesbian enters this field as the exception that proves the rule. It is for this reason that *Ellen*'s coming-out episode marks a unique moment in U.S. television history — both because it constitutes the first time the central character of a series was lesbian or gay, and also because it was the first time the central character came out as gay or lesbian midway through a series.

To understand the specific contours of the widespread (although not universal) negative reaction to this coming-out arc — beyond the obvious, blanket homophobia that might be directed at any mainstream lesbian or gay representation — requires a lesbian-specific analysis of the iconography that preceded it. For lesbians, the palette of images building in the '80s and '90s could be loosely described as lesbian chic, a trend in which sexuality and politics were particularly anxious undercurrents of lesbian representation.

The linking of lesbianism with broader issues like feminism (connecting straight and lesbian women together under the rubric of gender) that Torres notes in the '80s is a distinct difference between lesbian and gay representation of that period — one that critics have not always viewed positively. An exception to the 1-episode rule that Torres analyzes is *HeartBeat*, a short-lived 1980s dramatic series that featured a regular lesbian character. She suggests that the primary problem with representations of lesbians that took place in the '80s is that they universalize lesbianism, making the lesbian character "just like everyone else," without naming her specificity. For many critics, the missing specificity is her sexuality.[1]

For example, Hantzis and Lehr argue, as do many lesbian media critics, that representing lesbian sexuality is the primary way to combat heterosexism (108). They criticize *HeartBeat* for failing to integrate "her life as a lesbian" into the show (110). Explicit sexual activity is only one part of her life as a lesbian, however, and there are many ways the show could have depicted lesbian life: by representing lesbian-specific cultural and political history, by depicting homophobia and heterosexism, or by not replicating heterosexism in the structure of the show, among other solutions. Simply to call for signs of sex would lead to an inadequate remedy to the quandary lesbian characters face in mainstream media. This becomes evident when considering the lesbian chic phenomenon of the early '90s which illustrates the limitations of a focus on sexuality as the mark of lesbianism.

By the early '90s, gays and lesbians were being represented in U.S. popular culture with increasing frequency and confidence. Straight America suddenly appeared able and willing to tolerate a multitude of stories about some parts of Queer America — stories of a very specific sort. Critics have noted the ambiguity behind the images and styles that make up the culture and representation of lesbian chic. Chic print advertising presents feminine, yet slightly androgynous women in ambiguous poses that appear to frame them as couples. The images are open enough to attract both lesbian and heterosexual interest, making them more commodifiable (Clark; Lewis and Rolley). This feminine androgyny, drawing on the fashion styles of young, white, privileged, urban lesbians, rapidly spread out into the mainstream. In addition to this ambiguity of sexual identity, another key feature of lesbian chic is its sexualization of the figure of the lesbian. While many critics have analyzed chic as a depoliticization produced through asexual images that reduce lesbianism to a commodified lifestyle (Clark; Schwartz), I would argue that chic is a hypersexualized phenomenon. Some images may emphasize the chic lesbian's class status over her sexuality, but sexuality remains a central component of the entire chic phenomenon, alongside postfeminism (Cragin).

The only explanation I can think of for the above critical position is that it seems to emanate from an *apriori* commitment to the notion that lesbianism is primarily sexual.[2] When critics say the chic lesbian image is asexual, I think what they mean is that it is fairly "delesbianized," i.e., stripped of visual references to lesbian culture, politics, history, aesthetics, and sexuality. The "lesbians" that are left seem hardly different from a coupling of two heterosexual women, as with "femme films" (Holmlund). In fact, despite their blurring of lesbian identity, and removal of this identity from its cultural context, the image of the chic lesbian remains profoundly sexual. Certain aspects of lesbianism (or fantasies of it) have for many years been a part of American popular culture, from pornography to high art. The sexualization of lesbianism does not seem to provide any guarantee of resistance to heterosexism, as some critics would suggest. On the contrary, it seems just as likely to facilitate heterosexism and co-optation by converting politics into a commodity (Hennessy). As with all attempts at celebrating aspects of a formerly abject countercultural trend (and here the parallels to feminism and postfeminism are strong), the anxiety invoked by this reappraisal of lesbianism is barely beneath the surface.

That is to say, despite the emphasis on aesthetics and consumption, an anxious political current undergirds lesbian chic. I would argue that the lesbian chic phenomenon cannot be properly understood without locating it within the current cultural context of postfeminism. The central characteristic of the mainstream media coverage of the chic subculture is its preoccupation with feminism, and specifically, with lesbian/feminism. Apart from instances in which the vilification of radical or lesbian feminism is made explicit in chic representations, a more subtle way of obscuring the troubling political aspects of lesbianism occurs through the representation of an ideal — the apolitical femme. Her valorization is almost always accompanied by her lesbian/feminist foil. As Deborah Schwartz explains,

> The recent flurry of articles on hip lesbians ... isn't about documentation ... it's about creation: building a better lesbian, one palatable enough for mainstream consumption ... a line is drawn between the fab lesbians of today and those cruddy old dykes of yore. We meet the lesbian Goofus and Gallant [34].

This newer image exchanges an association of lesbianism with feminist politics for an association with sex appeal, youth, fashion, and conspicuous consumption. Good lesbians, we are meant to understand, embody the aesthetic and ideological standards of traditional femininity. Good lesbians are interested not in sexual politics, but simply in sex itself.

The Monster in the Narrative

It is within this context that popular culture became fascinated with sexualized, feminine lesbians, yet continued its hostility toward lesbian affiliation with feminist politics that the sitcom *Ellen* emerged. The events surrounding the show's development and demise lend insight into the political context behind lesbian television representation, as *Ellen* stumbled over every unspoken line between the acceptable and the taboo. It failed to avoid politics, and perhaps more importantly, it failed to provide the titillation required to excuse its liberal politics.

While earlier representations framed lesbianism as a topic, one that was at best tangential to generic conventions, on *Ellen*, lesbianism emerged from within a preexisting heterosexual narrative. This key difference may explain many of the difficulties the series experienced, both artistically and politically. Just as homosexuality comes from within heterosexuality, Ellen's inner lesbian adult developed out of an earlier heterosexual childhood of sorts. Like the timid gay newbie whose incessant hinting tests the waters in search of a safe reception, as early as September, 1996, Ellen DeGeneres began publicly joking that her show's main character, Ellen Morgan, might soon be revealing that she is "Lebanese" or "left-handed," and the show's producers announced that they were considering having the character come out (Mifflin B3).

After many months of speculation and anticipation, the infamous coming-out episode aired on April 30, 1997, and *Ellen* became the first U.S. television show with a lead character who was openly lesbian. While other shows have had gay or lesbian secondary characters as a part of larger ensembles, the presence of a lesbian lead character foregrounded homosexuality as an issue and more openly advocated for it. Because *Ellen* commanded greater attention, it provoked greater outrage than earlier lesbian and gay TV characters, and the backlash included bomb threats (Handy 81), viewer boycotts, affiliates' refusals to air the episode, withdrawals of corporate sponsorship (de Vries 20), and even a full-page ad in *Variety* by Jerry Falwell and Phyllis Schlafly (4/30/97). Despite five Emmy nominations and one win, *Ellen* was canceled at the end of its next season. The widespread consensus was that, since the coming-out episode, the show had become "too preachy" and "too gay," although DeGeneres alleged, and a network executive admitted, that the show floundered under a complete lack of promotion (Cagle 30, 32).

Where did this unusually high level of animosity come from? Why did this representation of lesbianism provoke so much fascination and so much heated rebuke? I would argue that it came from within. If, as Schwartz suggests, the iconography of lesbianism sections off Lesbian Goofus from Lesbian Gallant, then Ellen Morgan pulled a fast one on the public by blurring the boundaries between the two. But as with so many lesbian childhoods, this one was not without certain clues.

Ellen had problems from the outset. The show's focus on a single woman and her group of friends lacked narrative tension. Perhaps this is because the representation of heterosexual romance is such a common narrative convention that its absence leads to a lack of dramatic tension for viewers (Stacey). One critic writes:

A major problem has been the indistinct character of Ellen Morgan, who seems to drift wackily through each show without ever offering much in the way of believable motivation, even in the elastic sense that usually applies to sitcoms [Handy 82].

Because the story lines were rarely anchored to the usual heterosexual plots of dating drama, and relationship problems, Ellen Morgan seemed without a social context. The sense of "drifting" reflects the fact that story lines could not develop across episodes, as this would require a more involved representation of relationships.[3] Various solutions to the show's emotional flatness were proposed, including one network executive's suggestion that the writers "juice up" the show by having Ellen get a puppy (82).

The lack of heterosexuality (or, at least, of successful heterosexuality, as Ellen was occasionally shown dating men, although usually with disastrous results) seems to be due in large part to the casting of the lead role. DeGeneres was deeply involved in the writing of the episodes and the development of the character, which seems to be largely based on the persona she presents in her stand-up comedy act. After two seasons of awkward chemistry with male characters, DeGeneres insisted that the dating story lines be stopped. While she stated that the reason for this was her disinterest in creating a show about relationships, writers reported that she felt uncomfortable taping the romantic scenes (Handy 79, 82). Whether due to a personal discomfort with heterosexuality or to a discomfort with having to closet her character (by putting Ellen Morgan into situations that seemed unnatural for the character in order to fit sitcom convention), the show struggled to create a space for an Ellen that was not heterosexual, yet not explicitly lesbian.[4]

The comings-out of Ellen Morgan and Ellen DeGeneres were parallel and intertwined, both in timing and in style. In the coming-out episode, (which was entitled "The Puppy Episode," in reference to the executive's suggestion above), Ellen Morgan struggles to say the words that discomfort her, then accidentally blurts them into an airport microphone, broadcasting her lesbianism through an electronic medium far wider and louder than she had intended. DeGeneres has said that the decision to have her character come out was based upon her own personal need to come out, that she was tired of the effort involved in maintaining the closet as a public figure (80). While it might seem odd that an actor who wanted to come out personally would need to have her character come out in order to do so, DeGeneres appears to have linked the performance of heterosexuality in her personal life to her professional performance so that both closets became intolerable. Ironically, if she were out in her personal life, the performance of a straight role on her show may have been less problematic for her, but because she linked the two closets together, her personal closet seems to have hampered her ability to creatively develop her character.

Ellen Morgan's coming out was a great personal relief to DeGeneres (80), although it came as no surprise to the other characters in Morgan's world or to many of her gay and lesbian viewers. The euphoria at the end of the season was short-lived, however, as the development of the next, now with an openly lesbian main character, quickly ran into problems. The question of how to make a character gay without being "too gay" proved to be a difficult one. This difficulty was compounded by the ambivalence of DeGeneres and the show's producers toward the representation of homosexuality.

Ellen's *Inner Adult*

I have argued that mainstream images of lesbians are often divided into binary opposites: angry politico vs. apolitical (sexualized) femme. How then to explain the developmental shift in the character of Ellen Morgan? She was not able to fulfill the sexualized function of most chic images, yet she was initially not on the side of the angry, political lesbian either. What allowed her to function as a nonsexualized, nonpolitical (semiotically closeted) lesbian was another binary underlying the first: adult/child, as children are said to progress in their moral and emotional development from pleasure-oriented narcissism to more outwardly focused knowledge of the world. Similarly, John Hartley has argued that audiences are "paedocratized" by television producers, who assume they are childlike (230). He argues that the medium itself is inherently paedocratizing: that its need to appeal to the widest possible audience results in an address that is simple and childlike. It appeals to us not as citizens seeking information, but as children seeking pleasure through fun, energy, constant movement, emotional reflexes, simplicity, and a lack of literacy or ideas (232).[5]

I would argue that DeGeneres has been successful in the mainstream as a stand-up comedian and comedic actress because her style of humor draws on this paedocratizing tendency.[6] The persona she presents onstage clearly draws to some extent on her own personality, yet it must be considered a performance. She presents only select elements of her self, emphasizing them repeatedly, to create a recognizable, stylized persona. In this case, DeGeneres' persona consistently represents her as a naive, childlike person who is stumbling through her attempts to perform and understand adulthood. While this is not the only comic mode that appeals to American audiences, it is a mode that offered space for DeGeneres to draw upon a partially autobiographical style of humor while remaining closeted.

This childlike persona carried over into the sitcom as well, where mainstream America could watch Ellen Morgan each week and laugh at her foibles, or relate to her inability to master herself and her situation. The glaring lack of (stable) heterosexuality for her character and in her comedy could be explained by the innocent, tomboyish, childlike frame of her extratextual and textual personae. Before the point at which she came out, Ellen Morgan seemed either unable to get a man or too immature to want one (Yescavage and Alexander 23). In a world in which female adulthood is predicated upon the attainment of heterosexual relationships and motherhood, Ellen refused (or was unable) to grow up. The transition was therefore abrupt when Morgan suddenly asserted her adulthood by laying claim to the label lesbian.

The naming of Morgan's lack of heterosexuality as lesbian awakened the adult specters of sexuality and politics, both of which would undermine the childlike, bumbling elements of the character, which were the foundation of her likeability. From the outset, DeGeneres and the producers made it clear that there would not be a lot of heated discussion of issues, nor would there be a lot of heated lesbian relationships. After her character came out, DeGeneres insisted there would not be any kissing between women, because "*Ellen* won't become the lesbian dating show" (Handy 85). Executive producer Dana Savel explained the show's continuity:

> Ellen Morgan is still in a very heterosexual situation. Almost all her friends are heterosexuals. If one of the other characters has a guy that they're interested in, she's the first to say "Omigod, he's hot" [85].

The desire of the creators was that the main character's lesbianism would not disrupt the show's formula, but it was inevitable that Ellen Morgan would be reinterpreted, as the very elements that sustained her likeability were now being radically reframed and associated with elements that many in the culture find distinctly unlikable.

And DeGeneres herself seemed to find many elements of lesbianism unlikable. In an interview just before the coming-out episode aired, she described coming-out to her father. He asked if she was going to "go all flamboyant," and she responded, "Yeah, Dad, I'm going to completely change. I'm going to start wearing leather vests. I'm going to get one of those haircuts that they all have" (86). The "they" marks a telling distance between herself and lesbians, and in her remarks, DeGeneres often seemed to view lesbians with the same discomfort and hostility that many heterosexuals do. For example, when asked if she was angry that more gays and lesbians in Hollywood had not come out, she replied:

> I didn't do it to make a political statement. I did it selfishly for myself and because I thought it was a great thing for the show, which desperately needed a point of view. If other people come out, that's fine. I mean, it would be great if for no other reason than just to show the diversity, so it's not just the extremes. Because unfortunately those are the people who get the most attention on the news. You know, when you see the parades and you see dykes on bikes or these men dressed as women ... I don't want them representing the entire community [86].

She described her first lesbian experience at 18 as "someone else's idea — I was freaked out even by the thought of it," and did not come out to herself until her thirties (86). She stated that if she had a choice, she would never choose to be lesbian, because "No one in their right mind would choose something this hard" (*The Oprah Winfrey Show*, 4/30/97).

All of these elements, when taken as a whole, suggest that the actress who created and portrayed the first lesbian main character on U.S. television was at the time highly uncomfortable with and ambivalent about her own lesbianism. This changed, however, over the summer. Between the coming-out episode and the development of the new, openly lesbian *Ellen*, DeGeneres seems to have gone through a period of personal growth where she shed her shame and became increasingly political. For example, before the coming-out episode, she had reassured everyone that there would be no relationships or kissing, yet by the time the Fall 1997 season began, she was demanding that Ellen be allowed to have a relationship (de Vries 25) and was infuriated when the producers planned to film the back of her head during a lesbian kiss (Cagle 32). When asked about this discrepancy, she explained, "I changed. I grew up. Because when I talked to you last year, I didn't even realize the internal homophobia and the — the shame that I was still dealing with" (*Prime Time*, 5/6/98).

DeGeneres had pressured ABC not to renew the series and agreed to return only reluctantly (de Vries 22). It was the hundreds of letters she received from gay teens who had been considering suicide that politicized her and made her return to the show (Cagle 31). At the same time that ABC was assuring the public it would be taking "baby steps," Ellen was faxing in scripts all summer, pressuring them to "make Ellen more of an adult, to make the stories more real" (de Vries 24). ABC had begun with a paedocratized woman-child and wanted to keep her that way, yet DeGeneres' personal maturation led to a split between the once-fused character and author, which threatened the show's formula for success. In an atmosphere in which the open acknowledgment of homosexuality is charged with politics, "it was a bolder statement than she imagined — and thoroughly at odds with her awkward, please-like-me TV persona, which ABC was counting on to carry the show" (Cagle 31). In the space of one year, DeGeneres went from:

> I understand the not understanding of it. Because I didn't understand for a long time, and I'm still struggling to — I have the same problems [with homosexuality] that a lot of people do [Handy 86].

to:

> I can understand why someone looks at it and is a little uncomfortable because they're not used to seeing it. You know, it must've been uncomfortable for some white people to see some black people walk

into a restaurant that they weren't supposed to be in. It's conditioning [*Prime Time*, 5/6/98].

This abrupt attitudinal shift was clearly one for which the general public was not ready.

Because the struggle over the production of the post-coming-out series was so public, it provides insight into the parameters that shape gay and lesbian representation on television. While it is not impossible to create sitcom characters that are both legitimately gay and compatible with the sitcom format (for example, *Will & Grace* springs to mind), it is certainly difficult. Anna McCarthy has noted that the coming-out episode and subsequent season of *Ellen* were pulled in two directions: by the network's desire to market the character's coming-out as a must-see event (with the expectation that after this event, the show would return to its routine, nonpolitical serial narrative) and by DeGeneres' own desire to integrate the political results of the event into a new kind of narrative, where gayness is a part of everyday life, not an issue to be debated. As she soon discovered, the event of her queerness emerging from within, rather than being appended to the side, was too constitutive and too explosive to be recontained. The ambivalence toward lesbianism and politics that DeGeneres repeatedly expressed helps explain the show's jerky, chaotic narrative ends.

The final episodes represented lesbianism as both irrelevant (just one particular aspect of identity among many) and expressly the "point." But that is the very way homosexuality often is. Some days it seems to be the very essence of what one is, and other days an empty label.[7] The shift *Ellen* represented — from the invocation of a distant margin as a means of shoring up a center, to the revelation of the constitutive marginality of the center itself— marked a startling turning point in television history. However earnest and homosexual her appeal, in many ways its presence at the very heart of the likeable child was fairly queer indeed. DeGeneres might have been content to reside within the confines of the open secret for another 40 years if it were not for the relentless heterosexualizing gaze that prodded her into speaking her sexuality.

Coming out is, after all, a result of heterosexual practices more than homosexuality. It is not queers' unsolicited burdening of others with our secrets, but the relentless incitement to discourse, as Foucault put it, that makes it nearly impossible to ignore or fail its terms without aggressively articulating a narrative break. Given that heterosexuality is a regime that attempts to categorize and understand each self by matching it to its opposite gender/sex, coming out might best be understood as the process of one side dragging out the dirty truth, not the other side revealing it. The hypocrisy of the system is that the eventual result of the endless harassment is what is condemned, rather than the process that provokes it. Heterosexuality wants to see itself reassured and reflected back in every instance and image. After several years of narrative pressures and pained attempts to give the "right" answers, Ellen simply told inquiring minds what they didn't want to know.

Notes

1. For example, Torres 179; Moritz "Old Strategies" 136; and a roundtable discussion of the subject (in terms of *Ellen*) at the 1997 Queer Frontiers conference, published in Boone et al.

2. As Patricia White has noted, "a lesbian specter can be said to have haunted feminist film theory" (72). I would argue even more specifically that a lesbian/feminist specter could be said to have haunted many arenas of feminist and lesbian inquiry. The recurring legacy of the sex wars and lesbian/feminist linkages of lesbianism and feminism appears to me to be a noticeable reticence on the part of critics to describe lesbianism as anything other than primarily a form of sexual desire. See Cragin for more on ambivalence toward lesbian/feminism in academic feminism.

3. By comparison, *Seinfeld*, the highly successful sitcom that *Ellen* appears to have been based upon (from its basic premise as "a show about nothing" down to the boppy bass line between scenes) didn't evoke the same sense of flatness. Romance is so intrinsically intertwined with our expectations of women's narrative possibilities that its absence is far more noticeable with women than with men. This is one example of a gender difference that needs to be attended to when analyzing queer media. While homophobia is shared by gay men and lesbians equally, I would argue that heterosexism may impact lesbians even more intensely than gay men because of their gendering as women (see Whisman for a similar argument.)

4. See Shugart for a detailed reading of the various mechanisms of ambiguity in *Ellen*.

5. Some of Hartley's assumptions may now be outdated, as television has changed dramatically since his analysis was written. For example, he argues that television avoids acknowledgment of racial and class differences which may be potentially divisive, focusing instead on childlike pleasures as a common ground we can all identify with (232). While television certainly does fail to acknowledge racial

inequality and class inequality, its address has become increasingly diversified, as factors such as the advent of cable have led to the identification of subaudiences (Moritz "American Television" 36). In addition, others have argued convincingly that television doesn't avoid anxiety, but rather courts it (Mellencamp; Doane). Yet, with these modifications, his argument essentially holds, as television emphasizes nonrational or noninformational elements over others.

6. This essay argues that paedocratization on *Ellen* is primarily achieved through the avoidance of coming out. For an interesting variation on this position, see Straayer's analysis of Monika Treut's *Virgin Machine*, which argues that the coming-out narrative itself leads to paedocratization (23–41). I agree entirely with her argument that coming-out is not enough, that it leaves lesbian texts always back at the beginning, viewing life from the perspective of a neophyte. What I'm suggesting is that in its paedocratized stage, *Ellen* failed to achieve even that inadequate form of politics.

7. Or, as Judith Butler puts it, "To write or speak as a lesbian appears a paradoxical appearance of this 'I,' one which feels neither true nor false.... How is it that I can both 'be' one, and yet endeavor to be one at the same time?" (13, 18).

Works Cited

Abelove, Henry, Michele Barale, and David Halperin, eds. *The Lesbian and Gay Studies Reader.* New York: Routledge, 1993.
Bark, Ed. "Ellen Back to Humor Home Base." *Dallas Morning News* 26 July 2001: 33A.
Boone, Joseph, et al., eds. *Queer Frontiers: Millenial Geographies, Genders, and Generations.* Madison: University of Wisconsin Press, 2000.
Butler, Judith. "Imitation and Gender Insubordination." *Inside/Out: Lesbian Theories, Gay Theories.* ed. Diana Fuss. New York: Routledge, 1991. 13–31.
Cagle, Jess. "As Gay as It Gets?" *Entertainment Weekly* 8 May 1998: 26–32.
Clark, Danae. "Commodity Lesbianism." Abelove, Barale and Halperin, 186–201.
Cragin, Becca. "Post-Lesbian-Feminism: Documenting 'Those Cruddy Old Dykes of Yore.'" *Carryin' on in the Lesbian and Gay South.* John Howard, ed. New York: New York University Press, 1997. 285–327.
de Vries, Hilary. "Ellen DeGeneres: Out and About." *TV Guide* 11 Oct. 1997: 20–27.
Doane, Mary Ann. "Information, Crisis, Catastrophe." *Logics of Television: Essays in Cultural Criticism.* Patricia Mellencamp, ed. Bloomington: Indiana University Press, 1990. 222–239.
Ehrenstein, David. *Open Secret: Gay Hollywood, 1928–1998.* New York: William Morrow, 1998.
Foucault, Michel. *The History of Sexuality.* Vol. 1. 1978. New York: Vintage, 1990.
Handy, Bruce. "Roll Over, Ward Cleaver." *Time* 14 Apr. 1997: 78–86.

Hantzis, Darlene, and Valerie Lehr. "Whose Desire? Lesbian (Non)Sexuality and Television's Perpetuation of Hetero/Sexism." Ringer 107–121.
Hartley, John. "Invisible Fictions: Television Audiences, Paedocracy, Pleasure." *Television Studies: Textual Analysis*. Gary Burns and Robert Thompson, eds. New York: Praeger, 1989. 223–243.
Hennessy, Rosemary. "Queer Visibility in Commodity Culture." *Cultural Critique* (1995): 31–76.
Holmlund, Christine. "When Is a Lesbian Not a Lesbian? The Lesbian Continuum and the Mainstream Femme Film." *Camera Obscura* 25.26 (1991): 145–178.
Lewis, Reina, and Katrina Rolley. "Ad(Dressing) the Dyke: Lesbian Looks and Lesbians Looking." *Outlooks: Lesbian and Gay Sexualities and Visual Culture*. Eds. Peter Horne and Reina Lewis. New York: Routledge, 1996. 178–190.
McCarthy, Anna. "'Must See' Queer TV: History and Serial Form in Ellen." *Quality Popular Television*. Eds. Mark Jancovich and James Lyons. London: BFI, 2003. 88–102.
Mellencamp, Patricia. *High Anxiety: Catastrophe, Scandal, Age & Comedy*. Bloomington: Indiana University Press, 1992.
Mifflin, Lawrie. "Title Character in *Ellen* May Come Out as Gay." *New York Times* 16 Sep. 1996: B3.
Moritz, Marguerite J. "American Television and the Creation of Lesbian Characters." Doctoral thesis. Northwestern University, 1991.
_____. "Old Strategies for New Texts: How American Television Is Creating and Treating Lesbian Characters." Ringer 122–142.
Ringer, Jeffrey, ed. *Queer Words, Queer Images: Communication and the Construction of Homosexuality*. New York: New York University Press, 1994.
Schwartz, Deb. "The Days of Wine and Poses: The Media Presents Homosexuality Lite." *Village Voice* 8 June 1993: 34.
Shugart, Helene. "Performing Ambiguity: The Passing of Ellen DeGeneres." *Text and Performance Quarterly* 23.1 (2003): 30–54.
Stacey, Jackie. "'If You Don't Play You Can't Win': *Desert Hearts* and the Lesbian Romance Film." *Immortal, Invisible: Lesbians and the Moving Image*. Tamsin Wilton, ed. New York: Routledge, 1995. 92–114.
Straayer, Chris. *Deviant Eyes, Deviant Bodies: Sexual Re-Orientations in Film and Video*. New York: Columbia University Press, 1996.
Torres, Sasha. "Television/Feminism: HeartBeat and Prime-Time Lesbianism." Abelove, Barale and Halperin. 176–185.
Whisman, Vera. *Queer by Choice: Lesbians, Gay Men, and the Politics of Identity*. New York: Routledge, 1996.
White, Patricia. *Uninvited: Classical Hollywood Cinema and Lesbian Representability*. Bloomington: Indiana University Press, 1999.
Yescavage, Karen, and Jonathan Alexander. "What Do You Call a Lesbian Who's

Only Slept with Men? Answer: Ellen Morgan: Deconstructing the Lesbian Identities of Ellen Morgan and Ellen DeGeneres." *Lesbian Sex Scandals: Sexual Practices, Identities, and Politics*. Dawn Atkins, ed. New York: Haworth Press, 1999. 21–32.

About the Contributors

Robert Benjamin Bateman Robert Benjamin Bateman is a Ph.D. student in English language and literature at the University of Virginia in Charlottesville. His scholarly interests include twentieth century British literature, literary theory, and cultural studies.

Rebecca Clare Beirne Rebecca Clare Beirne is currently a Ph.D. candidate at University of Sydney, Australia, writing her dissertation on lesbian representation in contemporary culture. She has previously published an article called "Queering the Slayer-Text: Reading Possibilities in *Buffy the Vampire Slayer*," and has presented papers on issues in lesbian representation at several conferences.

James Black James Black is director of tutorial services at Susquehanna University, a private undergraduate liberal arts institution in Selinsgrove, Pennsylvania. His work allows him to play the roles of administrator and educator in various ways, often merging the two: mentoring and tutoring students; promoting academic support programs; co-teaching a course on peer education theories and practices; providing faculty development opportunities regarding the teaching of writing. He holds a master's in English with an emphasis on creative writing from the University of Missouri at Columbia. His scholarly/research interests currently lean toward issues relating to writing, narrative, and identity.

Becca Cragin Dr. Cragin, an assistant professor of popular culture at Bowling Green State University in Bowling Green, Ohio, received her Ph.D. in women's studies from Emory University in Atlanta in 2002. She co-chaired the steering committee of "Queering the South," the first Southern queer studies conference and recently completed an ethnographic study of lesbian and gay television talk show viewers. Her research examines the representation of feminist and queer issues in film and television, and her publications include "The Study of Gender in Culture: Feminist Studies/Cultural Studies" in *Handbook of the Sociology of Gender* (primary author with Wendy Simonds) and "Post-Lesbian-Feminism: Documenting 'Those Cruddy Old Dykes of Yore'" in *Carryin' On in the Lesbian and Gay South*.

Richard J. Conway Richard J. Conway holds a B.A. in English and philosophy and an M.A. in film studies from University College, Dublin. He is currently a member of the Dublin Queer Studies Seminar and has particular interests in filmic and televisual (re)negotiations and (re)imaginations of established normativity and the ontological safety these media provide. He currently works as a journalist and creative editor and has recently produced an explorative magazine for *BeLonG To*, Dublin's first lesbian, gay, bisexual, and transgender youth project.

Guy Mark Foster Guy Mark Foster is assistant professor of English at the University of California, Santa Barbara. He has published essays and fiction in *Radical Philosophy Review, Lambda Book Report, Ancestral House: The Black Short Story in the Americas and Europe* as well as *Brother to Brother: New Writings by Black Gay Men* (1991). He is presently working on a book entitled *Made in America: Interracial Desire in Postwar U.S. Literary and Popular Culture*.

W. C. Harris W. C. Harris is an assistant professor of English at Shippensburg University in Shippensburg, Pennsylvania, where he specializes in early and nineteenth-century American literature as well as gay and lesbian studies. His essays on Edgar Allan Poe, Walt Whitman, Beatrix Potter, and William James have appeared in *American Literary History, The Walt Whitman Quarterly Review, Arizona Quarterly*, and *Victorian Review*. Recent work on topics including Christian Science and reconstruction; homosexuality and antifederalism in Charles Brockden Brown; and utopian fantasy in gay liberation writing has been presented at national and regional conferences. His short story "The Wrong Kind of Queen" appeared in *M2M: New Literary Fiction* (2003).

James R. Keller James Keller is professor of English and director of the Honors College at Mississippi University for Women. He is the author of three previously published monographs: *Princes, Soldiers, and Rogues: The Politic Malcontent of Renaissance Drama* (1993); *Anne Rice and Sexual Politics: The Early Novels* (McFarland, 2000); and *Queer (Un)Friendly Film and Television* (McFarland, 2002). He has a forthcoming book, entitled *Eminem—The Bubble-Gum Anti-Christ: From Shady to Encore*, and another, entitled *Hunger Artists: Food, Film, and Culture*, is currently being written. Keller has recently coedited with Leslie Stratyner a collection entitled *Almost Shakespeare: Reinventing His Work for Film and Television* (McFarland, 2004). Keller has published more than 35 articles on a variety of topics, including early modern literature, African American literature, modern and contemporary drama, gay and lesbian studies, film, and cultural studies.

Kelly Kessler Kelly Kessler holds a Ph.D. in radio-television-film from the University of Texas at Austin, where she served multiple terms as the cocoordinating editor of *The Velvet Light Trap*. Her current work investigates both the mainstreaming of lesbianism in contemporary television and film and shifting generic codes and articulations of masculinity in the Hollywood musical. Kessler's work on lesbian film can be found in a recent issue of *Film Quarterly*.

About the Contributors

Margaret McFadden Margaret McFadden is an associate professor and director of the American studies program at Colby College in Waterville, Maine, where she teaches popular culture and queer studies. Her essays have appeared in *The Journal of American History* and *The Journal of American Culture*, and she is completing a book on gender and sexuality in 1930s popular comedy.

Margo Miller Margo Miller received a B.A. in gender studies from the University of Chicago and an M.A. in media, technology, and society from Northwestern University. She is currently enrolled in Northwestern's Ph.D. program in screen cultures. Her work focuses on the queer arrangements of single television characters, particularly in sitcoms during the postwar period.

Danielle Mitchell Danielle Mitchell is an assistant professor of English at Penn State Fayette, the Eberly Campus, where she teaches courses in composition and literature. Her work typically blends her interests in cultural studies, rhetorical theory, queer studies, and composition theory.

Esther Peeren Esther Peeren completed undergraduate degrees in English and comparative literature at the University of Groningen in Holland and a masters in women's studies at the University of Oxford. She is currently a third year Ph.D. candidate at the Amsterdam School for Cultural Analysis (University of Amsterdam), working on a dissertation tentatively titled "Bakhtin and Beyond: Intersubjective Identities in Popular Culture." The dissertation takes such Bakhtinian theoretical concepts as the chronotope, excess of seeing, dialogism, speech genres, translation, and carnival and explores the ways they relate to individual and group identities in popular culture (television series and films) and how they correlate with other theoretical frameworks.

Christopher Pullen Christopher Pullen is a lecturer in media, gender, and performance at Bournemouth Media School, Bournemouth University in England. His research interests relate to the representation of minorities within television and film, specifically focusing on confessional documentary and contemporary drama.

Leslie Stratyner Leslie Stratyner is a professor of English at Mississippi University for Women, where she teaches courses on medieval and Anglo-Saxon literatures, oral formulaic theory, and epic and myth. Dr. Stratyner is coeditor of the collection *Almost Shakespeare: Reinventing His Work for Film and Television* (McFarland, 2004) and has published and given papers on subjects as varied as Elvis, the medieval romance, *The Odyssey*, *The Dream of the Rood*, and *Star Trek*. She lives in Columbus, Mississippi, with her husband and her daughter.

Index

Abjection 65, 69
"Accent" 63–69, 72
ACLU 144n
Activism 31, 32, 67, 114, 119, 190
ACTUP (AIDS Coalition to Unleash Power) 1, 2
The Advocate 23, 31–32, 36, 38n, 56n
African-Americans 24, 25, 102, 105, 107–108
AIDS (Acquired Immune Deficiency Syndrome) 2, 13, 48, 67, 124, 152
All My Children 87
Alley, Kirstie 13
Althusser, Louis 110
The Amazing Race 30
An American Family 160–161, 176
American Family Association 124
Amos 'n' Andy 24–25
Androgyny 196
Are You Being Served? 76
Arendt, Hannah 14, 15, 18n, 19
Assimilation 4, 5, 21, 29, 30–31, 39n, 43–44, 45, 46, 52, 53, 54, 55, 66, 71, 102, 114, 126, 135, 141
Athletics 187
Atlas, Charles 182
Ausiello, Michael 44, 56, 73, 74
Austen, Jane 45

Babuscio, Jack 80, 83
Bakhtin, Mikhail 5, 60, 61, 65, 68, 69, 70, 71–72, 74, 75, 76, 79–80, 82–84, 162, 167, 175
Barrie, Dennis 125, 126
Bataille, George 17
Bateman, Robert Benjamin 4, 9–19, 209
Bawer, Bruce 47, 56, 56n
BBC 66, 76
Bech, Henning 10, 19
Beirne, Claire 5, 43–58, 209
Bersani, Leo 183, 191
Bigotry 109
Bisexuality (GLBT) 1, 2, 10, 20, 21, 29, 30, 31, 40n, 85, 86, 87, 91, 92, 95–96, 113, 179, 180, 190

Black, James 6–7, 177–192, 209
Blacks 66, 99–112
Bordo, Susan 182, 191
Bourdieu Pierre 69, 74
Bourgeois 14–15, 93
Bowers v. Hardwick 20
Boy Meets Boy 7, 160–176
Bruni, Frank 131, 145
Buchanan, Pat 124
Buffy the Vampire Slayer 87
Burke, Phyllis 181, 191
Butch 138–140, 144n, 189
Butler, Judith 16–17, 19, 60–61, 65, 68, 69, 74, 183–185, 191, 206n

Cagney and Lacey 194
Camp 25–26, 31, 32, 34, 36, 55, 77, 80, 89, 190
Capitalism 17, 18, 49, 50, 91, 144n
Capsuto, Steven 131, 145
Carlson, Marvin 162, 175
Carnival 5, 75, 76, 78, 79–83, 162, 167, 170, 171
Censorship 72, 115, 121
Chaiken, Ilene 113, 125–126, 128
Chambers, Samuel 103–104, 111
Chasin, Alexandra 22, 39n, 42, 57
Cheng, Cliff 183, 191
Chic, Lesbian 195–197, 200
Chodorow, Nancy 181, 191
Christian 6, 56n, 114, 115, 116, 118, 119, 123, 124, 125, 127
Clark, Danae 13, 18n, 19, 57, 206
Class 86, 130, 138, 144n, 206n
The Closet 43, 200
Cohen, Cathy 106, 111
Collis, Rose 131, 145
Colonization 65, 143
Color Blindness 100–102, 108, 110–111
Coming-Out 67, 147, 161, 193, 195, 198, 199, 202, 203, 204, 206n
Commodification 3, 13–14, 50–51, 52, 95, 161, 173, 196
Consumerism 4, 13, 17, 23, 26, 51

213

Index

Conway, Richard J. 5, 75–84, 209–210
The Cosby Show 76
Cragin, Becca 7, 193–208, 209
Crimp, Douglas 126

Dandy 12
David, Larry 148
Dawson's Creek 87
Deconstruction 17, 44, 78, 79, 83, 89
DeGeneres, Ellen 193, 198, 199–203
Derrida, Jacques 65, 74
DINK (Dual Income No Kids) 22
Discrimination 2, 55, 128, 142
Diversity 24, 29, 43, 45, 46, 54, 55, 138, 189
Divorce 95
Durdale, Alonso 23, 42, 176
Dynasty 87

Eaton, Mike 80–81, 84
Economics 4, 22, 93–97, 137
Effeminacy 6, 15, 16, 30, 31, 33, 147, 148, 156, 167, 181, 183, 190
Ellen 7, 143, 193–208
Engels, Frederick 94, 98
The Enquirer 85
Entertainment Weekly 130, 144n
ER 77
Erotophobia 11, 13
Eskridge, William 47, 56n, 57
Etheridge, Melissa 86
Ethnicity 100, 130, 152
Ettelbrick, Paula 138
Experiment: Gay and Straight 173, 175, 176

Faludi, Susan 181, 182, 185–156, 191
Falwell, Jerry 124, 198
Family 86–87, 88, 94, 95, 97, 106, 108, 117–119, 123, 125, 126–128, 133, 141
Father Knows Best 76
Fausto-Sterling, Ann 181, 191
Felski, Rita 12, 19
Femininity 15–16, 89, 139, 148–149, 181, 183, 184, 188, 196, 197
Feminism 56n, 85, 118, 144n, 193–197, 205n
Femme 138–139, 144n, 189, 196, 197, 200
Fetchit, Stephen 24
Fetish 43, 100, 143
Feuer, Jane 66, 74, 82, 84, 145
Fineman, Martha 85, 98
Finley, Karen 124
Flax Jane 108, 111
Fleck, John 124
Foster, Guy Mark 6, 99–112, 210
Foucault, Michel 11, 19, 39n, 162, 175, 206
Frazier 149
Frederick, Latisha 30
Free speech 115

Freud, Sigmund 17
Friends 6, 39n, 81, 130–131, 133–146, 147–148, 149, 151, 153, 159
Frohnmayer, John 124, 128
Fundamentalism 6, 114, 116, 127, 128

Gay-bashing 47, 87–88, 178, 179
Gender 2, 5, 7, 10, 15, 16, 17, 23, 25, 56n, 78, 86, 89, 90, 102, 104, 105, 108–110, 147, 149, 162, 180, 183, 184, 187, 188, 189, 190, 193, 195, 205
Giddens, Anthony 173–174, 175
Giltz, Michael 31, 42
GLAAD (Gay and Lesbian Alliance Against Defamation) 6, 87, 143, 145, 177, 178, 179, 180, 187, 190, 191
Golden Girls 194
Goldstein, Richard 21, 22, 26–27, 31, 34, 36, 42, 88, 98, 190, 191
Good Times 131
Gray, Herman 66, 74, 102, 111, 144n, 145
Grote, David 132, 134
Grotesque 167
Grounded for Life 81–82
Guys and Dolls 156

Hall, Stuart 103, 111, 175
Harris, W.C. 4, 20–42, 210
Hartley, John 200, 205n, 207
HBO/Home Box Office 6, 99, 102
Heart-Beat 195
Hedonism 56n
Helms, Jesse 121, 124
Henderson, Russel 40n
Heterosexism 109, 195, 196, 205n
Heterosexuality 2, 3, 4, 6, 9, 10, 11–18, 20, 22–29, 31, 32–34, 36, 61 43, 44, 45, 54, 55, 64, 66, 72, 77, 78, 87, 88, 90, 94, 97, 107, 109, 131, 133, 135–142, 144n, 145n, 148, 149, 150, 154, 155, 156, 165, 168–173, 179, 181–184, 186, 188, 194, 196, 197, 199, 201, 202, 204–205
Himmelstein, Hal 132, 134, 145
Holleran, Andrew 89, 98
"Homo-genization" 10
Homophobia 2, 7, 11, 14, 21, 24, 28, 40n, 44, 47, 49, 50, 51, 52, 64, 86, 87–89, 101, 104–106, 109, 126, 127, 144n, 156, 178, 180, 183, 184, 186, 190, 193, 195, 203, 205n
Homosexual panic 40n
Homosocial 79, 87, 148, 157
hooks, bell 105–106
Hughes, Holly 124
The Human Rights Campaign (HRC) 56n, 96, 98
Humanism 14, 15, 48

Identity 16–17, 21, 30, 44, 46, 49, 51, 54, 63, 89, 103, 105, 107–110, 126, 138, 143, 148, 151, 156, 157, 160, 161, 162, 165–166, 167, 172, 173, 174n, 184, 196
Integration 31
Invisibility 4, 142, 144n
"Ironic Dismissal" 6, 147–158

Jagose, Annamarie 89, 98
Jarina, Fred 30
Jews 14, 107
Jhally, Sut 178
Jhaveri, Hemal 29–30, 31, 39n, 42
Johnson, Ben Patrick 32, 35, 39n, 42
Julien, Isaac 106, 112

Kanner, Melinda 20, 23, 24, 26–29, 35, 37, 40n, 42, 88, 98
Kate and Allie 194
Keller, James R. 1–7, 210
Keller, Wade 178, 190
Kelly, Christopher 24, 28–29, 33, 38n, 39n, 40n, 42
Kessler, Kelly 6, 130–146, 210
Kimmel, S. Michael 181, 183, 184, 188, 191
King, Rodney 107
Kipnis, Laura 94, 98
Krutnick, Frank 76, 81, 84

The L Word 6, 113–129, 194
Lambda Legal Defense and Education Fund 98
Lawrence et al. v Texas 20, 38n
Leavitt, David 30, 42
Lesbiphobic 54
Liberation 3, 11, 88
"Linguistic Stratification" 60
Lipman, Daniel 63
Loud, Lance 160–161, 174, 176

Mad About You 6, 130–131, 133–146
Mapplethorpe, Robert 124, 125
Marriage 5, 17, 21, 32, 39n, 43, 50, 55, 56n, 78, 79, 85–90, 93–97, 127, 134, 136–137, 138, 140–141, 145n, 153, 154, 186
Marx, Karl 4, 13, 18n, 19
Masculinity 5, 6, 7, 15, 16, 75, 76, 77–80, 82–83, 90, 139, 147, 148, 149, 150, 151, 158, 167, 180–190
Materialism 4, 23
McCarthy, Anna 204, 207
McClelland, John 178, 179, 191
McFadden, Margaret 6, 113–129, 211
McKinney, Aaron 40n
Medicalization 67
Melrose Place 87
Metrosexual 10

Meyer, Richard 126, 128
Midler, Bette 156
Miller, Jonathan 178, 192
Miller, Margo 6, 147–159, 211
Miller, Tim 124
Mimesis 132
Les Miserables 150
Misogyny 12, 54, 183, 184
Mitchell, Danielle 5, 85–98, 211
Monogamy 90, 94, 116, 135–138, 186
Monster's Ball 108
Moritz, Marguerite 131, 145, 205n, 206n, 207
Motherhood 94, 133, 134, 136–138, 201
MTV 164, 176
Multiculturalism 66
Munt, Sally 50, 57

NAACP 101–102
Naficy, Hamid 63–65, 68, 73n, 74
National Endowment for the Arts 124
The National Gay and Lesbian Task Force 56n
Nazis 107, 152
Neale, Steve 76, 81, 84
The New Republic 56n
New York Times 85, 178, 186
Newcomb, Horace 132–134, 144n, 146
Nock, Stephen 186, 188, 192
Normal, Ohio 4
NYPD Blue 87

The Odd Couple 157
Oklahoma 147
The Oprah Winfrey Show 202
Orecklin, Michele 179, 192
OUT 23, 130, 144n

"Paedocratizing" 200–201, 203, 206n
Parnaby, Julia 91, 98
Parody 178
Pathologization 67
Patriarchy 189
Pedophilia 47, 120
Peeren, Esther 5, 59–74, 211
Performativity 6, 10, 16, 65, 87, 110, 160–176
Phalen, Peggy 142, 146
Pluralism 66
Pollack, William 187, 192
Pornography 17, 48, 63, 117, 119, 120, 122, 123, 125, 196
Potts, Leanne 30, 32, 42
Prime Time 203–204
Privilege 9, 93–97, 110, 138, 183, 186
Pro Wrestling Torch 178
Promiscuity 45, 47, 56n
Pullen, Christopher 6–7, 160–176, 211

Index

Queer As Folk 2, 5, 11, 24, 43–58, 59–74, 194
Queer Eye for the Straight Guy 4, 9–19, 20–42, 86, 173, 174, 176, 194
Queer Nation 44, 51, 56n

Race 6, 86, 92, 99–112, 130–131, 138, 162, 205n
Racist 119
Radical Fairies 1
Raphael, Ray 188, 192
The Real World 7, 161, 163–165, 172–173, 174n, 176
Reality television 6–7, 11, 31, 160–176
Religious Right 113, 114, 117, 120–121, 123, 128
Representation 9, 67–68, 69, 72, 73n, 76, 117, 130–131, 138, 195, 197
Riggs, Marlon 124, 144n, 146
Road Rules 164
Robertson, Pat 124, 125
Roof, Judith 189, 192
Rosanne 87, 130, 131
Ross, Douglas 168
Russo, Vito 174, 175

Sadomasochism 125
Sappho 130
Savel, Dana 201–202
Sawyer, Terry 20, 22, 23, 26, 39n, 40n, 42
Scalia, Antonin 35
Schechner, Richard 162, 175
Schlafly, Phyllis 198
Schwartz, Deborah 197, 198, 207
Scopophilia 17
Seinfeld 6, 147–159, 205n
Seinfeld, Jerry 148
"Semantic Elasticity" 69
Semiotics 144n, 200
Seomin, Scott 177–180, 187, 189, 190
Serrano, Andres 124
Shales, Tom 30
Shepard, Matthew 40n
Showtime 59, 113
Sisters 67
Situation comedy 5, 6, 7, 75, 76, 77, 79, 80–84, 130–146, 147, 149, 150, 151, 152, 156–157, 193, 197, 199, 201, 204
Six Feet Under 6, 30, 99–112
Smackdown 177, 178, 179
Soap 87
Sodomy 13, 20, 45, 46
Somerville, Siobhan 104, 109, 112
"Speech Genre" 61, 63, 68, 69
Spin City 87, 130
Spivack, Gayatri 67, 74
Sports 187
Stacey, Judith 97, 98

Stallybrass, Peter 162, 171, 175
Steele, Bruce 32, 35, 42
Stereotype 4, 9, 14, 15, 20, 21, 24–6, 28–36, 39, 40n, 45, 47, 49, 52, 56n, 64, 72, 88, 89, 109, 139, 142, 149, 151, 155, 161, 165, 167–171, 177, 179, 180, 182, 183, 189
Stonewall 1, 29
Strayner, Leslie 1–7, 211
Stuever, Hank 188–189, 192
Subaltern 67–68
"Subaltern Insurgency" 67
Subjectivity 85, 89, 91, 108, 161, 174
Sullivan, Andrew 39–40, 42, 47, 56n, 57
Survivor 7, 144n, 161, 164–166, 172, 174n, 176

That's My Mama 131
Thirtysomething 67
This Life 66
Thompson, Bob 28
Three's Company 20
Time 179
Today 178, 181
Torres, Sasha 194–195, 205n, 207
Transgendered (GLBT) 1, 2, 20, 21, 29, 30, 31, 40n, 86, 87, 91, 95–96, 179, 190
Transgression 161, 173
Tropiano, Stephen 131, 146

USA Today 125

Vaid, Urvashi 46, 58
Vance, Carole 126
Van Gogh, Vincent 126
Variety 198
The Village Voice 21
Visibility 1, 2, 22, 24, 43, 110, 117, 121, 126, 130–131, 142–143, 147, 158, 161, 165, 185, 189
Voyeurism 143

Walters, Suzanna 88, 98
Warner, Michael 21, 33, 37, 39n, 40n, 42, 46, 48, 58, 126–127, 129
The Washington Post 30, 178
Weinke, Chris 183, 192
Weston, Kath 127, 129
What's Happening 131
White, Allon 162, 171, 175
Wilde, Oscar 26
Wildmon, Donald 124
Will & Grace 2, 4, 5, 11, 18n, 24, 30, 38n, 39n, 66, 75–84, 85–98, 130, 143, 144n, 204
The Wizard of Oz 55
World Champion Wrestling (WCW) 179
World Wrestling Entertainment, Inc. (WWE) 177–178, 179, 188–189
Wrestling 177–192

www.ingramcontent.com/pod-product-compliance
Lightning Source LLC
Chambersburg PA
CBHW032054300426
44116CB00007B/737